Remembering Cosmopolitan Egypt

Remembering Cosmopolitan Egypt examines the link between cosmopolitanism in Egypt, from the nineteenth century through to the mid-twentieth century, and colonialism. Although it has been widely noted that such a relationship exists, the nature and impact of this dynamic is often overlooked. Taking a theoretical, literary, and historical approach, the author argues that the notion of the cosmopolitan is inseparable from, and indebted to, its foundation in empire.

Since the late 1970s a number of artistic works have appeared that represent the diversity of ethnic, national, and religious communities present in Egypt in the nineteenth and early twentieth centuries. During this period of direct and indirect European domination, the cosmopolitan society evident in these texts thrived. Through detailed analysis of these texts, which include contemporary novels written in Arabic and Hebrew as well as Egyptian films, the implications of the close relationship between colonialism and cosmopolitanism are explored.

This comparative study of the contemporary literary and cultural revival of interest in Egypt's cosmopolitan past will be of interest to students of Middle Eastern Studies, Literary and Cultural Studies, and Jewish Studies.

Deborah A. Starr is Associate Professor of Modern Arabic and Hebrew Literature at Cornell University. Her research and teaching interests include contemporary literature and film, minorities of the Middle East, cosmopolitanism, postcolonial studies, and urban studies.

Routledge Studies in Middle Eastern Literatures

Editors: James E. Montgomery
University of Cambridge

Roger Allen
University of Pennsylvania

Philip F. Kennedy
New York University

Routledge Studies in Middle Eastern Literatures is a monograph series devoted to aspects of the literatures of the Near and Middle East and North Africa both modern and pre-modern. It is hoped that the provision of such a forum will lead to a greater emphasis on the comparative study of the literatures of this area, although studies devoted to one literary or linguistic region are warmly encouraged. It is the editors' objective to foster the comparative and multi-disciplinary investigation of the written and oral literary products of this area.

Postcard titled "Cairo – Native Quarter" (Lichtenstern & Harari)

Remembering Cosmopolitan Egypt

Literature, culture, and empire

Deborah A. Starr

Routledge
Taylor & Francis Group

LONDON AND NEW YORK

First published 2009
by Routledge
2 Park Square, Milton Park, Abingdon, Oxon OX14 4RN

Simultaneously published in the USA and Canada
by Routledge
270 Madison Ave, New York, NY 10016

Routledge is an imprint of the Taylor & Francis Group, an informa business

© 2009 Deborah A. Starr

Typeset in Times New Roman by
Value Chain International Ltd
Printed and bound in Great Britain by
MPG Digital Ltd, Bodmin, Cornwall

British Library Cataloguing in Publication Data
A catalogue record for this book is available from the British Library

Library of Congress Cataloging in Publication Data
Starr, Deborah A., 1968–
   Remembering cosmopolitan Egypt : literature, culture, and empire /
Deborah A. Starr.
      p. cm. – (Routledge studies in Middle Eastern literatures; 21)
   Includes bibliographical references and index.
   1. Egypt–Civilization–Western influences. 2. Egypt–Fiction. 3. Cairo
(Egypt)–Fiction. 4. Alexandria (Egypt)–Fiction. I. Title.
   DT70.S73 2009
   962´.04–dc22
                                                          2008040870

ISBN13: 978-0-415-77511-3 (hbk)
ISBN13: 978-0-203-88136-1 (ebk)

For Dorothy and Jerome Starr

Contents

Figures

Acknowledgments

Although the image of the solitary writer toiling in seclusion persists, no piece of writing is produced in isolation. Over the years as I have conducted the research and undertaken the writing of this book, I was very lucky to have the support and encouragement of many family members, friends, and colleagues, as well as the financial support of several institutions and foundations.

Of the many people to thank, I would like to begin by expressing my gratitude to those who read and commented on part or all of this manuscript at various stages in its development, as well as those who have served as ongoing interlocutors as I have refined my thinking on the issues discussed in these pages. These include: Ross Brann, Michelle Campos, Shai Ginsburg, Sabine Haenni, Kim Haines-Eitzen, Barbara Mann, Bruce Robbins, Laurence Roth, Sasson Somekh, and Robert Vitalis. Their insights have enhanced this manuscript. Any errors to be found in the pages that follow are my own.

Most of this book was written while I was teaching in the Department of Near Eastern Studies at Cornell University. I consider myself very lucky to work in such a collegial environment. I would like to thank my colleagues and the department staff for all they have done to support me, and my graduate and undergraduate students for challenging my thinking in innumerable ways. Research conducted during my years at Cornell has benefited from the generous support of the Department of Near Eastern Studies. I am also grateful for the support I received as a fellow at the Society for the Humanities at Cornell in Fall 2002. I would like to thank my fellow fellows, and particularly, Dominick LaCapra, the director of the Society at the time, for the valuable feedback I received during the course of the seminar.

Another institution that has played a significant role in fostering and supporting the development of this project is my undergraduate *alma mater*, the University of Pennsylvania. I would particularly like to thank my undergraduate mentor Roger Allen for not only sparking my interest in Arabic literature many years ago, but also for his ongoing interest in the development of my scholarship. I also would like to thank him for helping to shepherd this manuscript through the review and editing process in his capacity as coeditor of Routledge Studies in Middle Eastern Literatures. In addition to my undergraduate years in Philadelphia, I had the great fortune to spend the 2004–5 academic year at the Center for Advanced

Judaic Studies at Penn. I am grateful to the Center for its generous support, and for creating an intellectually generative and productive scholarly environment. I was also fortunate to be surrounded by an inspirational group of colleagues. I would particularly like to acknowledge those individuals who served as interlocutors, critics, and mentors outside of our weekly seminars: Alan Mintz, Marc Caplan, Bryan Cheyette, Kathryn Hellerstein, Sheila Jelen, Michael Kramer, Scott Lerner, Anita Norich, Laurence Roth, Anita Shapira, and Lilane Weissberg. I would also like to thank the Middle East Center at Penn for inviting me back to participate in a symposium on Cosmopolitan Egypt in February 2007—a forum that also proved engaging.

The intellectual work represented in these pages began during my years as a graduate student in the department of Comparative Literature at the University of Michigan. I am very grateful for the time my faculty mentors spent with me and the close attention they paid to the development of my scholarship. In particular, I would like to thank my dissertation chair, Carol Bardenstein, and my dissertation committee members, Sasson Somekh, Anton Shammas, and Anita Norich. During those years, the mentorship of scholars at other institutions also shaped my thinking on the issues that came to form the basis of this book. I would like to thank Ammiel Alcalay, Leonard Cassuto, Sidra Ezrahi, Hanan Hever, and Laurence Silberstein for all they taught me about scholarship and mentorship, and for their interest in my work during those formative years and since. I also received the generous support of the University of Michigan Dean's Dissertation Grant, as well as a Dissertation Fellowship from the National Foundation for Jewish Culture.

I would also like to thank Edwar al-Kharrat and Ibrahim Abdel Meguid for generously taking time to meet with me during my visits to Egypt in July 2002 and March 2003, and for providing me with material that made this project possible. I am grateful to Ronit Matalon for spending time with me and my students during her visit to Cornell University in February 2004 and during my visits to Israel. And most recently, I thank Nadia Kamel for undertaking the journey to Ithaca in March 2008 to screen her film at Cornell Cinema.

There are innumerable people I first met in Egypt who helped to shape my understanding of contemporary Egyptian literature and intellectual life. I am grateful to the following individuals for their friendship and for helping to broaden my understanding of Egyptian culture: Iman Mersal, Nagwa Hedayet, Ibrahim Hamid, 'Ala Khalid, Ahmed Taha, Safaa Fathy, and the late Osama Dinasaury.

I would like to commend the staff of Cornell's Olin Library for maintaining such a rich collection of materials, and for their tireless efforts to help hunt down references. Many thanks are also due to Munther Younes and Ragy Ibrahim for their assistance in helping me unlock and interpret nuanced passages in Arabic texts and films. I also thank Nicole Brisch for her assistance in translating an article in German. I would also like to thank Joe Whiting and Suzanne Richardson and other staff at Routledge Press for seeing this book through.

A section of Chapter 4 is reprinted with permission from a previous work "Recuperating cosmopolitan Alexandria: Circulation of narratives and narratives of circulation," *Cities* 22, no. 3 (2005): 217–228, Elsevier.

It is difficult to put into words my gratitude to my family for believing in me over the years it took to research and write this book. I would like to thank my sister, Rebecca Starr, for being both an incisive reader—always encouraging me to strive for clarity—and an inspiration by example through her courage and perseverance. Over the years, my biggest cheerleaders have been my parents, Dorothy and Jerome Starr. I am very grateful for their ongoing, enthusiastic encouragement.

My greatest thanks are due to my husband, Elliot Shapiro, who, by my side, has lived with this book over the last several years. I have benefited enormously from his comments and insights, as well as his continuous support and encouragement. I am also grateful for everything he has done to make it possible for me to spend the long hours necessary to complete this project. In this venue I can only begin to thank him for all the ways his presence has enriched my life, and for the ways his involvement—as reader, critic, interlocutor, editor, companion, and friend—have enriched the contents of the book before you.

1   Introduction

Making the cosmopolitan native

Postcards produced for European visitors to collect or send home tell a great deal about how Westerners perceived foreign locales. By the turn of the twentieth century a thriving postcard business in Egypt catered to European visitors. Some images featured archaeological relics, others modern buildings. Images voyeuristically gave their consumers access to secret domestic spaces and exotic religious rituals. Postcards peeked into the harem, revealing bare breasts, a projection of desire.[1] Another commonly reproduced image was the "native" street scene. These vertical images peered down a narrow street bordered by buildings that feature local architectural elements. The visual lines of the buildings converge on the center of the frame where, in many representations, the minaret of a mosque rises above the roof line (Figures 1.1 and 1.2).

Sometime between 1909 and 1912 the Cairo Postcard Trust, also known as Lichtenstern & Harari, one of the major producers of postcards in early twentieth century Egypt, published a somewhat unusual postcard. The title on the back of the card reads, "Cairo – native quarter" (Figure 1.3). Like other postcards of "native" street scenes in Cairo from the early twentieth century, this print of a hand-drawn image features a domed mosque with a tall, elegant minaret, framed by a narrow street. Canvas stretched across the alley provides shade to the shop-lined street below. Male figures dressed in flowing robes, *galalib*,[2] mill around the alley, some deep in the shadows of the covered market, others emerging into the bright sunlight. The upper floors of the buildings bordering the street leading to the mosque feature *mashrabiyya*, intricate wooden lattice window screens.

Surprisingly, this postcard features a second visual axis. In the foreground, cutting across the mouth of the alley runs a broad commercial street. In contrast to the modest *mashrabiyya* overlooking the alley, on the side facing the main street, the buildings feature inviting open balconies accessed by louvered doors. The shops lining the main street are identified by signs in both Arabic and Roman script. The wide thoroughfare is bustling and full of life. A man on a camel rides down the street just ahead of a donkey cart carrying several women cloaked in *milayat*, traditional black shawls. A child hawks newspapers to passersby. Not surprisingly, more men than women populate the street. Their clothes are varied, offering clues

Figure 1.1 Postcard titled "Cairo – In the Arab Quarters".
Source: Livados & Coutsicos

Figure 1.2 Postcard titled "A Street in the Native Quarter of Cairo".
Source: Eastern Publishing Company

Figure 1.3 Postcard titled "Cairo – Native Quarter".
Source: Lichenstern & Harari

to their social status, profession and region of origin: one man from the educated upper classes sports a *tarbush* accompanied by a Western blazer worn over a *gallabiya*, another dons a turban over his *tarbush* and wears a flowing clerical robe, and the head of a third man is covered with a white *kufiya*.

In the foreground of the frame amidst the movement stand two still figures, a man and a woman. In contrast to those around them, they appear in elegant Western dress—high fashion of the 1910s. The woman wears a high-collared dress with a tight bodice and a full sweeping skirt, and on her head sits a wide-brimmed hat. The man, wearing a blue blazer, demonstrates his good manners by holding his straw boater deferentially behind him as they speak. Another man in Western attire, a brown jacket and bowler hat, casually picks his way through the crowd, heading generally in their direction.

The presence of Westerners in the frame could be said to domesticate the scene for the postcard's consumers: visitors to Egypt and their family and friends back home. The image proclaims the exotic locale safe for a respectable Western woman. The signs in English render the city navigable. The representation of the commerce advertised in Western languages familiarizes the city. Borrowing a turn of phrase from Timothy Mitchell, one could say that the postcard renders Cairo legible to the Western consumer accustomed to the marketplace of the "world-as-exhibition."[3]

Mitchell's approach to interpreting representations of urban space in *Colonising Egypt* provides a possible model for reading this image as a metaphor for the colonial ordering that made Egyptian society legible, and thereby governable, to Europeans. According to this reading, in order to gain perspective on the cramped native quarters, one must step outside into the wide commercial street of the "Western" city. Without this perspective, the narrow alleys and the people bounded within them remain illegible to the Western eye. The mosque peeks out from the alley framed by familiar-looking buildings with Mediterranean-style facades and English-language signs. The postcard represents the Egyptian past—the Islamic architecture and narrow street—as a "world enframed." The *mashrabiyya* overlooking the alley resist penetration—they block out the male gaze and block in the women relegated to the domestic space—whereas the open porticoes facing the commercial street illuminate the dark corners of the interior. The obscure, shadowy, unknowable, impenetrable, and ungovernable past represented by the alley gives way to the brightness, clarity, and order of modernity. The image, read thus, offers a metaphor for enlightenment, secured by British military protection.

However compelling such a reading is, it only tells part of the story. This interpretation of the image is predicated on the existence of zones of separation: areas safe and familiar to European visitors and conquerors alike juxtaposed with strange, exotic areas made familiar when they are enframed as consumable objects. The urban expansion of Cairo begun in the 1860s under the Khedive Ismaʻil , who provided this separation. Upon returning from a visit to Paris, Ismaʻil ordered the construction of a new city—alongside the old—designed on a European model and by European architects. This construction created what is frequently described as two cities: one medieval and Islamic, the other modern and Western. But the wide commercial street in the postcard looks neither like the cramped alleys we expect in the "native quarter" it is said to represent, nor the grand, belle époque architecture of the Western city.

The postcard rather depicts buildings of mixed character in which Eastern and Western elements coexist. The structures in the foreground have two façades, one marked by *mashrabiyya* and the other by open porticoes. These elements are situated contiguously in the same building. The two faces meet at the corner, the crossroads. The signs are bilingual, suggesting the patrons of the shops are of mixed origins. Architecturally and linguistically, then, "native" and "foreign" are depicted as intertwined. Read thus, the image depicts a border zone—a point of contiguity, contact, and métissage.

On second viewing we note that the Western woman's back is turned to the covered market of the alley and the shops along the wide commercial street. The man, with his eyes trained on his interlocutor, is shown in profile. The comportment of the two characters suggests that this "native" street may not be intended for their gaze. The same could be said of the other Western figure in the image. They are all depicted as participants in the street scene, not observers of it, and as such they cannot easily be said to function as mediators of the consumer's gaze. Travel literature of the period frequently describes Egyptian merchants and guides thronging around foreign tourists in the native marketplace. In the postcard, by contrast, the "locals" appear to find the Westerners' presence unremarkable.

The artist has gone to great lengths to depict the city's diverse population in a single frame: *effendiyya*, merchants, and barefoot children; a *shami*[4] and a *shaykh*; men, women and children. Perhaps the presence of these three Western figures in the image is not to be read as anomalous, but to be seen as part of the diversity of Egyptian life represented in the postcard. Read this way, the image sits somewhat at odds with the title of the postcard, "Cairo-native quarter." Could the postcard be positing diverse local subjectivity as an alternative to nativeness, narrowly defined? What would it mean to suggest that this entire scene represents a kind of nativeness: nativeness not constructed in binary opposition with "foreignness," but a nativeness that embraces difference?

Details about the production of the postcard provide some insight into its representation of nativeness. Joseph Lichtenstern, a Viennese Jew who had immigrated to Egypt in 1895, founded a publishing company under his own name in 1899. In 1902 he took on David Harari, a Syrian Jew, as his business partner, and "Lichtenstern & Harari" was born. When the partnership dissolved in 1912, the business was sold to a Hungarian citizen, Max Rudmann, another central European postcard publisher in Cairo.[5] These businessmen arrived in Egypt during an extended period of immigration that attracted Ottoman subjects and foreigners seeking economic opportunity. Although many of these merchants, like Lichtenstern himself, did not integrate into Egyptian Arab society, nor seek Egyptian nationality, they started business and settled in Egypt. Although he would never become an Egyptian citizen, Lichtenstern lived out his life in Egypt and is buried there, as is his daughter who passed away in 1996.[6] Although neither Lichtenstern nor the members of his family would have considered themselves to be Egyptian in either the cultural or legal sense of the term, they nevertheless called Egypt home.

Although they laid no claim to Egyptian national identity, they nevertheless were local residents who identified with their chosen city. The image on the postcard that includes Western figures in its depiction of "nativeness" could be said to emerge from this experience.

The Cairo Postcard Trust under its various names published many representations of "native" people, places, and events in Egypt, most of them representing the more typical exoticizing idiom of the genre (Figure 1.4). By contrast, the hand-drawn image on the postcard entitled "Cairo – Native Quarter" is unique and quite personal. The image literally writes Lichtenstern and his business into the city. The building to the immediate left of the alley displays signs for "Lichtenstern & Harari" and "The Cairo Postcard Trust." The other signs indicate that businesses in the district were operated by other central Europeans. One store sells Törley, Hungarian sparkling wine widely exported in the early part of the twentieth century. Another sign advertizes the services of a Wilhelm Hochstein.

The site represented in this image is believed to be 6 Shari' Disuqi, the company's headquarters during the period in which the postcard was produced.[7] The office was located in one of the earliest Westernized business districts, near the former Jardin Rosetti, an area that forms a wedge between the medieval Frankish quarter and the modern district of Azbakiyya.[8] The representation of this location in the postcard visually foregrounds the intermixing of cultures and classes. The diversity represented in the image undermines the native–foreign binary presumed by the postcard's title: "Cairo–native quarter." Instead, the postcard depicts a distinctly cosmopolitan construction of "nativeness." By cosmopolitan, I mean that the image represents identification with a place and with a collective as a "voluntary affiliation,"[9] not governed by legal definitions of nationality, nor by commonly held conceptions of national identity. In popular parlance, when one speaks of "cosmopolitans" in Egypt, the term refers exclusively to Europeans and Europeanized foreign minorities who resided in Egypt from the middle of the nineteenth century to the middle of the twentieth century. Although the image represents a diverse Cairo cityscape that includes figures in Western dress, it is not the presence of these figures alone that warrants the label "cosmopolitan." The image's cosmopolitanism destabilizes parochial constructions of identity. The broad sense of the collective depicted in the image avoids homogenization; it rather acknowledges, and deliberately portrays difference.

The postcard, as we have seen, is a product of the nexus between demand driven by the colonial encounter, and supply produced by a cosmopolitan society. However, the Timothy Mitchell-inspired interpretation of the image as the representation of a world enframed and domesticated for foreign consumption occludes its cosmopolitan content and what could be called its cosmopolitan mode of production. The terms offered by postcolonial theory provide necessary, but not sufficient, tools for understanding the interplay between the various ethno-religious and ethno-linguistic groups present in Egypt from the middle of the nineteenth century to the middle of the twentieth century. Much writing about this period in recent years, taking a cue from Edward Said's *Orientalism* and *Culture and Imperialism,* and Timothy Mitchell's *Colonising Egypt,* offers

Figure 1.4 Postcard titled "Cairo Native Street".
Source: Cairo Postcard Trust

explorations of the methods, terms, signification, and lasting impact of colonial domination on Egyptian society and culture.[10] Said's and Mitchell's work, and the works of others following their lead, have contributed a great deal to our understanding of the unequal East–West encounter. But, for better or for worse, these narratives have come to dominate the study of Egypt's recent past. Postcolonial approaches to the study of Egypt's history, in general, tend to overlook the cosmopolitan narrative. In particular, the narrative of Egyptian anti-colonial resistance to foreign rule tends to flatten distinctions between agents of the European powers and Europeanized foreign minority residents. *Remembering Cosmopolitan Egypt* argues that intertwined with the narrative of colonial encroachment and anti-colonial resistance is a repressed narrative about how resident minorities came to be viewed as resident aliens; or rather, how resident minorities came to be associated with the European powers.

This book foregrounds the cosmopolitan, reading it against and through the colonial experience. Cosmopolitanism in Egypt developed out of imperial rule (Ottoman and British) and was shaped by the East–West encounter; however, cosmopolitanism is neither reducible nor equivalent to colonialism. Through readings of texts that, like the postcard, thoughtfully and self-critically portray Egypt's cosmopolitan past, *Remembering Cosmopolitan Egypt* explores the ways in which cosmopolitanism and colonialism are inherently intertwined.

The texts discussed in the following chapters—unlike the postcard of the "Lichtenstern & Harari" offices, an artifact from the cosmopolitan era—were produced decades after the demise of the foreign minority communities. My analyses focus on texts by Arabs and Jews produced in Arabic and Hebrew, which began to appear in the late 1970s. The works that I have chosen to discuss emerge in cultural environments characterized by disillusionment with their respective national myths. Although clearly influenced by the writings of E. M. Forster, Constantine Cavafy, and Lawrence Durrell, the works discussed in *Remembering Cosmopolitan Egypt* also represent a re-orientation of the myths of Cosmopolitan Egypt. These works demonstrate nuanced understandings of the relationships among individuals, communities, the state, and the colonial power. These texts not only portray intercommunal relations within Egypt, but also interrogate the impact of the colonial encounter on Egyptian cosmopolitanism.

To talk about cosmopolitanism, one must contend with its foundations in and indebtedness to empire. However, as already noted, the study of empire can obscure or flatten expressions of the cosmopolitan. *Remembering Cosmopolitan Egypt* brings the cosmopolitan to the fore while recognizing its close interrelationship with empire. In the next section of the chapter, I map the relationship between the cosmopolitan and empire as articulated in contemporary critical theory. Although many theorists have noted that a relationship exists between the cosmopolitan and empire, the nature of that relationship remains under-explored. I examine the various articulations of this relationship not so much to produce a singular understanding but rather to draw out its multiplicitous nature—a range of colonial–cosmopolitan expressions that are mirrored in the texts discussed in following chapters.

In the section that follows, I trace the rise and fall of cosmopolitan society in Egypt in the context of colonial encounter while also examining other factors shaping Egyptian society. Understanding how foreign minority communities were perceived over time, and how their legal status shifted from the mid-nineteenth to the mid-twentieth centuries, can tell us a great deal about the multiple factors that came to play in the development of Egyptian national consciousness. As already noted, European colonialism only goes part of the way to explaining the emergence of a cosmopolitan society, and the success of the Egyptian anti-colonial struggle only partially explains its demise. In the final section, I introduce the literary texts and films discussed in the following chapters and outline the organization of the book.

Cosmopolitanism and empire

The term "cosmopolitanism" has seen a resurgence of popularity in a variety of academic disciplines and the popular media since the mid-1990s. Scholars of Mediterranean port cities have employed the term to describe cultural, linguistic, and religious diversity amongst residents and transient populations in urban environments. Political scientists and social theorists frequently draw upon Immanuel Kant's essays "Idea for a Universal History with a Cosmopolitan Purpose" and "Perpetual Peace," particularly when discussing transnational governance of the European Union and immigrant rights. Anthropologists tend to focus on the cosmopolitan subject—a person or group with multiple, flexible affiliations. Among literary and cultural critics whose writings variously reference the Stoics, Kant, Marx, and Gramsci, the term reflects a political commitment to anti-parochial transnationalism. Within and between these various approaches there is much debate about what the cosmopolitan signifies, to say nothing of the diverse valences attached to it. It is, of course, not surprising that a term that valorizes transnationalism and multiple affiliations would itself become so multiply affiliated that it risks losing all distinction as a concept. What, then, to make of the cosmopolitan, and why continue to use it?

What prompts me to stake a claim in this book for an overused and overdetermined term is its much-noted but under-theorized foundational element—its relationship, historically and conceptually, with empire. Several texts by philosophers as well as literary and cultural critics note that cosmopolitanism develops out of metropolitan philosophers' intellectual reckoning with imperial expansion. In an essay that reflects upon philosophical engagements with the notion of the cosmopolitan, Amanda Anderson offers a definition that in her view remains consistent across the various periods and contexts in which it has been employed: a "cultivated detachment from restrictive forms of identity."[11] Nevertheless, although the definition has remained consistent over time, the particularities of the "restrictive forms of identity" from which thinkers were cultivating detachment differed. Anderson writes:

> In antiquity, with the initial elaborations of cosmopolitanism by the Cynics and Stoics, cosmopolitan detachment was defined against the restricted perspective and interests of the polis. In the Enlightenment, it was defined against

the constricting allegiances of religion, class, and the state. In the twentieth century, I think we can fairly say that it is defined against those parochialisms emanating from extreme allegiances to nation, race and ethnos.[12]

Anderson also notes that during these three periods—antiquity, the Enlightenment, and the twentieth century—earlier forms of attachment came to be viewed as local, confining, and parochial in the face of expansion or reconfiguring of empire. Indeed, as Anderson and others have demonstrated, it is through the experience of empire that the notion of the cosmopolitan develops, and through the expansion and perpetuation of empire that the cosmopolitan retains significance in cultural or philosophical discourse. One could even go so far as to say that cosmopolitan philosophy cannot exist without empire.[13]

"In the context of Stoical cosmopolitanism," Anderson writes, "the sense of an expanded world traces to Alexander the Great's program of cultural fusion and his far-reaching world conquests."[14] In other words, according to Anderson, cosmopolitan philosophy originates with and in response to the possibilities inherent in empire—the cultural fusion made possible by military conquest. Scott Malcomson provides further articulation of the complicity between cosmopolitan knowledge and centers of imperial power in antiquity. Malcomson writes that cosmopolitans in the ancient world "most of them influenced by Stocisim, took their universal citizenship as a license either to withdraw from the world or to master it."[15] As examples of the two extremes, and the points of contact between them, he cites a reported exchange between Alexander the Great, the conqueror, and Diogenes the Cynic, a recluse, before the former set off on his military escapades. This meeting, for Malcomson, suggests the point of departure for a long history of complicity between cosmopolitan knowledge and imperial expansion and administration. He maintains that "Stoic cosmopolitans were first among the ranks of ancient geographers and ethnographers; they were likewise prominent among the defenders of empire, particularly during the Roman Empire."[16] In other words, the success of empire rested on the production of cosmopolitan knowledge in the metropole.

As Anderson notes, when the notion of the cosmopolitan resurfaced in Enlightenment philosophy, it also emerged out of confrontation with new conquests. She writes:

In the eighteenth century the opening up of trade routes and the advancement of imperial ventures caused powerful self-interrogation among thinkers in Europe. The results of such interrogations often appear naively unaware of their own imbrication in relations of power, or their relation to the logic of capitalist expansion, as instanced in the common Enlightenment view that international commerce would foster world peace.[17]

Kant, whose writings on cosmopolitanism, as already noted, have influenced many contemporary theorists, offers perhaps the most prominent example of this kind of thinking. Geographer David Harvey provides a sustained analysis of what Anderson refers to as "naiveté" in Kant's writings, particularly in his infamous *Geography*. Although scholars have often dismissed *Geography*, unpublished during Kant's lifetime, Harvey argues that it is central for understanding the philosopher's body of work in general, and his conception of geography and cosmopolitanism in particular. Although, as Harvey notes, Kant himself opposed colonialism, his writings on cosmopolitanism shared the prejudice and belief in European cultural superiority common among "fervent defenders of universal reason and of universal rights at that time."[18]

Water Mignolo also posits a cosmopolitanism indivisible from European colonialism, although he arrives at this conclusion through a different line of reasoning. Mignolo maps the development and consolidation of the notion of "the West" in modernity, noting that coloniality is both "the hidden face of modernity and its very condition of possibility."[19] For Mignolo, Enlightenment philosophy, along with capitalist expansion in the Atlantic, served as twin vehicles for consolidation of the West as a discursive construct that links it "intrinsically" to colonialism and by extension to cosmopolitanism.[20] With the continued hegemony of the West— both in terms of the continued geopolitical dominance of "the West" and in terms of the concept's continued dominance as a term of critical analysis—one must continue to deal with the legacy of colonialism and its cosmopolitan offshoot.

The return of "cosmopolitanism" as a critical discourse in the late twentieth century emerges out of theorists' confrontation with the legacies of colonial encounters and the rise of neo-colonialism. Discussions in "New Europe" about immigration and citizenship rights for former colonial subjects in the metropole revolve around the notion of "cosmopolitanism" as reflected in the works of Seyla Benhabib and Julia Kristeva.[21] In the United States, the rise of a politically engaged or activist contemporary theories of cosmopolitanism—evident in Martha Nussbaum's essay in the *Boston Review*, or the writings of Bruce Robbins—could be characterized as attempts to conceive of individual agency or networks of affiliation on a global scale as a counterpoint to the homogenizing effects of late-capitalist globalization.[22] Whether as a reckoning with Europe's colonial legacy or a response to American neo-colonialism, cosmopolitanism in its contemporary idiom positions itself in opposition to colonialism.

However, Timothy Brennan argues that contemporary theorists of the cosmopolitan exhibit a similarly uncritical and presumably unwitting relationship to neo-colonialism as their eighteenth century predecessors did to colonial expansion in their day. In *At Home in the World*, Brennan outlines and savagely critiques a cosmopolitan ethic and aesthetic among self-congratulatory intellectuals and academics. He deflates a faddish embrace of "hybridity" and "transnationalism," arguing that cosmopolitanism theories presented by various critics as progressive or revolutionary reflect instead "a decidedly mainstream position, solidly in the conventional liberal center of the American intellectual scene."[23] Further, he suggests that thinkers such as James Clifford, Martha Nussbaum, Paul Rabinow, and Bruce Robbins, despite their "frankly—even belligerently—anti-imperial"[24] stance, share more with American neo-colonial politics and the economics of globalization than they acknowledge.

Whether one accepts Brennan's argument, or the contentions of the theorists he critiques, there is no disagreement among the various parties that cosmopolitanism bears some relationship to empire. Whichever theorist or body of literature one relies upon, one can characterize the relationship between the cosmopolitan and neo-colonialism at the turn of the twenty-first century as oppositional, dialectical, or complicitous. Empire provides a necessary condition for the rise of cosmopolitanism as a critical discourse, and, in turn, cosmopolitanism as a concept provides a means of engaging with the implications of empire and its lasting legacy.

Empire also provided the conditions under which cultural, ethnic, and linguistic diversity thrived in port cities of the Eastern and Southern Mediterranean—a cultural phenomenon that has also been labeled "cosmopolitan."[25] A body of scholarship exploring Mediterranean cosmopolitan history arose simultaneously with, but independently of, the rise in cosmopolitanism as a theoretical discourse. Although the interrogation of a transnational notion by historians and theorists emerges from the same cultural imperatives and the same milieu of the European and American academies, the signification of the term differs. In contrast to the interests of the theoretical discussions of "cosmopolitanism," historical works privilege the city as "cosmopolis"—identifying it as a universal space in which people and cultures come into contact. To the extent that "cosmopolitanism" in its theoretical formulations offers a utopian vision of a postnational Europe or models for transnational agency, it is prescriptive; for historians who use the term to characterize urban intercommunal contact of a particular historical period, the term is largely descriptive. For the latter, "cosmopolitanism" implies a situatedness at odds with the universalist valences in its theoretical formulations.

Historians of (former) Ottoman port cities have been particularly engaged in exploring the social history of cosmopolitanism in the nineteenth and twentieth centuries.[26] Ethno-linguistic or religious communal identity underpinned the social structure in these cities where endogamy and communal cohesion were the rule, but where individuals interacted in commercial exchanges, in municipal governance, and in what was by the nineteenth century a burgeoning public sphere. Although intercultural contact existed at multiple levels of the society, the term "cosmopolitanism" is most frequently applied to the upper classes who interacted at the exclusive social clubs and the European cafes, and who sent their children to Western-style schools. The ease of movement within the boundaries of the Ottoman Empire had a significant bearing on the flow of immigrants to the port cities as they grew in the late nineteenth century. The culture of religious tolerance and diversity was underpinned by the Ottoman *millet* system that defined the role of non-Muslim minorities in society, and granted protection. Whereas the appearance and initial growth of cosmopolitanism in these cities was fostered by the Ottoman Empire, its character was influenced by European imperial interests in the region.[27] Throughout the nineteenth century, European powers were gaining influence over the Egyptian economy and Egyptian governance. European powers, together with the Ottoman authorities, put an end to Mehmed Ali's imperial aspirations in 1840. In 1879, after years of growing debt to European financiers, European powers intervened and demanded that the Ottoman Sultan dismiss the Khedive Isma'il. In 1882 Britain occupied Egypt. The existence of empire—both the declining Ottoman empire and the ascendant European empires—provide the conditions under which the cultural interactions that scholars have termed "cosmopolitan" flourished.

The writings of Robert Ilbert, one of the foremost scholars of Ottoman port cities, uses the term "cosmopolitan" circumspectly. He writes, "at the heart of Mediterranean cosmopolitanism is perhaps merely the contact between its groups, the assertion imposed by the city to 'live together.'"[28] He continues, "If one means by cosmopolitanism the coexistence of groups, languages and origins, and if the Mediterranean past is reduced to diversity and mixing, then these cities were cosmopolitan at the end of the nineteenth century."[29] Throughout his work, Ilbert consistently utilizes the term "cosmopolitanism" (*cosmopolitisme*) in this very narrow sense—describing interactions between discrete religious, ethnic, and linguistic groups (terms which were not mutually exclusive and indeed often overlapped) in an urban sphere.

Ilbert's definition of "cosmopolitanism" goes from narrow to downright provincial—in both a literal and figurative sense—in his discussion of Alexandria. According to Ilbert's characterization of Alexandrian society, leading members of the discrete ethno-religious communities held seats on the Municipal Council, which exerted significant influence over matters of economic investment and urban planning, and mediated disputes that arose between and among members of the different communities. In his view, Alexandrian cosmopolitanism was, "the aggregation of interests imposed by a Levantine bourgeoisie on the fluid national contours and consolidated by a communal system that granted notables a place of predominance."[30] As such, he contrasts Alexandria's communal structure with the American "melting pot"[31]—a metaphor that itself has received much critical scrutiny—and he distinguishes Alexandria's largely Mediterranean character from the broader ranging diversity of Paris and New York.[32] What bound the communities together, according to Ilbert, was shared concerns about life and commerce in their city.[33] Civic pride, in Ilbert's view, commanded Alexandrians' loyalty, not the nation—neither Egypt nor the myriad of other nations with which Alexandrians identified.

Ilbert's characterization of Alexandria as an urban community ("*communauté citadine*") with its dependence on communal identity, is built upon a commitment to coexistence that transcends parochial identifications. Ilbert and other historians ascribe the demise of these communities to the rise of parochial nationalisms by the mid-twentieth century: Egyptian anti-colonialism, Greek irredentism, fascism, and Zionism. In other words, "cosmopolitanism" as a characterization of urban diversity in Ilbert's writing and the works of other historians, functions as the antithesis of parochial nationalism.

Indeed, Ilbert's definition of cosmopolitanism prompts the question of whether it is accurate to describe this social model as "cosmopolitan" at all. It could, rather, be characterized as "pluralist" according to David Hollinger's interpretation of the term. For Hollinger, pluralism, "respects inherited boundaries and locates individuals within one or another of a series of ethno-racial groups to be protected or preserved," whereas cosmopolitanism "favors voluntary affiliations" and "promotes multiple identities."[34] In the period under consideration, Egyptian cities housed diverse populations with strong communal and religious identification, although they shared a hybrid cultural identity that transcended these communal boundaries. However, "pluralism" has its own drawbacks as a term intended to capture the nature of social structure and intercommunal interactions in Egyptian cities. In addition to Hollinger's definition of the term, "pluralism" connotes a participatory and multi-vocal system of governance—characteristic of the United States but not Egypt. Further, one suspects that historians have another reason for preferring the term "cosmopolitan" to "pluralist" or other adjectives to describe the social phenomenon. Despite the documentary evidence of clear limits to the nature and extent of interactions between members of different groups in Mediterranean port cities, historians like Ilbert have perhaps continued to employ the term "cosmopolitan" as means of signaling their rejection of the parochial nationalisms that undermined the societies they describe with such affection, even nostalgia.

Critics of this body of scholarship read the privileging of the "Mediterranean" as a new form of Eurocentrism and the exploration of the "cosmopolitan" as a form of colonial apologia.[35] Indeed, much of the scholarship thus critiqued focuses on the foreign and minority communities in the port cities while excluding the social, cultural, political and intellectual streams circulating among the majority population.

My decision to adopt the term "cosmopolitan" to describe this cultural phenomenon in Egypt is not intended to suggest an uncritical affinity for a Eurocentric view of Egypt. Nor should it be read as valorizing the hybrid cultural expression of urban foreign-minorities while excluding Egyptian Arab culture and history. To the contrary, more than half of this book discusses Egyptian cultural production in Arabic—contemporary works that reinvestigate Egypt's cosmopolitan past. These imaginative works display a keen awareness that colonialism fostered Egypt's cosmopolitan society, yet demonstrate a nuanced understanding of the distinctions among communities. Moreover, they differentiate between the social roles of the foreign minorities and the colonial powers. *Remembering Cosmopolitan Egypt* sets out neither to demonize nor to valorize the colonial–cosmopolitan era in Egypt. Nor does it demonize nor valorize efforts by the writers and filmmaker under discussion to reckon with this past. Rather than coining a term to describe the presence of foreign-minorities in Egyptian cities, or attempting to find a more accurate, less-flawed substitute, in *Remembering Cosmopolitan Egypt*, I have chosen to retain the word "cosmopolitan." Unlike other terms, "cosmopolitan" is inseparable from its foundation in and reflections upon empire. The term highlights a key tension essential for understanding both the cultural phenomenon and its representation in literature and film.

Mapping the cosmopolitan in Egypt: from minorities to foreigners

While *Remembering Cosmopolitan Egypt* examines reminiscences about Egypt, it would not be entirely accurate to say that this study is about the "imagined community"[36] of the Egyptian nation or the modern state of Egypt, although it has bearing on both. This book is about representations of a largely extraterritorial phenomenon that existed within the boundaries of Egypt against and through which Egypt has come to define itself.[37]

In this section, I trace how Ottoman era notions of communal difference such as *millet* and *ta'ifa* were replaced by the oppositional, binary discourses majority–minority and native–foreigner, signified by the rise of the terms *aqaliyya* and *ajnabiyya*, respectively. These transformations in the social positioning of the transnational, polyglot Levantines can be mapped alongside the intertwined processes of immigration and shifting political, legal and cultural constructions of nationality in Egypt through the nineteenth and early twentieth centuries.[38] While I am not suggesting that the residents of Egypt prior to the rise of national identity were an undifferentiated population, the nature of the differentiation between groups— and the values attached to them—shifted significantly from the mid-nineteenth to the mid-twentieth century. I also do not read as inevitable the rift between the minority communities and Egyptian majority culture that widened into an unbridgeable gulf. Rather, it was a process that developed out of particular historical circumstances.[39] This story has only partially been told, but it is one that deserves further study and further integration into the questions about the formation of the Egyptian nation which drive much contemporary scholarly inquiry.

In Cairo under Ottoman rule prior to the nineteenth century, there were communities of non-Egyptian Muslims—Turks, North Africans, and *shawam*—and non-Egyptian non-Muslims—Greeks, Jews, Armenians, and Christian *shawam*.[40] These populations were considered Ottoman subjects—as were Egyptian Muslims and Copts. Non-Egyptian Muslims constituted part of the larger Islamic *umma* but were distinguished from the local populace by language in the case of the Turks and dialect in the case of the North Africans and *shawam*. Resident Christians and Jews were granted protection by the Sultan through the *millet* system, which provided administrative organization of their communities while offering autonomy of religious practice in exchange for communal taxes. The Turkish term *millet*, derived from the Arabic *milla*, signified "religious community" in the general sense, taking on particular reference to the religious communities of Christians and Jews in the nineteenth century.

In the Ottoman Arab lands, another administrative term, *ta'ifa* (pl. *tawa'if*), was also used to distinguish between self-defined, self-governing denominations within a *millet*.[41] The *tawa'if* included communities that shared religion, language, or geographic origin, as well as practitioners of specific trades, which often tended to break down along communal lines.[42] In Cairo, members of the distinct groups tended to cluster in the same districts of the city. According to André Raymond, *tawa'if* were "organized like semi-administrative entities placed under the management of shaykhs," communal leaders, providing the backbone for Ottoman urban administration.[43]

It would be anachronistic to refer to these communities in Ottoman times as "foreign," "diasporic," "transnational" or even "extra-territorial" before modern conceptualizations of "nation" (*demos*) or "ethnicity" (*ethnos*) became accepted cultural and legal terms in Egypt.[44] Through much of the nineteenth century, one cannot speak of a territorially bounded, ethno-linguistically defined Egyptian national identity against which these communities—Muslim and non-Muslim alike—could be viewed as "foreign." In the nineteenth century, members of the *tawa 'if* were considered Ottoman subjects.

As we learn from Ernest Renan, although nations are constituted by commonality, that commonality is forged through forgetting. Prior differences must be forgotten for the successful rise of the common collective identity known as the nation. The failure to forget leads to disastrous consequences in the age of the nation. In his writings on the nation, Renan relegates the Ottoman Empire to the past even before its dissolution. In his opinion, the cause of its downfall was its failure to create a unified national identity out of the diverse populations. In his 1882 essay "What is a Nation?" Renan writes:

> The Turkish policy of separating nationalities according to their religion ... brought about the downfall of the east. If you take a city such as Salonika or Smyrna, you will find there five or six communities each of which has its own memories and which have almost nothing in common.[45]

Sadly, the history of Turkish nation formation proved Renan correct. In the Armenian genocide and the massive Greek–Turkish population exchange, inassimilable groups were destroyed or expelled. Not only was the memory of these populations erased from the national imaginary, but also the memory of that erasure.

There are many limitations to Renan's thesis in this essay, most notably his monolithic vision of national identity. As documented and interpreted by Edward Said, Renan's portrayal of Eastern culture as always already moribund is consistent with his earlier philological writings about Semitic languages and his attitude toward Islam.[46] Contrary to Renan's assertion, the Ottoman *millet* system did not "separate *nationalities* according to religion." At the time he was writing, "nationalities" were in the process of forming along geographic lines, out of Ottoman provincial divisions or in a more localized way through the relationship between cities and their hinterlands. European penetration into the region also shaped the nascent national identities. European notions of nationalism had an impact on local intelligentsia and political leadership. Further, as discussed in greater detail below, European efforts to gain local influence contributed to driving a wedge between communities.

When nations were formed out of the former Ottoman lands, the *tawa 'if* were excluded from national identity only insofar as they came to be seen as foreign or identified with foreign interests. In Egypt, some groups distinct from the majority Arabic-speaking Muslim population were assimilated into the national identity. For example, Copts, the descendents of the Christian inhabitants of Egypt prior to the rise of Islam, share with the majority Muslim population language, local customs, and relationship to the land, and, as such, were integrated into the national imaginary.[47] Nubians—an ethnic group identified with Nubia, a region now divided between Southern Egypt and northern Sudan—were also accepted as Egyptian. However, their integration grew out of Egypt's territorial interests, and was affected at great cost to Nubian culture in a process consistent with the description Renan provides of centrally imposed nation formation.[48] Although both groups, Copts and Egyptian Nubians, have been subject to institutional and informal forms of discrimination, they are nevertheless considered Egyptian in terms of national identity and legal nationality.

In the process of nation formation, the differences between the majority Egyptian Arab Islamic culture and the other resident groups, however, were sharpened. Whereas some members of the *tawa'if* assimilated into Egyptian culture and obtained Egyptian nationality, they were never successfully integrated into the Egyptian national imaginary as a collective. As a result, by the middle of the twentieth century the majority of Greeks, Italians and Jews had left Egypt. In other words, according to Renan's terms, the differences between the Egyptian nation coming into being and members of these *tawa'if* proved "unforgettable."

This process of differentiation is always an important component of nation formation. Drawing upon the work of postcolonial critic Homi Bhabha, Timothy Mitchell writes, "the nation is made out of projects in which the identity of the community as a modern nation can be realized only by distinguishing what belongs to the nation from what does not, and by performing this distinction in particular encounters."[49] Under this formulation, the national self is constructed through its collective encounter with otherness. Whereas Egyptian nationalist discourses identify the European colonial powers as the "others" against which their struggle was defined, I maintain that there were multiple processes of differentiation occurring roughly simultaneously.

Europeans were only one significant collective of "others" with whom Egyptians increasingly came into contact from the mid-nineteenth century onward, and about which much has been written. A small number of Europeans resided in Egypt in the late eighteenth century, and several hundred more arrived with the French occupation under Napoleon in 1798,[50] although few Egyptians had direct contact with the French.[51] Mehmed Ali's industrial expansion drew foreign investment to Egypt, increasing immigration. However, even as immigration increased following the 1860s, contact between Egyptians and foreigners was limited to the urban economies of Cairo and Alexandria, as well as the Suez Canal zone.[52] Contact also took place outside of Egypt as Egyptian envoys were sent to Europe.

Another group of "others" against which Egyptian identity was being forged in the early nineteenth century were Turkish-speaking Ottoman Arab elites. These elites included Ottomanized Egyptians, who, like the Ottoman rulers, adopted an "imperial, universal but Istanbul-centered" identity distinct from the local "rooted" Arab Egyptian culture shared by non-elite Muslims and Copts.[53] Some members of the "*tawa'if*" were also counted among the Ottoman Egyptian elite. Christians of Coptic, Armenian, Greek, and other European origins held posts in the administration of Mehmed Ali, who governed Egypt from 1805 to 1849.[54]

The *tawa'if*—who were neither Ottoman Arab elites nor representatives of the European powers—constitute a third collective that must be considered in the discussion of the formation of Egyptian national identity. The presence of these groups shaped the development of Egyptian national identity. However, this influence has been occluded by the over-determination of the anti-colonial national struggle. By the mid-twentieth century Egyptian nationalists came to view minorities as compradors to colonialism, collaborators with the colonial regime. For this reason, the narrative of their departure became subsumed under the narrative of Egyptian victory over European colonialism. It is beyond the scope of this study to map the full impact foreign minorities had on Egyptian nation formation. However, in what follows I outline some of the processes by which the differentiation between *tawa'if* and Egyptians took place.

Khaled Fahmy's description of the early stages in the formation of Egyptian national identity implicitly offers insights into the beginning of the process by which the *tawa'if* became "foreign." Fahmy attributes a significant role to the army in the creation of a collective Egyptian nation. Arabic-speaking Egyptian men served together as foot soldiers in Mehmed Ali's army with no possibility for promotion, as senior ranks were reserved for Turkish-speaking Ottoman elites. For these men, army service was brutal. Even those who did not serve lived in fear of forced conscription. Women and children were affected by the separation from men in their families who served in the army for long periods of time. According to Fahmy, army conscription "helped to homogenize the experience of these thousands of Egyptians in a manner that was crucial in the founding of their 'imagined community.'"[55]

Non-Muslim Egyptians, *ahl al-dhimma*, were not subject to conscription. Thus, they did not participate in the experience through which the imagined community of Egypt was being forged. In other words, in addition to marking the beginning of Egyptian national identity, as Fahmy argues, conscription could also mark the beginning of a "national" and not exclusively religious rift between the Egyptian Muslim majority and the non-Muslims in their midst.

By the middle of the nineteenth century, the administrative structure of the *millets* had undergone significant changes, which according to Kemal Karpat, undermined the autonomy of the *millet*, replacing it with a "new and direct relationship between the individual and the state based on rights and obligations that stemmed from the individual's status as citizen of the Ottoman state."[56] This restructuring, according to Karpat, changed the relationship between the religious and ethnic communities, creating a power dynamic of minorities and majorities.[57]

In the 1860s Egypt experienced economic growth that accompanied the cotton boom. During this period the small communities of *tawa'if* and foreign nationals with a longstanding presence in Egypt, like *shawam*, Greeks, and Italians, were augmented by immigration. Various factors contributed to the ebb and flow of immigration through the late nineteenth century and into the twentieth century. The general trend over the period until the 1920s was a population increase among foreign minority communities partially attributable to immigration.[58] Some immigrants like *shawam* and Jews from the Arab world were Arabaphone and could easily integrate into the existing communities and into Egyptian society. However, while Greeks, Armenians, and Sephardi Jews from Turkey could integrate into their own ethno-religious, linguistic communities, assimilation into Egyptian Arab culture was more difficult. Many of these immigrants never mastered Arabic and never sought to integrate into Egyptian Arab society, even when families remained in Egypt for several generations. Instead, a hybrid Levantine culture flourished, in which French punctuated by expressions from the various communal languages served as the lingua franca, and European fashions dictated tastes. As a result the evident foreignness of Levantine culture shaped Egyptians' attitudes about the resident minority communities. Immigration, thus, played a significant role in driving a wedge between the longstanding integrated minority communities and majority Egyptian culture.

The perception of minority communities as foreign solidified along with definitions of Egyptian nationality and national identity. In 1892 the Egyptian government issued the first in a series of decrees that began to carve out a definition of local subjecthood independent of Ottoman legal categories.[59] However, Egypt was still subject to the terms of treaties signed by the Ottomans with foreign governments. In particular, a set of treaties originating in the sixteenth century between the Ottomans and European powers known as the Capitulations dictated the legal status of foreign nationals. Originally designed to protect Christian merchants traveling to or residing in Ottoman lands, the Capitulations granted extra-territorial legal protection to foreigners and exempted them from taxation.

Since as early as the seventeenth century, European powers interpreted clauses in the Capitulation treaties with the Ottoman Empire to grant them the right to protect the interests of particular religious minority communities: the Russians claimed rights to intervene in internal Ottoman affairs to protect the interests of Orthodox Christians, while the French claimed such privileges over the Catholics, and the British over the Druze and Jews of the Levant. Positioning themselves as champions of minority rights in the Middle East, they were able to increase their power and influence in Ottoman lands. In its most extreme application, the protection of minorities served as a pretext for French and British military intervention to further their colonial interests. The concern expressed by an eighteenth century French traveler to Egypt, Claude-Étienne Savary, about the poor treatment of Europeans there provided some justification for the French occupation of Egypt.[60] Nearly a century later, the British invasion of Egypt in 1882 was also partially justified by the need to protect foreigners and Christian minorities in the wake of a riot in Alexandria was characterized as interethnic violence.[61]

Foreign consuls were authorized to grant citizenship to their protégés, and some did so quite liberally. The Ottoman administration viewed the practice as a targeted denaturalization of its subjects, undermining the empire's territorial and judicial integrity. The Protection Law (1863) and the Ottoman Nationality Law (1869) were promulgated to counter this "nationality drain."[62] These laws sought to check the power foreign governments wielded over the populations most likely to seek foreign nationality: Armenians, Syrian Christians, Jews, and Levantine Greeks. In other words, from these laws we can see that Ottoman Porte wanted to maintain the *tawa'if* as its subjects.

However, in spite of these laws, the system for granting foreign nationality continued to be abused. The countries granting citizenship to local residents gained important resources and contacts, whereas recipients of nationality were granted the special privileges extended by the Capitulations. By the latter decades of the nineteenth century, according to David Landes, "the passport became a commercial commodity rather than a warranty of nationality."[63]

Under the terms of the Capitulations, legal cases involving a citizen of a Capitulatory Power were handled by the appropriate foreign consul rather than by the local court system. In 1875, during Egypt's growing debt crisis, France and Great Britain prevailed upon Egypt to accept a new, consolidated system of Mixed Courts.[64] Under this arrangement legal cases involving European residents—including cases involving disputes between Europeans and Egyptians—fell under the jurisdiction of the Mixed Courts. Needless to say, this situation was not popular with Egyptians, particularly since European governments extended nationality disproportionately to non-Muslims.[65]

In the first quarter of the twentieth century, the Egyptian nationalism that arose in resistance to colonial rule was marked by a desire to implement democratic self-rule founded upon pluralist principles. The ideals of the era could be summed up by the slogan popularized by the leaders of the 1919 Revolution: "Religion is for God, and the nation is for the people." This pluralist spirit was evident in the Egyptian nationality law first drawn up during this era. This law included in its definition of Egyptian nationals all Ottoman subjects habitually resident in Egypt at the start of the First World War.[66] Passage of the Egyptian nationality law, long under deliberation, was delayed until 1929.[67]

The 1929 nationality law marked an optimistic, if belated, development for non-native former Ottoman subjects long resident in Egypt. The mood in the country had begun to shift away from the "utopian expectations" of the 1919 Revolution, under "the dual impact of depression and repression" according to historians Israel Gershoni and James Jankowski.[68] Joel Beinin also describes how the "secular-liberal, territorial conceptions of the nation" gave way to pan-Arab and Islamist nationalism beginning in the 1930s.[69] He notes that Egyptians were disillusioned with failures of the Revolution, apparent in their country's limited autonomy and the continued British military occupation. Egyptian public opinion was also shaped by the conflict in Palestine and the rise of Fascism and Communism in Europe.[70]

Egyptian concerns over the privileges granted to foreign nationals were partially redressed in 1937 at the Montreux Convention, when Egypt succeeded in reaching accords with the twelve remaining Capitulatory Powers to abolish the Capitulations. The treaties included a provision that, although foreigners were to be subject immediately to Egypt's laws and to taxation, cases involving foreign nationals could continue to be tried in the Mixed Courts, during a transition period of 12 years, after which authority would revert to the Egyptian legal system.

Although the terms of the Montreux treaties removed the legal privileges granted to foreign residents of Egypt, their economic dominance remained intact. Foreign nationals owned a disproportionate number of major companies in the Egyptian economy and held a disproportionate number of management positions in those companies.[71] A visible segment of the non-native, unassimilated immigrant population achieved great financial success. Because of the European proclivities—and often European citizenship—of these capitalists Egyptians came to view minority businessmen as foreign agents acting against the interests of the state. However, according to Robert Vitalis, the view that capitalists with foreign nationality were undermining state welfare was exaggerated, as was the assumption that Egyptian capitalists were serving the nation.[72] Nevertheless, the visibility of the foreign *haute bourgeoisie* served as a lightening rod for Egyptian frustrations.

Not all immigrant minorities achieved the level of success of their communities' elites, and not all members of the *haute bourgeoisie* were foreigners. It was not only at private clubs, European pâtisseries and the opera that members of Egypt's varied ethno-linguistic populations interacted. Examining police records in Alexandria from the 1860s and 1870s, Khaled Fahmy demonstrates that less exclusive cafés, bars, and markets were also sites of contact—and sometimes conflict—between the working classes, including Egyptians and members of minority ethnic and religious communities.[73] Nevertheless, Egyptian public opinion of a relatively small group of foreign minority capitalists shaped their views of the entirety of the foreign minority community.

In 1947, two years before the dissolution of the Mixed Courts, a law was enacted effectively setting quotas on the number of foreign nationals in any company's employ. The law stipulated that 75% of the salaried positions and 90% of the workers employed by any company in Egypt should hold Egyptian nationality.[74] The Egyptianization of the economy undercut the benefits granted to capitalists and industrialists of foreign nationality, diminishing their economic opportunities.

Many Egyptian Jews and non-native former Ottoman subjects who were eligible for Egyptian nationality had not sought or received citizenship when it was first extended. In the 1930s and 1940s when the shift in legal status of foreigners made Egyptian nationality a desirable commodity, it became increasingly difficult to obtain. The applications of many minority residents who were technically eligible for citizenship were denied.[75] As a result, following the promulgation of the 1947 Law, foreign nationals and minorities without Egyptian citizenship were confronted with diminished employment opportunities.

Robert Mabro has suggested that by this period one could segment into four distinct groups the population of those formerly known as *tawa'if* under Ottoman urban administration.[76] These groups were defined by national and cultural affiliations. Arabic-speaking immigrants who arrived prior to the mid-nineteenth century became fully integrated into Egyptian culture. Members of these assimilated Arabic-speaking groups, such as the North Africans long resident in Egypt, were ultimately granted Egyptian citizenship. The second group comprised immigrants who arrived during the late nineteenth century and early twentieth centuries from Ottoman lands and sought Egyptian citizenship. This group includes *shawam*, Levantine Greeks, Armenians, and Jews who integrated into Egyptian culture. Some members of these first two groups of minorities and immigrants embraced the emerging Egyptian national identity and were visible in its body politic. The third group was comprised of immigrants of Ottoman origin who obtained European nationality via the "nationality market." By and large, this group did not integrate into Egyptian society, but rather identified with Levantine European culture. Finally, there were immigrants who arrived in Egypt with European nationality, such as Italians, Maltese, and Greeks from Greece, who never relinquished their national identities or cultural affiliations.

The 1952 coup d'etat by the Free Officers did not initially have a significant impact on the legal status of the foreign and minority residents of Egypt.[77] However, the final blows to these communities were dealt by the new regime under the leadership of Gamal Abdel Nasser after he became the president of Egypt in 1954. Following the 1956 Suez Conflict in which Israel invaded the Sinai Peninsula in collusion with Great Britain and France, Egypt expelled British and French citizens from its soil. The Jewish community in Egypt had already been diminishing in the wake of the establishment of the state of Israel and the first Arab–Israeli war. After 1956, the majority of the remaining Jews left Egypt.

In the years following the Suez Conflict the Egyptian regime implemented a number of reforms to the economy. Two initiatives had a significant impact on the remaining foreign minorities: the further Egyptianization of business in 1958 and the nationalizations of companies in the early 1960s. Although the nationalizations did not specifically target minority-owned businesses, the remaining foreign communities were significantly affected. The nationalizations were the final blow to the stalwarts of those communities who had remained in Egypt despite the decreasing tolerance of foreigners. Egyptian nationality did not, as it turned out, guarantee a future for minorities in Egypt, as national ideology and public policy turned against the foreign minority presence. By the mid-1960s, the population of foreign minorities in Egypt had dwindled. Egypt's so-called cosmopolitan era had come to an end.

The preceding narrative demonstrates how in the late nineteenth and early twentieth centuries European interests enabled non-Muslim Ottoman subjects, including many recent immigrants to Egypt, to gain foreign nationality, granting them extra-territorial rights and privileges not available to the majority population. European Colonialism played a defining role in enabling the minorities with foreign nationalities to flourish, and to succeed economically. Conversely, anti-colonial nationalism played a role in the demise of cosmopolitanism in Egypt. However, "cosmopolitanism" in Egypt is not reducible to a battle between European colonial powers and Egyptian anti-colonialists. Indeed, to read the period this way produces a flattening caricature of *comprador haute bourgeoisie* that occludes a nuanced understanding of the phenomenon in all its diversity. Rather, cosmopolitanism in Egypt must be explored in a broader framework that takes into account its Ottoman origins as well as its connection to British colonial rule in Egypt. Likewise, the demise of cosmopolitanism in Egypt in the middle of the twentieth century needs to be understood in the context of the rise of a range of parochial nationalisms and divided loyalties in wartime—the Second World War, the Arab–Israeli war of 1948–49, and the Suez Conflict—and not just as a result of anti-colonialism. Furthermore, studies like Khaled Fahmy's investigation of Egyptian police records in Alexandria, are needed to write Egyptians and members of other classes into the Eurocentric narrative of "cosmopolitanism" in Egypt, and to write the resident minorities into the narrative of Egyptian history.[78]

Representations of Cosmopolitan Egypt

As Timothy Brennan has noted, literary works identified by critics as "cosmopolitan" frequently represent a narrow aesthetic that constitutes a new canon of hybrid, transnational, postcolonial literature. Works in this group are often "critical of the West but only as those whose sympathies finally belong here," while simultaneously distancing themselves from national liberation movements.[79] He notes that works of Arabic literature, like their Asian and Lusophone counterparts, are often excluded from curricula and anthologies of cosmopolitan literature. He sarcastically explains their omission as follows:

> Not all regions lend themselves equally to cosmopolitanism's particular allure. From the outset the role of interlocutor can be played mainly by those who write in a European language, who resist thematizing colonialism from a socialist point of view, or who avoid expressing themselves in difficult-to-assimilate genres like the oral poem, the song lyric, or the locally situated essay.[80]

Approaches to the study of "cosmopolitan" literatures that privilege such discourses continue to dominate the field, in spite of Brennan's critique. Recent works such as Rebecca Walkowitz's *Cosmopolitan Style*[81] and Neelam Srivastava's *Secularism in the Postcolonial Indian Novel: National and Cosmopolitan Narratives in English*[82] focus primarily, if not exclusively, on works produced in English in the metropole.

Remembering Cosmopolitan Egypt seeks to shed light on a cosmopolitan phenomenon reflected in a different set of literary and artistic works—works that do not fit the rubric Brennan outlines. The texts discussed in the following chapters were not produced in Western languages for consumption in the metropole, although most are available in translation.[83] These works, produced in Arabic and Hebrew, all interrogate the structures of empire that underpin cosmopolitan society.

It is these two criteria—language and exploration of the interrelationship between the colonial and cosmopolitan—that have shaped the selection of texts analyzed at length in the chapters to follow. There are many notable literary works, thus, for which I do not provide close readings, although references to these texts are scattered throughout the pages that follow. Perhaps the most notable omission is Lawrence Durrell's *Alexandria Quartet*, the most well-known and influential literary representation of cosmopolitan Alexandria—a work that has already been the subject of many academic studies. Although some scholars have begun to examine the corpus of poet Edmond Jabès in the context of his early life in Egypt,[84] it remains to some future scholar or scholars to consider the significance of the cosmopolitan discourses in the Francophone works of Andrée Chedid, Paula Jacques, and Robert Solé. A discussion of the Italian works of Giuseppe Ungaretti and Fausta Cialente, as well as the Greek works of Constantine Cavafy and Stratis Tsirkas, among others, are also unfortunately beyond the scope of this work.

The choice to devote this book to a study of creative works in Arabic and Hebrew also provides a second, significant subtext to this book. My thinking in developing this project has been influenced by the work of Ammiel Alcalay, whose sweeping study, *After Jews and Arabs: The Remaking of Levantine Culture*, explores not only the conditions of coexistence that existed throughout the Levant for close to a thousand years and the factors involved in its demise, but more significantly, a myriad of literary texts produced in this environment or nostalgic for it. This present volume is an attempt to examine closely a small constellation of the larger universe his work reveals.

Additionally, as Alacaly notes, "For the last hundred years, the protracted conflict between Zionism and Palestinian nationalism has retroactively affected, in one way or another, most historical, cultural, political, and social discourse on Arabs and Jews in general."[85] This assertion is certainly true for any discussion of Egyptian cosmopolitanism, not only as it pertains to the history and literature of Egypt's Jewish population. In the choice of texts, *Remembering Cosmopolitan Egypt* acknowledges the significant impact the Israeli–Palestinian conflict has had on the region and the lives of its inhabitants. However, it also attempts to look beyond the reductive terms of the conflict to a cosmopolitan past shared by Muslims, Christians, and Jews in nineteenth and twentieth century Egypt. Alcalay has eloquently written that, "as the conflict in Palestine completely collapsed into a confessional war between essentialized 'Jews' and 'Arabs,' an appalling shade began to block the rays of light once clearly refracted through the Levantine prism."[86] The texts discussed in this book, whatever the political position of the various authors on the Israeli–Palestinian conflict, all attempt to illuminate that lost world.

The first four chapters of the book explore Egyptian representations of cosmopolitan Alexandria produced since the late 1970s. All of these works investigate the impact of mid-twentieth century events—the Second World War, the Free Officers Revolt, the Suez Conflict—on the city's culture and society. Although nostalgic for elements of coexistence and tolerance, these works are also critical of the colonial system in which cosmopolitanism thrived in Egypt.

Chapter 2, Literary Alexandria, opens by mapping the representation of Alexandria in twentieth century Egyptian Arabic literature. Following the departure of the foreign minority communities from Alexandria in the 1960s, Egyptian literary representations of Alexandria were engaged with normalizing the image of the city to the national narrative. Edwar al-Kharrat's 1985 novel *City of Saffron* [*Turabuha za'faran*][87] marks the beginning of a rupture with this trend, ushering in a literary reevaluation of Egypt's cosmopolitan past discussed in Chapters 3 and 4.

The following chapter Edwar al-Kharrat's Poetics of Memory offers a close analysis of *City of Saffron* along with its companion work, *Girls of Alexandria* [*Ya banat iskandariyya*] (1990).[88] The discussion of these novels tracks an evident shift in representations of cosmopolitan Alexandrian society. *City of Saffron* portrays interactions between the protagonist's Coptic family and their Muslim neighbors. Popular resistance to British rule is also depicted as an interconfessional alliance between Copts and Muslims. By contrast, *Girls of Alexandria* paints a broader, more inclusive picture of Egyptian identity. In the novel, a diverse array of Egyptian residents are involved in anti-colonial resistance, as evidenced by the protagonist's underground communist cell. *Girls of Alexandria* explores the dialectical relationship between colonialism and cosmopolitanism through this broader social perspective as well as through the frame of a universal political discourse.

In Chapter 4, Polis and Cosmos, I examine two novels by Ibrahim Abdel Meguid. Both texts open with the outbreak of war and explore the possibilities of cosmopolitan coexistence through a frame of conflict. *No One Sleeps in Alexandria* [*La ahad yanam fi al-iskandariyya*] (1996)[89] is set in the period between the start of the Second World War and the defeat of the Afrika Korps at al-Alamein in 1942. The portrayal of cosmopolitan society in *No One Sleeps in Alexandria* is fraught with intercommunal strife, the resolution of which is situated, I argue, in a pluralist nationalism distanced from colonial influence. The second novel, *Ambergris Birds* [*Tuyur al-'anbar*] (2000),[90] depicts the repercussions of the 1956 Suez Conflict on the citizens of Alexandria—Egyptians and foreign minorities alike. While *Ambergris Birds* romanticizes intercommunal relations, it too critiques both the colonial system that fostered cosmopolitan society and the regime of Gamal Abdel Nasser that oversaw its demise. Attempting to recreate a cosmopolitanism untainted by colonialism, the novel seeks out precedents within Arab Islamic culture and history.

Whereas the previous chapters discuss texts seeking a counterforce to parochial nationalism, Chapter 5, Why New York?, explores texts that engage cosmopolitanism in a transnational idiom. In particular, this chapter discusses Youssef Chahine's autobiographical films: *Alexandria ... Why?* [*Iskadariyya ... lih?*] (1978), *An Egyptian Story* [*Hadduta misriyya*] (1982), *Alexandria Again and Forever* [*Iskandariyya kaman wa-kaman*] (1990) and *Alexandria ... New York* [*Iskadariyya ... New York*] (2004). I argue that over the course of the film cycle New York, a living cosmopolitan city, comes to supplant the absent Alexandria of the past. This transfer of identification, however, raises with it the specter of American neo-colonialism underpinning New York's cosmopolitanism. I argue further that throughout the film cycle the presence of Jews serves as an indicator of a society's cosmopolitan nature. However, this view is complicated—both on and off screen—by the terms of the Arab–Israeli conflict. This chapter also maps the development and transformation of Chahine's representations of Jews as he explores cosmopolitan society.

The Arab–Israeli conflict has shaped the experience of Egyptian Jews as well as the memory of the Jewish presence in Egypt. As Joel Beinin has noted, the beginning of peace negotiations between Egypt and Israel afforded Egyptian Jews, wherever they settled, an opportunity to reflect upon their repressed past.[91] The peace accords spawned Egyptian Jewish memoirs and fictional works in a variety of languages.

In the final three chapters of this book, I discuss works by Israeli authors who engage with this past as an opportunity to explore contemporary social issues. Like their Egyptian counterparts, these authors employ their representations of the past to critique parochial nationalism and to examine cosmopolitanism's colonial legacy.

Chapter 6, Gazing Across Sinai, addresses representations of Egyptian Jews in Israeli literature in the context of Israeli literary history. The 1970s also saw the consolidation and political mobilization of *mizrahiyut*, the collective identity of Jews whose families immigrated to Israel from the Arab Islamic world. The consolidation of Mizrahi identity and the emergence of Mizrahi literature frame my discussions of Egyptian Jewish literature in Israel.

Chapter 7, A Mediterranean Vigor that Never Wanes, continues with an analysis of Yitzhaq Gormezano Goren's *Alexandrian Summer* [*Qayitz aleksandroni*] (1978), one of the first Jewish literary works to appear in the wake of Egyptian President Anwar Sadat's visit to Jerusalem in 1977.[92] The novel's representation of bourgeois Levantine hybridity needles its presumed socialist-leaning, Ashkenazi readership. The novel, set in Alexandria during the summer of 1951, relates a conversion narrative from Islam to Judaism and back. Although conversion is treated as inherently incomplete, *Alexandrian Summer* hesitantly troubles the lines between self and other, disturbing the stereotyped binaries of Muslim and Jew, and of Mizrahi and Ashkenazi. This disruption of binaries is affected in the novel by the presence of a third term, the colonial power, which functions not as a mediator, but rather as a destabilizing force.

Chapter 8, Unmasking Levantine Blindness, discusses Ronit Matalon's novel *The One Facing Us* [*Ze 'im ha-panim elenu*] (1996).[93] The novel, framed by the visit of a teenage girl born in Israel to her uncle living in Cameroon, traces multiple generations of a Cairene Jewish family. The narrative interweaves the girl's discomfort with the inequities of life in postcolonial Cameroon with discoveries about her family who had dispersed over five continents after leaving Cairo in the 1940s and 1950s. This text also examines the notion of "Levantinism" introduced to Israeli society in the late 1950s by Egyptian Jewish essayist, Jacqueline Kahanoff. Matalon's novel extends Kahanoff's Levantinism to its various logical conclusions drawing out its indebtedness to, and complicity with, colonial discourses.

These texts, like the Lichtenstern & Harari postcard before them, represent a period in which a diverse population inhabited Egypt and circulated in the streets of its cities. However, these works go beyond mere nostalgic representation of coexistence. The contemporary literary works and films discussed in *Remembering Cosmopolitan Egypt* return to this past to explore the range of possibilities offered by the cosmopolitan. For some, fictionalizing this period allows the artists to question political choices—past and present. Others see in its anti-parochialism a means to counter militant religious nationalism. However, as all of the texts discussed in the following chapters acknowledge, the cosmopolitan, for all its hopeful possibilities, emerges out of empire. In reckoning with this legacy, these texts challenge readers to revisit the past and reconsider the implications for the present.

Part I

Colonial anxieties and cosmopolitan desires

2 Literary Alexandria

A tale of two statues

In 1938 the Italian community of Alexandria officially presented the city with a gift to celebrate the close relationship that existed between Italy and Egypt. The gift, a statue of the Khedive Isma'il, specifically commemorated the state visit of his son, King Fu'ad, to Italy in 1927—the first official trip of his reign.[1] The installation of the statue affected a repatriation of sorts for the exiled ruler—after Isma'il was deposed in 1879 he initially settled in Italy.[2] The Italian community of Alexandria had a particular fondness for Isma'il and his Italian-educated son, Fu'ad. Although Isma'il's grand vision for the reconstruction of Cairo was inspired by Haussmann's Paris, the Khedive showed a particular taste for Italian arts during his reign. He hired Italian architects and he commissioned an opera by Giuseppe Verdi to mark the opening of the Opera House during the celebrations that inaugurated the Suez Canal in 1869. Although the commissioned work, *Aida*, famously did not premiere in Cairo at the inauguration, the first performance featured another Verdi opera, *Rigoletto*.[3]

Consistent with Isma'il's reputation as a modernizer and Westernizer, the statue was placed in the heart of Alexandria's commercial center, adjacent to Manshiyah Square between the French Gardens and the sea. Elevated on a marble plinth, the statue was backed by a grandiose semi-circular marble colonnade in the idiom of Italian fascist architecture.[4] The statue stood with its back to the statue of Mehmed Ali on the other end of the French Gardens, which Isma'il himself had commissioned in 1868.[5] Isma'il's likeness faced instead toward the Mediterranean, to symbolize "Egypt turned toward the West."[6]

The unveiling of the statue by the Italian community of Alexandria had originally been set for 1935, during Fu'ad's reign, but was postponed because of the Italo–Ethiopian war.[7] The delay of the unveiling was unfortunate. Fu'ad died in 1936, so his son and successor, King Farouk, was the ruler present at the statue's dedication.[8] More significantly, between the original planned inauguration in 1935 and the unveiling in 1938, the Italian community in Alexandria—of which a significant proportion were Jewish[9]—had undergone a series of divisive shocks, particularly Italy's 1936 pact with Germany and its implementation of anti-Semitic laws in 1938.[10] Anouchka Lazarev notes that the timing of the gift intended to celebrate the symbiosis between Egypt and Europe is additionally steeped in irony; a year earlier the Montreux convention had repealed the Capitulations that underpinned the system of privileges granted to European residents of Egypt and set a timetable for the abolition of the Mixed Courts that Isma'il had implemented during his reign.[11]

In 1966, 14 years after the Free Officer's Revolt deposed the last of the hereditary line of rulers from which Isma'il issued, his statue was removed from its plinth. In contrast to the Italians' rosy view of the Khedive, Egyptian nationalists recall Isma'il's financial ineptitude, which brought about Egypt's increasing dependence on the West. When Isma'il ascended to power in 1863, he inherited an internationally financed national debt of three million pounds that the treasury had accrued under his predecessor Sa'id to finance the construction on the Suez Canal. During his reign, Isma'il continued borrowing from European financiers. In 1875, to avert a bankruptcy crisis, Isma'il sold Egypt's shares of the Suez Canal Company to the British government. This act drew Great Britain into Egypt's financial affairs, and is considered a stepping stone to British domination of Egypt. Isma'il was deposed by the Ottoman Sultan in 1879 under pressure from the British and French governments. Three years later Great Britain asserted its desired control by invading Egypt and holding the country under military occupation.

It is not uncommon, of course, for revolutionary regimes to topple the statues of former rulers. However, the fate of Isma'il's statue could be said to encapsulate not just the changing ideologies of the state, but also the changing perception of the country's cosmopolitan past. In the years between the fall of the monarchy and the removal of Isma'il's statue, the majority of Egypt's foreign minority communities had emigrated. According to the refigured national narrative of the new regime, Alexandria's cosmopolitanism was equated with the excesses of the bad old days of foreign domination. From the renaming of streets to the removal of statues of discredited former rulers, Alexandria's public face was made to conform to the new ideologies of the state. Institutions, monuments, and buildings that reflected the colonial-cosmopolitan era were neglected.[12] Alexandria was transformed from cosmopolis to regional capital. The foreign minorities who had once resided in Alexandria, if recalled at all, were cast as compradors to colonial interests.

Once the statue was removed, the plinth and colonnade were recycled into a national monument more in keeping with the new ideologies of state—the tomb of the Unknown Naval Soldier (Figure 2.1).[13] As Benedict Anderson asserts, "no more arresting emblems of the modern culture of nationalism exists than cenotaphs and tombs of Unknown Soldiers."[14] Both monuments—the statue and the memorial—represent articulations of nationalism and visions of the nation. Representing a former ruler, the statue stood not only as a reminder of the nation's history, but also reflected a vision of the nation that accepted the multiple affiliations represented by the Italian Alexandrian community. The tomb, by contrast, privileges military memorialization over civilian memory—patriotism over pluralism.

For 32 years, Isma'il's statue sat unceremoniously on the grounds of the Husayn Subhi Museum of Fine Arts in Alexandria. In 1998, at the initiative of the newly appointed governor of Alexandria, 'Abd al-Salam Mahjub, the statue of Isma'il

Figure 2.1 Tomb of the Unknown Naval Soldier, Alexandria.
Source: Photographed by the author

was re-installed in central Alexandria.[15] The reappearance of the statue is not an anachronistic expression of royalist sympathies, but rather an act of restoring honor to the past—royal, colonial and cosmopolitan—that must be understood in the context of the transformation Alexandria experienced in the late 1990s.

Following the change in leadership of the Alexandria Governate in 1997, and in preparation for the opening of the Bibliotheca Alexandrina, the city underwent a facelift. Much of the renovation effort was aimed at restoring the built environment of the colonial cosmopolitan era, and recuperating the look, if not the feel, of Alexandria's modern cosmopolitan past.[16] These efforts were in part motivated by the city's desire to transform itself into a tourist destination. Lacking the dramatic ancient artifacts of Giza and Luxor, Alexandria has pinned its marketing effort on nostalgia for the lost cosmopolitan past—anchored by the library on the one hand, and the literary city of E. M. Forster, C. P. Cavafy, and Lawrence Durrell on the other. Ismaʿil's statue represents a cosmopolitan era artifact. Although it was too politically explosive to return the statue to its original place, its restoration reflects the Governate's interest in returning visibility to Alexandria's cosmopolitan past.

In 1999, one year after Ismaʿil's statue was re-installed, the remaining Greek community of Egypt, in conjunction with the Egyptian Greek diaspora and the Greek Patriarchate of Alexandria, presented the city with a statue of Alexander the Great mounted on his horse Boucephalus.[17] The Governate commissioned a local architect committed to the preservation and revitalization of Alexandria's cosmopolitan past, Mohammed Awad, to design and landscape the square in which it was to be placed.

The plan raised the hackles of a number of public figures, spurring a debate in the newspapers. Some objected to the installation of the statue on the basis that Alexander was, in effect, the harbinger of "foreign rule" that had dominated Egypt, in one form or another, until the 1952 revolution. Even more galling was that the statue of Alexander was to be placed in a square previously named for a national military hero, 'Abd al-Mun'im Riyad. Riyad, a Lieutenant General, who served in the 1948 and 1967 Arab Israeli wars as well as the 1956 Suez conflict, was killed in combat during the War of Attrition with Israel. One journalist summed up the opposition to the proposed square in his newspaper column: "Isn't it enough that the entire city bears Alexander's name even though he was a conqueror and an imperialist? Wouldn't it be more proper to install a statue of an Egyptian hero like 'Abd al-Mun'im Riyad or even of an Egyptian writer, thinker, literary personality or artist?"[18]

Once the statue of Alexander had been installed, there was further dissent. The designers of the plaza included two artifacts from the collection of the Greco-Roman Museum in Alexandria—a column and a small sphinx. Together these relics were intended to represent the cultures unified under the Ptolemaic dynasty founded by Alexander's leading general. The sphinx was placed on a low, polished granite slab in front of the elevated platform upon which the statue of Alexander sits, while the column stands behind the statue to the right (Figure 2.2). The unveiling of the layout once again incensed opponents who saw Alexander's horse poised to step on the sphinx—the foreign conqueror trampling on their Egyptian heritage.[19]

In the aftermath of the public outcry, Riyad, whose name was already affixed to streets or squares in many Egyptian cities, was honored with his own statue in the square named after him in Cairo, a major transportation hub in the shadow of elevated highways and a tangle of ramps situated behind the Egyptian Museum (Figure 2.3). Riyad's statue in Cairo was dedicated in July 2002 during a week of national celebrations marking the 50th anniversary of the Revolution. The statue of Alexander was officially dedicated in October 2002 in conjunction with the festivities surrounding the opening of the Bibliotheca Alexandrina. The inauguration of each of these statues of military men represents a distinct act of memorialization that reflects its own vision of the nation's past. The statue of Riyad, not unlike the Tomb of the Unknown Naval Soldier, valorizes the modern military from whose ranks Egyptian presidents have emerged since 1952. The statue of Alexander, like the Bibliotheca Alexandrina, reflects a desire to recuperate memories of the city's cosmopolitan past.

While the opposition to Alexander's statue and its placement explicitly addresses the Macedonian's legacy as both conqueror and founder, the debate also implicitly resists a belated act by the dwindling Egyptian Greek community to inscribe itself on the public face of the city. The dispute also signals that Egypt's cosmopolitan past remains contested on the grounds of its implicit colonial legacy. The narratives of this past, despite the official revival of interest in the cosmopolitan built

Figure 2.2 Statue of Alexander the Great, Alexandria.
Source: Photographed by the author

environment, continue to pose a challenge to the integrity of the Egyptian national imaginary.

In this chapter I map the depiction of Alexandria in literature to understand the multiple, often conflicting valences attached to Alexandria's cosmopolitan past. I begin by briefly discussing the myth of cosmopolitan Alexandria perpetuated by literature in Western languages from Plutarch to Lawrence Durrell. Many literary works about cosmopolitan Alexandria in European languages are unmoored from the physical spaces of Alexandria and detached from the realities of the Egyptians living there. As Robert Mabro notes, one would get the impression from this literature that the city was almost exclusively populated by foreigners and the occasional Westernized Copt or Egyptian Jew, even though Egyptians significantly outnumbered foreigners in the city throughout the entire period.[20]

In the second section, I turn my attention to the representation of Alexandria in Egyptian Arabic cultural production. This literary Alexandria contributes to the formation of the Egyptian national imaginary—initially reflecting the pluralist idiom of the day, and later affecting a nationalization and domestication of Alexandria's image. In the 1990s Egyptian writers rediscovered Alexandria's cosmopolitan past. Although the trend toward a re-investigation of Cosmopolitan Alexandria began in the years after the announcement of the plans to build the new library, and took root simultaneously with the renovation efforts in the city, this body of literature diverges from the commercialized nostalgia perpetuated by the Alexandria Governate. Unlike the marketing plan of the Governate—which consisted of symbolic, restorative gestures like installing statues and whitewashing facades—these texts challenge both Western literary memory of Alexandria

Figure 2.3 Statue of ʿAbd al-Munʿim Riyaḍ, Cairo.
Source: Photographed by the author

and embrace pluralist nationalism. Several of these texts also explicitly explore the dialectical relationship between cosmopolitanism and colonialism.

Literary Alexandria ad Ægyptum

The image of Alexandria as a cosmopolitan space in which people and cultures come into contact has been immortalized, shaped and mediated by its literary legacy. The founding myths of Alexandria lay out the terms that came to define the city and shape its representation in the cultural imaginary: cosmopolis, empire, and literature. Alexandria was founded by Alexander the Great in 331 BCE to celebrate the conquests that had unified the ancient world. In Plutarch's version of events, flour used to mark the boundaries of the "large and populous city" that was to serve as a "colony of Grecians" was eaten by an "infinite number of great birds of several kinds," an omen that the oracles interpreted to mean that the city "would not only abound in all things within itself, but also be the nurse and feeder of many nations."[21]

According to Plutarch's sources, Alexander was also a great lover of "all kinds of learning and reading, and Onesicritus informs us that he constantly laid Homer's *Iliad* … with his dagger under his pillow, declaring that he esteemed it a perfect portable treasure of all military virtue and knowledge."[22] This text of "all knowledge" ultimately leads Alexander to the future site of the city, a locale that "had neither an important past nor an abundant supply of good water to recommend it."[23] Rejecting the work of the "best architects"[24] who had already laid out the plans of the city elsewhere, Alexander instead followed the advice of Homer who had been "neither an idle nor an unprofitable companion to him during his expedition,"[25] and who turned out to be "besides his other excellences, ... a very good architect."[26] Homer appeared to Alexander in a dream, reciting from the *Odyssey* (IV), "An island lies, where loud the billows roar, / Pharos they call it, on the Egyptian shore."[27] That island became the site of Alexander's city.

Plutarch's narrative lays out the terms that shape the city's representation in the cultural imaginary: cosmopolis, universal knowledge, empire, and literature. In this narrative, literature plays a role in the founding of Alexandria, and serves to inscribe and perpetuate the myth of the cosmopolitan city.

Literature has also played an important role in creating, disseminating and immortalizing the image of Alexandria as a cosmopolis in the modern era. Alexandria is described by one reader of the city's Western cosmopolitan literature as "elegant," "glamorous and exciting,"[28] whereas another refers to it as "an out-planting of European civilization growing luxuriantly on the coast of Africa."[29] The city's long history of rich cultural interaction and literary production fed the imaginations of inhabitants of the modern city. Writers such as Constantine Cavafy, E. M. Forster, and Giuseppe Ungaretti produced their works about the city from within Alexandrian cosmopolitan society. Others like Lawrence Durrell, Fausta Cialente, Stratis Tsirkas, Robert Solé, André Aciman, Henri el-Kayem, and Harry Tsalas wrote about Alexandria from afar, mostly after the cosmopolitan era had ended.[30]

Lawrence Durrell is the author whose work has done the most to create and perpetuate the myth of Cosmopolitan Alexandria—Alexandria as "the capital of memory."[31] Yet, the note with which Durrell opens his novel *Justine*, the first installment of the *Alexandria Quartet*, represents a subtle act of deception. He writes: "The characters in this novel ... are all inventions together with the personality of the narrator, and bear no resemblance to living persons. Only the city is real."[32] We need not take him at his word. His Alexandria, constructed of language and image, is also an invention, one that has proven to be very durable. In his elegy to a lost city, as in the nostalgia literature that follows in its footsteps, memory, Mnemosyne, the mother of the Muses, spawns creativity, mimesis, representations of reality, but says nothing of the nature of "reality," nor, for that matter, of the "real" city.

One could say, then, that modern Cosmopolitan Alexandria is a chimera, an imaginary construct, a myth created and perpetuated in text. The Chimera of Greek mythology was a three-headed monster with features of a lion, a serpent, and a goat. According to Hesiod and later sources, she was slain by Bellerophon riding on the winged horse Pegasus.[33] In the medieval imaginary, she became a symbolic representation of evil, a trope reproduced in the Freudian interpretations of the myth. In modern parlance, "chimera" has become a generalized concept, taking on two different meanings, each deriving from the ancient myth, although neither has much to do with the monster herself. The most familiar, of course, is that of an imaginary construct, "a mere wild fancy," "an unfounded conception."[34] In biology, particularly plant biology, it refers to genetically different organisms coexisting, like what happens when the buds of one plant are grafted onto the roots of another.

Metaphorically, modern Cosmopolitan Alexandria is all of these things. She is an imaginary construct, a living city always in motion, portrayed as a whole entity comprising various unassimilated parts. She is not a hybrid, although through her wiles she is said to "corrupt" and "pervert." She is rather a patchwork of incongruities, made up of parts that never lose their distinctive character even as they are incorporated into a single (perhaps even monstrous) whole.

Through the ages, as a cosmopolis, Alexandria is viewed as fostering an unnatural grafting of one culture onto another. Conservative elements and cultural purists find this sort of cultural promiscuity threatening. In Jewish thought, Alexandria is first and foremost associated with the Septuagint, the much mythologized translation of the *Tanakh* into Greek—a text viewed by the Rabbis with some wariness as a symbol of the dangers of Hellinization and Christianity alike.

Alexandria also engenders sexual and cultural multiplicity. As Durrell writes:

> Five races, five languages, a dozen creeds: five fleets turning through their greasy reflections behind the harbour bar. But there are more than five sexes and only demotic Greek seems to distinguish among them. The sexual provender which lies to hand is staggering in its variety and profusion.[35]

Alexandria, like the Chimera, is gendered female, ascribed with evil intent. In the Egyptian nationalist re-telling of her downfall, she is the foreign seductress slain by the lance of the phallic state. For others, her seductive gaze, which had penetrated the smoke and flames that emanated from her mouth, persisted in memory long after her body—the cosmopolitan imaginary, not the city itself—had grown cold. After her demise the balladeers immortalized both the Chimera and her slayer, Bellerophon, in their verses.

Eglal Errera writes, "The myth of Alexandria, as served up by literature, so essentially nostalgic, could be just this: the continually renewed epitaph on a tomb that one refuses to seal."[36] Alexandria's mythology stands somewhat at odds with the city writers such as Forster and Durrell encountered and wrote about with disdain in both private correspondence and published work.[37] As Khaled Fahmy has extensively documented, representations of Alexandria in Western travel literature, correspondence and *belles lettres* during the city's supposed prime uniformly described the city's woeful state, bemoaning its decline. In other words, Western visitors to Alexandria view the city's condition as deterioration from some presumed past splendor.[38]

Alexandrian French historian Robert Ilbert sums up the import of Alexandria's cosmopolitan myth and its literary legacy as follows:

> From beach cabins to business to political combat, Alexandria speaks of a Mediterranean where everything was possible, frontiers counted for little and movement was unhampered; and all this goes some way to explaining the presence of an Alexandrian myth. This myth tells us nothing of Egypt but presents

another face of our own world, albeit a face beautifully distorted, thanks to literature, into that of an almost ideal town.[39]

In his articulation the myth "tells us nothing of Egypt." Rather, his vision, one shared by much non-Arabic literature of Alexandria, "presents another face of *our own world*." But what face, then, does Alexandria present of Egypt?

Literary Alexandria in Egypt

For Egyptians, modern Alexandria is an important site in the national, anti-colonial struggle. Alexandria served as the port of entry for both the French Expedition under Napoleon in 1798, and for the British occupying force following their bombardment of the city in 1882. The Revolution of 1919 was sparked by a popular demonstration in Alexandria. On July 26, 1952, King Farouk signed his abdication papers in Ras al-Tin Palace, and set sail from the port in his private yacht. Four years later Gamal Abdel Nasser announced the nationalization of the Suez Canal during a speech delivered in Manshiyah Square.

A number of important Egyptian Arab writers and artists who produced their work prior to the Revolution also issued from Alexandria's cosmopolitan society. Egyptian literary and cultural production of Alexandria during the first half of the twentieth century contributed to the creation of a modern Egyptian national imaginary. For example, the painter Muhammad Naji (1888–1956), who completed his education in France and circulated in Alexandria's Levantine society, was also deeply committed to the ideals of the 1919 Revolution. His art is dominated by national iconography, particularly in the pharaonic idiom of the day. One notable exception is his mural "The School of Alexandria" in the main hall of the Governate of Alexandria, "a monumental celebration of the rich amalgam of religious and cultural traditions to which modern Egypt is heir," which includes representations of Cavafy and the Italian poet Giuseppe Ungaretti on the "European" side of the frame.[40] Another notable artist of his class and generation from Alexandria was Mahmud Sa'id (1897–1964), a lawyer and jurist in the Mixed Court, who is perhaps most famous for his portraits of Egyptian women. Although his style shows European expressionist influences, he painted Egyptian subjects. The celebrated colloquial Arabic poet, Bayram al-Tunisi (1893–1961), who represents the other end of the socio-economic and artistic spectrum, reflects another face of Alexandrian cosmopolitanism. A descendant of an immigrant from Tunisia, al-Tunisi was raised among the fishermen and petty merchants in the Anfushi district. His poetry in the years following the First World War expressed resentment of the European privilege in his city, anti-colonial sentiment, and criticism of political and religious figureheads too closely allied with the British. Because of his political poetry he was exiled from Egypt from 1919 to 1938.[41] Although all three artists are products of cosmopolitan Alexandrian society, their works share a predominantly nationalist discursive frame—even when, in the case of Naji, the work acknowledges the nation's cultural indebtedness to European civilization. These divergent works represent a nationalism inflected with the pluralist ideals of the 1919 Revolution. Nevertheless, the Egyptian cast of their cultural production, and their vision of creating a modern national imaginary, distinguish them from their contemporaries writing in European languages.

In the years following the 1956 Suez conflict, foreign minorities began leaving Egypt in large numbers. The cosmopolitan society immortalized by Western literature disappeared. Within Egypt, as the national government consolidated its power in Cairo in the 1950s and 60s, Alexandria, along with its literary caché, declined in relative importance to the capital. Egyptian writers and artists flocked to Cairo. Shortly after the Suez conflict, President Gamal Abdel Nasser established the Supreme Council on Arts and Letters (*al-majlis al-a'la li-ri'ayat al-funun w-al-adab*), currently known as the Supreme Council of Culture (*al-majlis al-a'la lil-thiqafa*). In 1958 he established the Ministry of Culture. According to Richard Jacquemond, these institutions "assured the control and mobilization of intellectuals," granting the state a "virtual monopoly" over cultural production.[42]

During this period, the few Arabic literary representations of Alexandria attempt to figure an independent Alexandrian identity, or, rather, an Alexandrian identity of independence. For example, Naguib Mahfouz's *Autumn Quail* [*Al-Summan wa al-kharif*] (1962)[43] narrates the decline of a Wafd party functionary who holds a high level civil service job on the eve of the Revolution, and becomes an unemployed loafer after he is dismissed on grounds of corruption. Also, the novel simultaneously tracks the downgrading of Alexandria from the effective seat of government during the summer months prior to the revolution, to a sleepy place of refuge by the late 1950s. On the day of the military putsch in July 1952, 'Isa, the protagonist, travels to Alexandria to discuss matters with a party leader. By the end of the novel Alexandria, even in the summer, functions as a site of a-social, a-political refuge. 'Isa escapes there with his wife to remove himself from the social temptation to gamble with his friends, and to delay further his job search.

Shortly after his dismissal from the government post, 'Isa flees in shame from Cairo to the anonymity of Alexandria. Alexandria becomes the site of 'Isa's moral fall from grace, which accompanies his social and economic decline in the wake of the Revolution. Throughout the section of the book devoted to 'Isa's self-imposed exile in Alexandria, the city of refuge is associated with sex and death, or sex as death. The chapter announcing 'Isa's relocation to Alexandria begins, "Everything seemed to promise a deathlike repose."[44] In the course of his stay he solicits the services of a prostitute, Riri, who convinces him to let her live with him in his apartment for the duration of the winter.

The fleshpots of Alexandria are portrayed as a remnant of the city's colonial-cosmopolitan past. 'Isa completes his self-imposed exile by renting a furnished apartment in al-Ibrahimiyya, a predominantly Greek neighborhood. There he counts himself among the "strangers in a strange land."[45] Although Riri, the prostitute, is Egyptian, the proprietress of the café from which she operates is a Greek who "opened her café on [British] money."[46] It is in the midst of "foreigners," thus, although not through their direct influence, that 'Isa loses his moral grounding.

By the end of the novel 'Isa agrees to be normalized to the new Egypt—signaled by a return to Cairo, a return to employment, and a return to socially sanctioned domestic life. In the final scene 'Isa, steps out from the Wafdist shadow of Saʿad Zaghlul's statue in central Alexandria into the light of a new day, pursuing a figure of the future, the opportunity for a new beginning.

Alexandria, too, has changed. When ʿIsa returns some years after the 1956 Suez Conflict there is no mention of foreigners, or the establishments that bear their stamp. Even Riri, whom ʿIsa discovers running a cafe, has found legitimacy through marriage. Riri's husband has accepted her daughter, the product of her liaison with ʿIsa, as his own. Her past, like that of the city, has been quietly repressed through domestication.

Greek waiters, bartenders and pension owners continue to appear in Egyptian literature and film through the 1960s and 1970s. Their presence as lone figures fulfilling stereotyped roles throws into relief the dominant figurations of the postcolonial, ethno-linguistically defined nation. Naguib Mahfouz's 1967 novel *Miramar* offers one prominent example.[47] Set in a pension in the harbor city, the characters of *Miramar* are often read as representatives of different classes and ideologies within the new Egyptian order, reflecting the deep divisions in Egyptian society.[48] The tired, aging Greek mistress of the house, Madame Mariana, represents the dwindling foreign community, flattening its former diversity into one figure. Mariana is a faded reminder, like the hotel itself, of the excesses of a bygone era, and of the literary valorization of its perceived glories.[49]

The rift between the Western Alexandrian myth and Alexandria of the Egyptian imaginary widens following the 1967 Arab–Israeli war. A collection of short stories published in November 1967 entitled *Alexandrian Stories on the Battlefield* [*Qisas sakandariyya fi al-maʿraka*] asserts a militant, activist, and politically engaged Arab Alexandria, opposed to "colonialism, imperialism, and world Zionism in various political, economic, and cultural arenas."[50] Its sentiments of national and pan-Arab solidarity are framed by a situated localness of civic pride. The volume's contributors offer local articulations of shared national and pan-Arab rage.

The introduction to the volume traces the development of the community of Arabic literati in Alexandria. In their estimation, literary salons sponsored by the Association Egypte–Europe founded in 1932 fostered Arabic literary production in the city.[51] The editors seem to miss the irony of valorizing a culture of cooperation in a militantly anti-colonial text. With the dissolution of the association Egypte–Europe, literature in Alexandria becomes both discursively and structurally a national enterprise, marked by the increased governmental promotion of and support for networks of local writers' associations across the country.

Many writers and artists from Alexandria relocated to Cairo in search of intellectual community. Those who stayed in Alexandria, and in the other regions outside of Cairo, received recognition—and supervision—from the state with the establishment of local "cultural palaces" under the oversight of the General Organization of Cultural Palaces (*al-hayʾa al-ʿamma li-qusur al-thiqafah*) in 1969. Nevertheless, Cairo continued to set the tone—both artistically and administratively—for regional cultural production.[52] One product of this re-assertion of regional identity can be found in an Alexandrian literary and intellectual journal, *Waves* [*Amwaj*], founded in 1976 and published irregularly until 1986. The journal reflected a continued attempt to assert an alternative Alexandrian cultural identity by encouraging local literary production and investigating Alexandria's Arab Islamic literary and cultural heritage. Throughout its ten-year run, *Waves* published a single article about a non-Arabophone Alexandrian writer—a study of Greek poet Cavafy. The framing of this piece demonstrates the obscurity into which his work had fallen in Egyptian literary circles.[53]

Other works produced in the 1980s and 1990s privilege representations of Alexandria as a space for articulation of the national struggle. For example, 'Abd al-Fattah Rizq situates his 1984 novel, *Alexandria 47* [*Iskandariyya 47*] between the 'Urabi rebellion, and the dissolution in 1949 of the Mixed Courts under which foreigners in Egypt were granted legal privileges.[54] Jamil 'Atiya Ibrahim's 1997 novel, *Alexandria Papers* [*Awraq sakandariyya*], an installment in a series of works of historical fiction, narrates the events of the 1919 revolution.[55] An unstated subtext of these assertions of Alexandria's place in the national struggle is the negation of a cosmopolitanism that threatens national integrity.

However, in the 1990s Egyptian representations of Alexandria began to shift away from nationalist characterizations toward an exploration of the city as a cosmopolitan site.[56] In 1996 Muhammad Jubril, who had already written numerous fictional works set in the Alexandrian fishing neighborhood of Bahri, published *The Other Shore* [*al-Shati' al-akhar*],[57] a novel that portrays "warm relations that connect Greeks to the Egyptian people."[58] In 1997 Egyptian TV broadcast the first series of "Zizinia," a dramatic serial set in Alexandria during the Second World War. Written by Usama Anwar 'Ukasha, "Zizinia" explores the origins of Egyptian identity through its relations with resident foreign communities on the one hand and the foreign powers on the other.[59] In 1999 poet 'Ala Khalid founded the journal *Places* [*Amkinah*], which has published multivalent oral histories of the city.[60] In 2002 Jamal al-Qusas published a volume of poetry entitled *Alexandria: A Poetic Quartet* [*al-Iskandariyya: ruba'iyya shi'riyya*], in a clear nod to Durrell's famed novelistic quartet.[61]

This interest in the cosmopolitan past was also reflected in the number of translations in the 1990s of works by Western Alexandrian writers including Cavafy's entire *oeuvre*, Stratis Tsirkas's *Drifting Cities,* Lawrence Durrell's *Alexandria Quartet*,[62] and E. M. Forster's *Alexandria, A History and Guide*.[63] In 1998 excerpts of a previously unpublished memoir by a Swiss woman, Esther Zimmerli Hardman, who was raised in Alexandria, were translated from German into Arabic.[64] During this same period, the Arabic literary and cultural journals *Creativity* [*Ibda '*][65] and *Cairo* [*al-Qahira*][66] each published a special issue on Egyptian Francophone writers.

Some of the Francophone writers included in pages of these literary journals had lived in Cairo, as do many of the writers and translators involved in reviving interest in Egypt's cosmopolitan past. During the colonial-cosmopolitan era Cairo was, like Alexandria, home to a sizeable foreign minority community. Thanks to Khedive Isma'il's construction efforts, the heart of modern Cairo bears the imprint of Italian architects. However, the cultural memory of Cairo, the Muslim-founded capital city, is not as heavily laden with cosmopolitan imaginary as is Alexandria. Nevertheless, during the same period in which Alexandria's cosmopolitan heritage has received increasing attention in Egyptian letters, there has been a similar, if somewhat more modest, revival of interest in the influence of foreigners and minority communities in Cairo as well. Among the earliest such efforts, beginning to appear in the mid-1990s, are works by Anglophone writers published in Egypt that aim to record Cairo's modern history and that call for the preservation of its built environment.[67] Chief among those recording and disseminating Cairo's cosmopolitan history is Samir Raafat, who published two books on the topic beginning in 1995: *Maadi 1904–1962: Society and History in a Cairo Suburb*,[68] and *Cairo, the Glory Years*[69] a collection of essays many of which previously appeared in the Egyptian press. In 1999 the American University in Cairo Press published another text that documents Cairo's colonial-cosmopolitan built environment: Cynthia Myntti's *Paris along the Nile: Architecture in Cairo from the Belle Epoque*.[70]

Nostalgic representations of Cairo's colonial-cosmopolitan past have appeared regularly in works published by Egyptians abroad such as Leila Ahmed's 1999 memoir *A Border Passage*[71] and Samia Serageldin's novel *The Cairo House* published in 2000.[72] Cairo also features prominently in memoirs by members of the city's former foreign-minority communities as well, including Edward Said's *Out of Place*[73] and Lucette Lagnado's *Man in the White Sharkskin Suit*.[74]

However, at the time of writing, within Egyptian Arabic literature, reflections of Egypt's cosmopolitan past have been dominated by narratives set in Alexandria rather than Cairo, with one notable exception, 'Ala' al-Aswani's high-profile popular novel *Yacoubian Building* [*'Imarat Ya'qubiyan*] (2002).[75] In the novel, the architectural history of Cairo's downtown district serves as the central metaphor of Egypt's cultural change in the twentieth century. The novel's melodramatic plot lines ripped from Egyptian popular media, its voyeuristic glimpse at the sexual lives of the characters, and its frustration with rampant corruption struck a chord with the Egyptian readership. The novel achieved a level of popularity generally not enjoyed by works of literature.[76]

The novel relates Egypt's economic and social history through the Yacoubian building's history. When the building, financed by an Armenian millionaire and constructed by an Italian firm, opened its doors in 1934, the address on Sulaiman Pasha Street (now Ta'alat Harb Street) was very fashionable, attracting, "the cream of society," "ministers, big land-owning pashas, foreign manufacturers and two Jewish millionaires."[77] Following the revolution, "the exodus of Jews and foreigners from Egypt started and every apartment that was vacated by reason of the departure of its owners was taken over by an officer of the armed forces, who were the influential people of the time."[78] Metal storage lockers on the roof were converted into rooms for the servants, generally poor immigrants from the Egyptian hinterland. The composition of the building's residents underwent further transformation following the Open Door policy of the 1970s. As the wealthy classes moved out of central Cairo to newer, more fashionable suburbs, many apartments were converted into offices. Also, as the rooms on the roof changed hands, the ties between the two classes of the buildings' residents were severed.

Although the novel relies on the building as a metaphor for the changes undergone by Egyptian society, it does not relegate the impact of the cosmopolitan era to the city's architectural relics. Several principal characters are defined by their relationship to Egypt's past: Hatim Rashid, who serves as the editor-in-chief of the Francophone newspaper *Le Caire*, is the son of an Egyptian father, who was a jurist and former dean of the College of Law, and a French mother; Zaki Bey al-Disuqi, the son of a former Pasha, is an aging, French-educated engineer who under the new order refused to pay out bribes for contracts and is therefore relegated to living on family money; and Madame Christine Nicholas, an Egyptian Greek, owns Maxim's, a European-style café-bar.[79]

In contrast, Buthaina and Taha, young adults who grew up in the building's roof dwellings, represent the impoverished, post-cosmopolitan generation who account for the majority of Egypt's population in the early 1990s when the novel is set. The two had been childhood sweethearts. Over the course of the novel their romance flags after Buthaina is forced into the workplace following her father's sudden death, and after the academically accomplished Taha is rejected by the police academy because his father is a lowly doorman. Buthaina, subjected to demeaning sexual advances by her supervisors at a series of short-lived jobs, ultimately learns how to manipulate the system to her advantage. However, both her shame and her cynicism begin to affect her interactions with Taha. Meanwhile Taha, frustrated by the classism and corruption he encountered during his interview at the police academy, and alienated by the privileged students he meets at the university, finds increasing solace in religion, which also drives a wedge between the lovers. Taha falls in with a crowd of other poor students at the university mosque who ultimately introduce him to Sheikh Muhammad Shakir, a voice of radical Islam in Egypt. Thus begins Taha's transformation from boy-next-door to *jihadi*.

The central concern of the novel, to which the various subplots return again and again, is corruption in all its forms—moral decay that plays out in and around the decaying structure of the Yacoubian building itself. The narrative presents repeated incidents of the use of sex for power and sex for money. Both Malik, the Coptic tailor who insinuates himself into a room on the roof, and Dawlat, Zaki's sister, succeed in, at least temporarily, manipulating the legal system to their advantage through bribes and duplicity. However, the most striking examples of corruption implicate the government and its officers. Taha understands that a well-placed bribe would have secured his acceptance into the police academy. Haj Muhammad 'Azzam pays a hefty sum to buy a seat in rigged Parliamentary elections, and then must continue to pay off his superiors—indeed the novel implies that corruption goes all the way to the top of the executive branch—under threat of exposure of his involvement in the illicit drug trade.[80] Upon the outbreak of the Gulf War in 1991 'Azzam's powerful spiritual advisor, Sheikh al-Samman, is trotted out by the government to "explain the legal justification for the war to liberate Kuwait."[81]

In response to corruption and the resultant economic and social stagnation, in the novel the anti-government Islamists appear to claim the moral high ground. In contrast to the other characters in the novel, the Islamists are treated with a certain amount of respect. Throughout the novel the narrator frequently adopts a moralizing tone, passing judgment on the characters' behavior. For example, in addition to repeatedly referring to Hatim's homosexuality as "sinful" (*ithm*),[82] the narrator at one point describes the journalist's facial expression as "that miserable, unpleasant, mysterious, gloomy look that always haunts the faces of homosexuals."[83] Elsewhere the narrator adopts a cynical tone in his description of Kamal al-Fuli's corrupt ways, noting that while the lawmaker's "authentic talent … like so many talents in Egypt, has been diverted, distorted, and adulterated by lying, hypocrisy, and intrigue till [his] name … has come to represent in the minds of Egyptians the very essence of corruption and hypocrisy."[84] By contrast, the judgmental narrative voice is suspended in the passages describing the Islamist movement. Sheikh Shakir's appearance, a "face not without certain good looks, and wide, impressive, honey-colored eyes" is coupled with his upstanding comportment. He displays concern for his disciples' well-being: "he knew most of the students crowding around him, and shook their hands and embraced them, asking them how they were."[85]

Nevertheless, there are ruptures in the façade of purity that pervades the representation of the Islamic movement. Later in the novel Sheikh Shakir incites these same students to engage in illegal protests, knowing that many of them would be apprehended and tortured in prison. Upon their release, it is these broken souls, like Taha, who embrace the movement's militarist goals. As Sheikh Shakir points out, Taha's motives for joining *jihad* are somewhat suspect and impractical—he seeks personal revenge on the officer who tortured him.[86] Ultimately, on his first mission Taha's personal goals supersede that of the collective. When confronted with his torturer, Taha snaps, tipping off his target's security detail to the planned attack. The mission fails and Taha is killed in the process. Thus, the dead-end future proposed by the Islamist option is, as seen through Taha's experience, at least as bleak as the options provided to the other characters whose resistance to the everyday injustices of Egyptian society is less radical or violent.

By way of contrast, the final chapter of the novel maps out a path of hope for Egypt's future. After her various frustrating employment experiences, Buthaina is set up by Malak to serve as Zaki's secretary with the understanding that she would use her wiles to get him to sign away his apartment. When Buthaina, having fallen in love with Zaki, refuses to double cross him, Malak in consort with Zaki's sister, exposes their illicit affair. However, in the end Zaki, the 65-year-old descendent of the old ruling class, honorably marries Buthaina, the dewy maiden, a woman of the people. Their wedding ceremony held in Maxim's with guests from all walks of Egyptian society, also depicts the integration of the worlds they represent. As the party progresses, the barriers begin to fall: "The roof people were awe-struck at the poshness of the restaurant and its old European style but little by little the women started to break through this by means of mirthful conversations on the side and loud bursts of laughter."[87] After Madame Christine plays "La Vie en Rose" the crowd demands that the band play Arabic music, and the guests begin to dance. The final sentence of the novel expresses Zaki's embrace of Egyptian popular dance just as the crowd of roof-dwellers embrace him as one of their own: "Then little by little, raising his arms aloft, [Zaki] joined [Buthaina] in her dance, amidst the joyful laughter and cries of the others."[88] The novel's conclusion can be read as a vision for Egypt's future that requires not only an embrace of Egypt's cosmopolitan history but also a synthesis of the universalist ideals and pluralist nationalism of the old Wafd, as represented by Zaki on the one hand, and the hopes and dreams of Egypt's struggling youth, as represented by Buthaina on the other. Put another way, the novel proposes turning the eyes of those who wish to emigrate and seek their fortunes in Europe, like Buthaina and her contemporaries, toward the sources of cosmopolitanism within Egypt.

In the discourse of the novel, France is the privileged site of Egypt's cosmopolitan aspirations, past and present. There are traces of the former prevalence of the French language in Egypt such as the continued publication of Hatim's journal, *Le Caire*. Zaki and Dawlat's domestic spat is also peppered with French expressions.[89] European customs are also in evidence; the narrator notes how in years past downtown Cairo would be bedecked with European-style decorations for Christmas and New Year's Eve.[90]

However, unlike in the other texts to be discussed in the coming chapters, in the *Yacoubian Building*, Egyptian cosmopolitanism is largely divorced from its colonial past. Malak's appropriation of space on the roof is likened to the actions of a great colonial power, but the metaphor has little to add to the novel's representation of cosmopolitanism.[91] The only specific mention in the novel of Egypt's colonial history is oblique, buried in Sheikh Shakir's *khutba*: "Islamic law is ignored in our unhappy country and we are governed by French secular law, which permits drunkenness, fornication, and perversion so long as it is by mutual consent."[92] However, this passing reference is offered as a harangue against secular law within a call for the implementation of Islamic law, not an attempt to yoke cosmopolitanism to its colonial roots. Sheikh Shakir's strong anti-colonial sentiments are reserved for more contemporary concerns—the American and Israeli expansionist postures in the Middle East.

However, *Yacoubian Building* points to an important force driving the literary exploration of Egypt's cosmopolitanism. The burgeoning literary interest in Egypt's cosmopolitan past—Alexandrian or Cairene—arose during a period when the liberal institutions of the Egyptian state came under fire from two fronts. First, Islamist politicians and jurists were rising to influential ranks in both the legislative and judicial branches of government, undermining some of the structures of Egyptian civil society,[93] even as militant Islamic nationalists staged violent attacks on state institutions, intellectuals, and Copts.[94] Second, the government was pursuing further liberalization of the economy, which brought with it all the dislocations of neo-colonialism and globalization. The turn toward the "locally and conjecturally"[95] situated cosmopolitanism evident in Egyptian literature of the 1990s signifies a search for "cultivated detachment from restrictive forms of identity"[96]—a reaction against ethno-religious nationalism on the one hand, and homogenizing globalization on the other.

In the three chapters to follow, I investigate at greater length a selection of texts that represent neither the Western nor the Egyptian nationalist representations of Alexandria. These texts acknowledge that the colonial encounter is constitutive both of Alexandrian cosmopolitanism and of its demise. In Chapter 3, I undertake an analysis of the first of such texts—Edwar al-Kharrat's semi-autobiographical novels, *City of Saffron* (*Turabuha za'faran*)[97] and *Girls of Alexandria* (*Ya banat iskandariyya*).[98] In Chapter 4, I discuss two novels by Ibrahim Abdel Meguid's *No One Sleeps in Alexandria* (*La ahad yanam fi al-iskandariyya*)[99] and *Ambergris Birds* (*Tuyur al-'anbar*).[100] In Chapter 5, I explore the cycle of four autobiographical Alexandria films by Youssef Chahine. These works by al-Kharrat, Abdel Meguid, and Chahine assert that cosmopolitanism is inseparable from its imperial pedigree.

3 Poetics of memory
Edwar al-Kharrat

Alexandrian authenticity

The UNESCO-funded quarterly journal, *Diogenes*, published simultaneously in English, French, Spanish, Chinese and Arabic, is dedicated to exploring topics in philosophy and the humanistic sciences. In 2005 the journal published an issue on "Emerging Humanisms," to which the Egyptian novelist, translator and critic Edwar al-Kharrat contributed an article entitled "Cultural Authenticity and National Identity."[1] In this international platform, al-Kharrat stakes out a position for an Arab cultural pluralism that resists both separatism and homogenization.

Of the first term in his title, al-Kharrat argues that in the effort to define and preserve cultural authenticity in the Arab world one must refute "the onslaught of a pseudo-culture proffered by certain ruling sectors of the West that advocate consumerism," while simultaneously resisting "subjugation to ancestral dictates."[2] In contrast to some of the more conservative elements in Arab society, for al-Kharrat, cultural authenticity resides solely in local practices consistent with humanist ideals. He writes, "I would deem as authentic the liberating culture that sees its *raison d'être* in the quest for such values as reason, freedom and justice—no hackneyed concepts, whatever some postmodernists say."[3]

Like his conceptualization of "cultural authenticity," al-Kharrat's understanding of the second term, "national identity," too, appeals to an activist, politically engaged sensibility. National identity—defined as "diversity within unity"—is formed by the aggregation of diverse "subcultural constituents," which nevertheless see their culture as inseparable from common, dominant Arab Islamic culture.[4] Drawing upon these pluralistic principles, he calls for a "universality based on democratic determination, on the respect for individuation, on national and cultural differentiation where heterogeneity and mutual correlations can blend—a process that can dialectically reproduce itself."[5]

Such ideals are clearly evident in al-Kharrat's literary efforts and shape the representation of Alexandria in his poetic autobiographical novels, among the earliest literary expressions of the Egyptian exploration of Alexandria's cosmopolitan past traced in the previous chapter. Al-Kharrat's Alexandria in *City of Saffron* [*Turabuha za'faran*] (1985)[6] and *Girls of Alexandria* [*Ya banat iskandariyya*] (1990)[7] is populated by mostly working-class individuals from a diverse array of ethno-linguistic and religious groups. As for the struggle for liberty and freedom underpinning his conceptualization of both "cultural authenticity" and "national identity," the works' Coptic narrator and protagonist, Mikha'il, embraces Communism and joins the struggle against colonialism.

Al-Kharrat also sees his literary works as offering a "culturally authentic" corrective to the distortions perpetuated by Lawrence Durrell in the *Alexandria Quartet*. In a 1994 essay that serves as an introduction to *Iskandariyyati* [*My Alexandria*],[8] a volume identified as a "novelistic collage," al-Kharrat clearly outlines the ideological underpinnings of his literary efforts. For al-Kharrat, a text's authenticity derives in part from its relationship to place. In al-Kharrat's writings Alexandria is portrayed as a dream-place (*al-mawqi'-al-hilm*) filtered through, indeed, authenticated by personal experience.[9] Unlike other Arabic authors whom he accuses of treating location as "background décor"—he includes in this category Naguib Mahfouz whose Cairo trilogy is closely associated with the Gamaliyya neighborhood in which it is set—al-Kharrat sees his Alexandria as an integral part of "the novelistic act," not merely a place nor an object of representation.[10]

While Durrell's Alexandria, as al-Kharrat notes, is also filtered through personal experience, that experience is garnered solely in the cafés, homes, and diplomatic missions of the city's European residents. The limited nature of this experience and its foreignness contribute, in al-Kharrat's view, to the *Quartet's* inauthentic representation of the city. In particular, Al-Kharrat takes issue with Durrell's derisive depiction of Alexandria's Arab quarters—the working-class districts that he nostalgically depicts in his own novels. Al-Kharrat draws the reader's attention to two particularly objectionable passages, in which Durrell inexorably links the perceived filth and stench of Arab neighborhoods to base corporeality: in *Justine*, "the strident native quarter" is characterized by its "jabbing lights and flesh-wearing smells,"[11] while in *Clea*, "the earthen streets" of the Arab town are described as "smelling like a freshly dug graveyard" following the rain.[12] This Orientalist vision, evidenced additionally in the stereotypical portrayal of Egyptian characters, furthermore, functions for al-Kharrat as the antithesis of the liberatory politics that must underpin true "cultural authenticity."[13]

Even Durrell's portrayals of Alexandria's diversity draw al-Kharrat's criticism. Take, for example, one such passage from *Balthazar* in which the narrator muses on the city's cosmopolitan nature:

> The city, inhabited by these memories of mine, moves not only backwards into our history, studded by the great names which mark every station of recorded time, but also back and forth in the living present, so to speak— among its contemporary faiths and races; the hundred little spheres which religious or lore creates and which cohere softly together like cells to form the great sprawling jellyfish which is Alexandria today. Joined in this fortuitous way by the city's own act of will, isolated on a slate promontory over the sea, backed only by the moonstone mirror of Mareotis, the salt lake, and its further forevers of ragged desert (now dusted softly by the spring winds into satin dunes, patternless and beautiful as cloudscapes), the communities still

live and communicate—Turks with Jews, Arabs and Copts, and Syrians with Armenians and Italians and Greeks.[14]

Al-Kharrat objects to Durrell's separation of "Copts" from "Arabs" in his list of communities that "still live and communicate" in Alexandria. For al-Kharrat this textual elision—the substitution of "Arabs" for "Muslims"—is evidence of Durrell's remove from local, authentic Egyptian culture. Al-Kharrat, as already noted, insists on authenticity and collective identity deriving from the shared majority culture—an Arab Islamic culture with which Muslims, Christians and Jews alike identify. Thus for al-Kharrat, even Durrell's valorization of the city's diversity reveals distortions.

In what follows, I examine *City of Saffron* and *Girls of Alexandria* to explore and interpret al-Kharrat's "culturally authentic" and politically engaged representation of cosmopolitanism in Alexandria. Throughout the texts, one can sense how al-Kharrat engages with and disrupts Durrell's literary construction. In my analysis to follow, I argue that in these texts al-Kharrat transitions from an interplay dominated by binary relationships evident in *City of Saffron*—interactions between Copts and Muslims, and their unified resistance to British rule—to a broader, more inclusive vision of Egyptianness and the breadth and complexity of the Revolutionary struggle in *Girls of Alexandria*. Although both texts serve to counteract discourses of ethno-religiously defined nationalism, the latter grapples with inherent interconnection between colonialism and cosmopolitanism.

Cosmopolitan memory

Al-Kharrat was born in 1924 into a Coptic family in Alexandria, where he was raised and educated. He received a degree in Law from the University of Alexandria in 1946. From 1948–50 he was held in detention for involvement in revolutionary activities. He served in a variety of official capacities in both the Afro–Asian Peoples' Solidarity Organization and the Afro–Asian Writer's Association. In 1959, al-Kharrat published his first collection of stories, *High Walls* [*Hitan 'aliya*].[15] He was one of the founding editors of the influential avant garde journal *Gallery 68.*[16] His first novel, *Rama and the Dragon* [*Rama wa-al-tinnin*], appeared in 1980.[17] Edwar al-Kharrat has also contributed to the Egyptian literary and cultural sphere in his roles as critic, editor, and translator.

In his Alexandria "textual duet"[18] *City of Saffron* and *Girls of Alexandria*, al-Kharrat traces the childhood desires and meandering adolescent awakenings of Mikha'il, the novels' Coptic protagonist, and the author's alter ego.[19] Both texts represent Mikha'il's fragmented, free-flowing reminiscences and imaginary flights of fantasy. They skip easily from early childhood memories to political events, to knowledge and narrative insight gained over time. The dense, poetic texts both individually and together resist a clear chronological mapping. Indeed, al-Kharrat's reputation as an important and challenging writer in part rests on a writing style characterized by experimentation in language and form. Much of *City of Saffron* is devoted to character analyses of family members and neighbors who surrounded

Mikha'il in childhood. Mikha'il's sexual, political, and artistic awakenings described primarily in the second novel, *Girls of Alexandria*, correspond to the revival of Egypt's national struggle after the Second World War, in the period leading up to the 1952 Free Officer's Revolution.

Mikha'il is a character who appears in other works by al-Kharrat. Critic Ahmad Khurays argues that the character of Mikha'il is defined and redefined from text to text through his ever-shifting search for identity within national, confessional, and ideological contexts. From the perspective of his origins as a Copt to his embracing and then rejection of Marxist ideology, Mikha'il, according to Khurays, questions the bases of Egyptian identity in its various politicized incarnations.

City of Saffron is constructed as a series of intertwined reminiscences that simultaneously capture the perspective of the character Mikha'il as a youth, and an adult narrative voice speaking through the fog of memory. The text at times offers lucid description, and at others dream-like reverie. The events described in the text range from Mikha'il's early childhood to the years following the completion of his studies at the university.

The people and events described in the text are filtered through the character's experiences. As many narrative fragments in the text refer to events in Mikha'il's childhood, the scope of that experience is quite limited. At one point the narrator expresses the narrow world view of the young Mikha'il: "It seemed to him that the open square at al-Manshiyah—he was living in Ghayt al-'Inab—was not of this world. Because Ghayt al-'Inab was all the world."[20] Rather than cosmopolis, Alexandria is reduced to fragments—to neighborhoods and even buildings within them. The city as an entirety exists merely as an abstract concept represented through Mikha'il's youthful encounters with it. Although the environment Mikha'il inhabits in *City of Saffron* has a diverse population, the novel's representation of the city could be characterized as local and parochial, in other words, as the antithesis of the cosmopolitan.

Al-Kharrat's Alexandria is populated by a wide diversity of Egyptian Muslims and Copts: *fellahin*, Sa'idis and Nubians, laborers, and effendis. Somewhat less visible, but nevertheless present in the text are members of the foreign minorities: Greeks, Syrians, Italians, and Levantine Jews. What is notable about al-Kharrat's characterization of this diversity—Egyptian and foreign minority—is class. There is no representation in the text of the much mythologized Alexandrian *haute bourgeoisie*. Mikha'il is raised in the working-class district of Ghayt al-'Inab. His friends and contacts mentioned in the novel, including the foreign minorities, are neighbors or merchants who issue from the same class. The text describes Mikha'il's memory of the diversity that rendered "the world a rich place, a place of changing colour; a bit frightening, but fascinating."[21] One chapter opens with Mikha'il running to visit his Greek neighbour, Umm Toto. As the narrator relates from the distance of time: "For him, back then, differences between people were part of the natural course of things."[22] The text continues:

> He bought *foul* from 'the Turk,' whose big white moustaches were slightly yellowed at the tips by smoke; and he felt a certain awe when he entered the

houses of Muslim neighbours; and the Maltese constable, who roared down Tramway Street on his motorcycle …; and 'Amm Hasan the Tunisian, the milk-man, used to live in an alley behind them, keeping three buffaloes and a frisky white donkey in his house; he used to wear a spotless, butter yellow North African *burnous* whose hood he wore flung back behind his head.[23]

Viewed through Mikha'il's eyes as a child, the differences between these individuals are portrayed as "natural" and organic. This perspective represents a prenational construction of difference. There are no judgments or political undertones to the novel's representation of the city's diverse population.

This culture of coexistence serves primarily as a backdrop to the portrayal of congenial relations between Copts and Muslims, to which a greater proportion of the text is devoted. These narrative fragments represent commonality forged through parochial identification. Interactions between Mikha'il's family and their Muslim neighbors, for example, are cast not only in terms of neighborliness, but also in terms of religious exchange. Mikha'il fondly remembers his mother exchanging treats with Muslim neighbors on their respective holidays.[24] He also recalls accompanying Muslim children going house to house with lanterns during Ramadan.[25]

The narrator pointedly mentions that during her frequent conversations with her "bosom friend," the Muslim neighbor, Sitt Wahiba, Mikha'il's mother periodically swears "by Christ, the living Son of God."[26] Sitt Wahiba occasionally expresses devotion to her Coptic friend in terms of religious duty: "She would sometimes tell my mother that their Prophet had entrusted us to them, and that our prophet, Jesus, was also a prophet of Allah, like Moses and Abraham."[27] On the one hand Wahiba's words express concern for her friend, and on the other hand, represent an historical, patronizing attitude of Muslim responsibility toward *ahl al-dhimma*.

By the end of the chapter, however, this patronizing discourse is turned on its head, as the Christian characters demonstrate their capacity for benevolence and compassion. Sitt Wahiba begins to suspect the two Muslim women in the first-floor apartment purporting to be mother and daughter of engaging in prostitution, and she informs the police. On the night of the raid, the girl-prostitute, Husniya, seeks refuge with Mikha'il's family. Their protection of the girl is cast in terms of religious obligation. Mikha'il's father mutters: "Our Lord has commanded the protection of women from shame. May He so protect the women of this house."[28] The chapter ends with a dense, dream-like passage in which the narrator imagines Husniya, the saved prostitute next to him: "I embrace her with hands pierced by nails, my side stabbed by a lance; and seeping from my wound a few drops of blood."[29] In his dream, an expression of his own hubris, it is Mikha'il, as Jesus, who "saves" the wayward girl. Husniya, the Muslim prostitute, is thus likened to Mary Magdalene, who in the popular imagination has come to represent the repentant sinner saved by Jesus' teachings,[30] and who is by his side at the time of crucifixion, tends to his body in death, and was the first witness to his resurrection. The mutual beneficence extended between Copts and Muslims in these passages from *City of Saffron* is motivated by religious dictates characterized as reciprocal senses of moral superiority.

City of Saffron also highlights the shared educational experiences of Coptic and Muslim boys who attended Mikha'il's school. "Good at learning by heart" and "enthralled by the rhythm of the phrases," Mikha'il excels at reciting from the Qur'an, eliciting the praise of the Arabic teacher who exclaims, "Allah! That recitation was like chains of gold—may Allah make you prosper, my son."[31] When the students are split up for religion classes, Mikha'il expresses envy toward the Muslim students who would recite the Qur'an together "in a sonorous droning rhythm."[32] He enjoys the texture of Quranic Arabic, preferring the musicality of recitation to the study of Biblical narratives. His experience of learning his own religious heritage is, thus, framed by his introduction to Islamic texts and traditional Islamic learning.[33]

As Mikha'il reaches maturity, he becomes increasingly politically aware and involved in the anti-Imperial nationalist movement "which was at that time fermenting throughout the country."[34] This struggle, too, is undertaken by Egyptian Copts and Muslims together. One fellow revolutionary, Iskandar 'Awad, is identified as a Copt,[35] and another, 'Abd al-Qadr Nasrallah, a Muslim.[36] The national struggle, in its fragmentary representation in the novel, is a shared effort of Egyptian Muslims and Copts.

In keeping with the local purview of the novel, the scope of Mikha'il's political commitments is defined by lived experience, growing out of his encounter with British soldiers in the city. At one point he recalls a peaceful protest against British Imperialism that was violently—and fatally—suppressed by the authorities. At this demonstration he meets an activist who draws him into a secret cell.[37] The narrative refers to, but does not describe, demonstrations in which Mikha'il participated, strikes he organized and "pamphlets, analyses and manifestos" he wrote.[38] The text employs terms that signal his Communist leanings: interest in the working classes, surplus value, opposition to imperialism, and the emblem of the hammer and sickle. These oblique references to universalist communist discourse are locally circumscribed.

By contrast, in the second novel, *Girls of Alexandria*, political engagement is characterized as universal and cosmopolitan, reflecting both the national struggle and a wider purview of political activism. A passage from each of the novels describing Mikha'il's revolutionary activities demonstrate the shift in political frames of reference that takes place between the texts. In *City of Saffron* to support his family after the death of his father during the Second World War, Mikha'il accepts a job with the British military administration, and engages in small acts of defiance and resistance:

> While I was studying I worked at the British Navy depot in Kafr Ash'ari, as assistant storehouseman. I used to go down to the depot, passing by the Greek guard who stood at the huge iron door. I had pinned a black metal badge, with the word 'Evacuation' written on it in English, to the long blue jacket my mother had bought for me from the consignments of second hand clothes sent by the Americans as aid. I had no other jacket. I would take it off and hang it on a nail in such a way that the badge was clearly on view for all to see. I wore a white shirt and naval shorts issued by the depot. I drew the emblem of

the hammer and sickle, with the number four beside it in English numerals, and also the crescent moon and three stars on the thin wooden partition which separated the corner of the room, with its tin table, which was my office, from the office of 'Misterlee,' the storehouseman.[39]

Mikha'il inscribes the symbols of his revolutionary desire inseparable from his desire for Egyptian independence from British rule on the partition that divides him from his English manager, and which they share. The pairing of the crescent and stars of the Egyptian state with the hammer and sickle particularizes the universal ideals of Communism and the Fourth International.

In *Girls of Alexandria*, by contrast to *City of Saffron*, Mikha'il identifies with a broader range of Revolutionary movements and struggles against oppression. The vision of Revolution in this text grows out of the dialectic of the cosmopolitan as it appears in Karl Marx's *Communist Manifesto*. According to Rob Wilson's reading of Marx, "the 'bourgeoisie has through its exploitation of the world market given a cosmopolitan character to production and consumption in every country,'" while the "cosmopolitan framework liberates liberal-capitalist subjects from 'the old local and national seclusion and self-sufficiency' to the point that we can increasingly move beyond narrow-minded local and national frames."[40] As we have already seen in *City of Saffron*, Mikha'il opposes *bourgeois* cosmopolitan exploitation of local capital. However, unlike *City of Saffron*, *Girls of Alexandria* embraces and explores the full Marxist dialectic of the cosmopolitan, that also permits universalist, transnational political affiliation, and revolutionary activity.

Take, for example, a passage of unexpected anger that rips into a romantic scene. The opening chapter of the novel depicts a pastiche of memories of Mikha'il's childhood crush on his neighbor, Mona. The young love-struck Mikha'il has planned to meet Mona at the fish market. The following surprising passage disrupts the description of Mikha'il's tram ride to the market:

It was down by the big petroleum tank, where there was a leaping column of flame which never went out, that I saw the American soldiers. Powerful-looking, armed to the teeth, they were standing with their backs to us in a tense line on the beach, staring out to the sea. The English battleship towered white and immovable on the water. It had its guns trained on a smaller warship, and even at that distance I saw the Greek letters on the side and the red flag which fluttered from the pole as if it were defying death. And I saw a line of soldiers in helmets and transparent bullet-proof masks, soldiers bristling with weapons, blocking the narrow streets trodden by prophets and poets and dreamers in Jerusalem and Ramallah and Nazareth and al-Khalil, raking the crowds of children with machine-gun fire and hurling tear-gas cylinders. Soldiers surrounding the round granite monument which gleams by night in the middle of Tahrir Square, beating boys and girls with truncheons, spiriting prisoners of war away into stifling locked railway carriages bound for the mired and frozen trenches of Warsaw and Siberia and the gas-chambers of Dachau. Soldiers harrying the crowds of workers from the spinning- and weaving-mills in Mahalla, Kafr al-Dawar, Karmuz, hounding the students of law, medicine and all other faculties on Abbasiya Hill in Muharram Bey. Their small yellow tanks knew what they had to do; they shot bullets from their old-fashioned long cannons and hundreds fell in the great square outside the Winter Palace; the sirens of their black cars wailed as they were barricaded in front of the Sorbonne; they dragged trained and vicious dogs by their leather leads to maul black legs in Johannesburg or by the Mississippi.[41]

This jarring sequence moves swiftly across time and place, linking acts of violence sanctioned by intolerant and repressive political regimes. Throughout, the text insists on the speaker as witness. The narrator employs the same verb "I saw" (*ra'aytu*) to his witnessing of both the South African soldiers stationed in Alexandria during the Second World War, and the soldiers repressing riots in Palestine. In addition to "seeing" the soldiers in the present time of the narrative, the narrator, looking back over events, recognizes historical parallels, enacting multiply layered acts of witnessing.

In addition to this broader frame of reference for political engagement, *Girls of Alexandria* also represents a pluralization of the national, anti-colonial struggle. The text describes Mikha'il's involvement in a Revolutionary cell in the years following the end of the Second World War:

> Where did they go, the footsoldiers of the Alexandrian revolutionary circle of 1946? We used to meet Antoine at the Messageries Maritimes office in Sesostris Street after working hours. The door was opened for us by 'Amm Salih, the young Nubian porter who understood everything that went on and did not utter a word. On the French Roneo copier we printed out our pamphlets calling for evacuation, for the nationalization of the Suez Canal, for the defeat of subjugation, capitalist exploitation and underdevelopment; calling also for support to be given to the workers' strikes at the Bolvara factory and the spinning and weaving mills of Karmuz. Fattuh al-Qaffas typed them on to the silky transparent duplicating paper at the patent office owned by an old Maltese Jew, a paunchy man with a loud voice who immigrated to South Africa in 1948 leaving the office to his son-in-law. ... We printed the pamphlets in semi-darkness so that we would not be given away by lights burning in the company after hours. I took half of them to Zaki Ibrahim Sadduq, a Jewish boy who was Egyptian born and bred (*ibn al-balad*), a pure Alexandrian, and who worked at the Bolvara factory.[42]

The Lebanese Antoine, the Maltese Jew, and Zaki, the Alexandrian Jew, we later learn, are all compelled to leave Alexandria. It is worth noting that the Maltese Jew is mentioned in *City of Saffron*. However, in that context, he is described merely as Mikha'il's employer, the owner of the patent office where he found work translating "documents on chemistry and mechanics" after the British Navy Depot closed.[43] In keeping with the a-political representation of foreign minorities in the earlier novel, there is no mention of the Maltese Jew's sympathies for the revolutionary movement in which Mikha'il was involved, nor his willingness to let his office be used for typing pamphlets.

Girls of Alexandria, in its fragmentary structure and style, is built around lacunae; a presumption of absence permeates the text. Only traces remain of such friends, compatriots, and revolutionaries—some scattered across the globe, others languishing in prison, and many whose fate is unknown. Likewise, only traces of their identities remain. Thus, we find allusions to names of people who populated the landscape of Mikha'il's memory like Fattuh al-Qaffas and Zaki Ibrahim Sadduq—a mere testament to their absent presence:

> After 1956 they all left, nearly all of them, for Athens, Rome or Marseilles: Yvette Sassoon and Marcelle Sadduq, Stepho Orphanides, Despina Stamatopolo, Rita and her husband Pissas, Anastasia and her husband Dimitri Campanis, tough old Maria Simonides, Janine Birkowitz, Madeleine and Miryam and Antoine and Odette and Arlette.[44]

The recalling of names serves to inscribe into the text the diversity that once characterized the city. Yet, throughout the novel naming is treated with great suspicion. Names both reveal and conceal—they lie, distort, misidentify. At one point, Mikha'il relates how he loved from afar one of his classmates at the college of engineering—one of two women in the class. He plotted ways of revealing his secret love for her, but he did not know how to approach her, and he did not know her name. When a list of students was posted, he located what he thought to be her name, "Ihsan Nasri," which turned out to be, rather, the name of a boy. Naming, here, a case of gender misidentification, is cast as an ambiguous, indeed, unreliable address.[45]

Furthermore, although the novel distinguishes between and among the various minorities, it resists essentializing identity along the lines of affiliative communities. In *Girls of Alexandria*, Mikha'il is wary of his own name, and the way it belies his Christian origins, distorting or overstating the importance such identification plays in his identity.[46] Yet, he sometimes longs for the connections his Coptic name provides. During Mikha'il's years of political activity against British occupation, he and other revolutionaries take on nondescript assumed names as a precautionary measure, to protect their identities. Once when visiting a comrade in a rented room, he trips on the stairs. A Madonna-like Coptic woman rushes into the stairwell to make sure he is alright, and invites him in. While he is there, she relates to him how she baptized her son with the blood and milk of her breast when she feared he would die on a long train ride. He longs to reveal his given name, the name that immediately identifies his Coptic origins—and a name which he shares with the woman's infant son.[47]

He questions the signification of a name, its authenticity and validity. Yet, he simultaneously appears nostalgic for the loss. Through this encounter and the longing to make a connection with this simple, but pious woman, Mikha'il reveals his own conflicted identity, fallen somewhere between the realm of tradition, and revolution, each attempting to erase the other by acts of naming. Instead, he falls in the narrow corridor between the two realms. It is through this ongoing encounter in the text between his Coptic identity and Egyptianness, between religious tradition and revolutionary activity that Mikha'il becomes aware not just of the fragmentary nature of both memory and identity, but also of his own otherness.

This ambivalence carries over to the signification of dates in the text. An understanding of the passage above beginning "after 1956 they all left" hinges on the valuation attached the signifier "1956." There is no question that the date refers to the Suez Conflict. For al-Kharrat, the date represents a site of ambivalence, in contrast to Egyptian nationalist, anti-colonial interpretations. The events that irrevocably transform the fabric of Alexandrian society are here the result of the conflict between Colonialism and Egyptian Nationalism. Indeed, many of the people named in the passage mourning their departure from Alexandria are elsewhere identified in the text as having been involved in the national struggle. On the one hand, the Suez Conflict signals the Egyptian victory over Imperial interests. On the other hand, there is a simultaneous discomfort implied in the novel of the victory of Nasser's narrowly defined national identity that, in viewing the foreign-minorities as compradors, leads to their expulsion or departure from Egypt in the conflict's wake.

As the passage that begins by enumerating absent Alexandrians continues, the text further signals its refusal to engage in essentializing practices: "My enduring Ni'ma [Grace] my homeland my refuge in my permanent exile my one diamond in Athenios-*shari'* Fu'ad."[48] In the Arabic, as reflected in the English, the sentence is extremely unstable. The text refuses to equate any of the terms. We want the text to read: "My homeland *is* my enduring grace," or, "My homeland *is* my refuge." But the text resists those easy identifications, and the reference to the "diamond," the single precious, solid, material object in this shifting landscape remains unidentified. This highly ambivalent moment, like many others in the text, gives prominence to the unresolved issues of identification.

The passage concludes several lines later, following a free-flowing, sensual description of the lingering memory of sights, sounds, tastes, feels, and smells of Alexandria:

> You girl of Alexandria (*ya bint iskandariyya*) single however many you are; too many for me. You force me to silence. And in the end is there anything but silence, how ever long my Alexandrian songs are sung, silence to the end of time? O girls of Alexandria, your lips are sugar-sweet. Has the world filled up with yesterday? Yesterday brims over.

This recurring ode to the girls, or more accurately daughters, of Alexandria, represents an identification with placeness. Yet, as indicated by the preceding dream-like description, that placeness is literally utopian (i.e. no place), only accessible, like the unfulfilled desire the women represent, through overflowing, intangible sensuality of memory. In evoking silence, we are returned to the tangible absences represented by the names invoked at the beginning of the passage. The violent rift signified by the date "1956" empties the place and renders it silent.

Alexandria, in its multiplicity, as depicted in *Girls of Alexandria*, also functions as an analogue to the fragmentary representation of identity—both personal and national—the narrative proposes. *Girls of Alexandria* complicates the relationship between cosmopolitanism and colonialism by locating cosmopolitanism in memory and within a decentered, evacuated situatedness.

4 Polis and cosmos

Ibrahim Abdel Meguid

Between July 24 and 26, 1996, the Supreme Council for Islamic Affairs in Egypt hosted a conference entitled "Islam and the Future of Dialogue between Civilizations." Approximately 300 Muslim and Christian leaders attended the proceedings including the Grand Imam of al-Azhar, Muhammad Sayid Tantawi, and Pope Shenuda III, the leader of the Coptic Church. The goal of the conference, according to Hamdi Zaqzuq, the Egyptian Minister of Religious Affairs, was to deliver, "a message to the world to show that Islam is a religion of tolerance calling for peaceful coexistence between people and rejecting extremism and terrorism in all forms."[1] From an international public relations perspective, the event fizzled, generating meager interest in Western media.[2]

However, the organizers had at least as much interest in the conference's domestic significance as in its international impact. In the midst of what was already a four-year battle against Islamist militants, the Egyptian government had a political stake in backing—and granting a public platform to—voices of religious tolerance. Four years earlier, Islamist militants had launched a deadly wave of violence that continued to stir up interfaith tensions. The first of such raids occurred in May 1992 on Sanabu village in Upper Egypt, killing 14 Copts. Throughout the mid-1990s Islamist militants were also responsible for dozens of attacks on Egyptian security personnel and tourist enclaves, as well as on Copts. At the time of the conference over 1000 people—civilians, police officers, and suspected militants—had died in the violence. Accused of being "un-Islamic" by the militants, the regime utilized the conference to endorsed Islamic leaders who preached tolerance and moderation, rejecting the theology and tactics of the armed militants.

During the same month, a novel was published in Egypt that depicts warm Muslim–Coptic relations in 1940s Alexandria. Although the release of the novel had no direct relationship to the government-sponsored conference on interfaith dialogue, the book, too, was received as a reaction against intolerance and intercommunal violence. The novel, *No One Sleeps in Alexandria* [*La ahad yanam fi al-iskandariyya*],[3] follows the development of a friendship between a Muslim and a Copt who find work together on the railway lines. In 1941, as the North African front is taken up by the Germans, the two are sent to run the train station at al-Alamein. There, their interfaith friendship stands on the vanguard of the defense against Rommel's troops and Nazi intolerance.

The novel's humane depiction of interfaith relations was warmly received by critics. One critic, 'Abd al-'Aziz Muwafi writes that "contrary to what is actually happening as a result of the narrowing of personal horizons," the novel depicts "what brings people together rather than what separates them." At the climax of the novel, which he describes as "one of the most poignant moments in the Arabic novel," "passages from the Qur'an and the New Testament are interspersed," an indication, he argues, that the religious texts "bring people together rather than divide them."[4] Hala Halim states that "the overriding 'message' […] of the novel is that Muslims and Copts can and should coexist not only peacefully, but also displaying the values of neighborliness, amity and mutual support that they have generally shown in their relations."[5]

However, I maintain that to read the novel as a multi-cultural tract is to fall under the sway of the aphorisms the patient, folksy Muslim character, Majd al-Din, offers to pacify the anxieties of his naïve, uneducated Coptic friend, Damyan throughout the novel. The portrayal of coexistence in *No One Sleeps in Alexandria* is fraught with intercommunal strife. In what follows, I argue that the novel represents not an idealized model of coexistence, but rather a cosmopolitan, pluralist nationalism forged through interethnic conflict. The novel attempts to construct a vision of the cosmopolitan uncoupled from anti-colonial sentiment.

No One Sleeps in Alexandria by Ibrahim Abdel Meguid represents the first installment of a planned trilogy depicting the transformations Alexandria underwent through the mid-twentieth century. Abdel Meguid, who was born in 1946 in Alexandria and attended the University of Alexandria, began publishing short stories in the 1970s. The three volumes of the trilogy revolve around wars fought over Egyptian territory. *No One Sleeps in Alexandria* opens on the first day of the Second World War, and depicts the lives of the city's inhabitants under aerial bombardment as German troops advance through Egypt's Western Desert. The second volume, *Ambergris Birds* [*Tuyur al-'Anbar*] (2000),[6] begins with Israel's invasion of Sinai in October 1956, and maps the aftereffects of the Suez Conflict as well as the impact of domestic economic and social policies on the social fabric of Alexandria. The planned third installment is said to explore the rise of fundamentalist Islam in the city following the 1967 Arab–Israeli conflict.[7] These historical novels are notably anchored in the spacetime of Alexandria.[8] Alongside the narrative elements of the novels, the text offers intermittent surveys of Egyptian newspapers reporting political and economic conditions, quirky human-interest stories, demographic statistics, and film listings.

In the second section of the chapter, I discuss *Ambergris Birds*, the second novel of the trilogy. *Ambergris Birds* critiques both the colonial system that fostered Alexandria's cosmopolitan society and the regime of Gamal Abdel Nasser that oversaw its demise. Attempting to recreate a cosmopolitanism untainted by colonialism, the novel seeks out earlier precedents within Arab–Islamic culture and history.

Saving the city from itself—cosmopolitan patriotism

From the opening page, Ibrahim Abdel Meguid's *No One Sleeps in Alexandria* situates itself within and against the Western literary mythology of the city and its imagined cosmopolitanism. The epigraphs to the novel include a passage from the work of French surrealist poet, Paul Éluard, whose writing held great influence over Egyptian Francophone poets of the interwar period, from Lawrence Durrell's *Alexandria Quartet*, and from a poem by Cavafy.[9] The novel, however, does not merely reflect the received Western imagery of Alexandria as the epigraphs might indicate.

As one critic notes, the novel takes place within a topography eclipsed in the Western imagination of Alexandria, literally on the other side of the tracks, and on the other side of the Mahmudiyya canal, a landscape that "does not even figure in E. M. Forster's *Alexandria: A History and a Guide*."[10] Although foreigners and foreign minorities are represented in the text, as are British Commonwealth soldiers, the novel foregrounds the diversity of Egyptians living in 1940s Alexandria: Muslims and Copts, longstanding residents and newly arrived migrants, *sa'ayda* and *fellahin*. This diversity of Egyptians is more significant to the novel than the city's "cosmopolitan" nature evident in the Western literary myth of Alexandria.

The city's size and diversity contain the possibility of bringing destruction on itself, as evidenced in an additional epigraph to the novel. This passage calls into question the unintended repercussions of exponential growth, such as that Alexandria experienced in the late nineteenth and early twentieth centuries. During this period of expansion, the city attracted both internal migration and immigration, bringing together people and cultures and creating the city's much mythologized cosmopolitan society. This epigraph is taken from an ancient Babylonian myth. The swelling numbers of people on earth make a clamor loud enough to wake the gods. The gods inflict the people with disease to quite the din, but their numbers rebound. They finally succeed in silencing humanity by casting drought upon the land, followed by a devastating flood. The gods' "sleeplessness" resonates with the sleeplessness of Alexandria's inhabitants during night bombing raids during the Second World War that, like the mythic flood of the epigraph, wreaks destruction upon the city, rendering it silent. This epigraph also introduces the notion of the city's potential to bring destruction on itself—a recurring trope in the text, as I discuss below.

No One Sleeps in Alexandria maps dislocations of internal immigration—notably conflict between *sa'ayda* and *fellahin*, new arrivals and longstanding residents. At the beginning of *No One Sleeps in Alexandria*, the protagonist, Majd al-Din and his wife Zahra are banished from their village in the Delta in the wake of a blood feud that has nearly wiped out two families in the village. They seek refuge in Alexandria with Majd al-Din's brother, Bahi, whose philandering years earlier had been responsible for sparking the feud. Majd al-Din seeks work as a day laborer with intermittent success. One day the police raid a café frequented by unemployed laborers, arresting dozens of men for failing to present identity papers. In prison the Muslim Majd al-Din meets and befriends the Coptic Damyan, a native of Alexandria. Upon his release, he discovers that Bahi has been killed in a brawl between immigrants from the Delta and recent arrivals from upper Egypt.

When Majd al-Din arrives in Alexandria, he finds a burgeoning metropolis, populated by a wide diversity of humanity. The novel maps Alexandria's human geography as follows:

Among the foreigners (*al-ajanib*) were hundreds and thousands of adventurers, who came to the cosmopolitan city and made it a virtual tower of Babel. Among the Egyptians (*ahl al-bilad*) were thousands of castaways, like Majd al-Din, who preceded and would follow him.

The north of the city was no longer enough for the foreigners, so the poorest of them—Greeks, Jews, Italians, and Cypriotes—moved to some of the poorer neighborhoods, such as 'Attarin and Labban. They moved closer to and mixed with the Egyptians (*ahl al-bilad*), who lived in the south of the city. Majd al-Din had arrived in an Alexandria that was on top of the world. In addition to the European residents, there were soldiers from Europe and all the Commonwealth—and he, the expelled peasant.[11]

Although groups of different ethnic and geographic origins mixed in the southern districts of the city, the text maintains a distinction between the "natives" (*ahl al-bilad*) and the "foreigners" (*al-ajanib*). Difference, of any sort, is presented in the novel as immutable. The narrator's description of this cultural environment as "a virtual tower of Babel" underscores the utter incommunicability of difference.[12]

Throughout the narrative, intercultural contact re-inscribes difference. Majd al-Din's piety propels Damyan to reconnect with his own religious tradition, prompting him to turn to the Church in times of crisis.[13] So, too, in a secondary plot line that follows the relations between teenage sweethearts, a Muslim boy, Rushdi, and a Coptic girl, Camelia, articulated through their mutual love for French and English poetry. The poetic universal, too, fails to transcend cultural particularism. When their chaste relationship is discovered, Camelia is sent off to a convent in her family's village in upper Egypt. Through her cloistered life, Camelia quickly reaches a level of legendary holiness, becoming renowned for her healing powers. Rushdi, deprived of information about Camelia becomes convinced that she has been killed for the sake of her family's honor. He wanders the Egyptian countryside, living off the land and with its people, in search of her body.[14] Ultimately, when Rushdi discovers Camelia's whereabouts and visits her at the convent, they confirm the necessity of their separation in the interest of her continued dedication to the Church, and his desire to pursue an education in France. In other words, rather than ending in violence—the death of either or both of the lovers—the novel resolves the tensions caused by interfaith romance with mutual respect.

In contrast to these friendships forged through difference, elsewhere in the novel difference slips into discord. To his Coptic neighbor with whom he maintains amicable relations, Majd al-Din expresses the view that discord is both universal and inevitable, "Discord exists in every era between every group."[15] But, it is to the city that the devolving of discord into violent conflict is ascribed. The city's self-destructive nature, according to the narrative, dates back to its ancient history:

[Alexandria's] inhabitants, after the death of Antony and Cleopatra, numbered three hundred thousand free citizens and an equal number of slaves. But

Alexandrians were fond of cockfights and writing verses that made fun of the rulers. That was why, when Napoleon Bonaparte conquered it, its inhabitants numbered only eight thousand.[16]

Left to their own devices, Alexandrians act recklessly—endangering themselves through high-risk gaming, or high-stakes verbal sparring. In the present time of the narrative, this self-destructive tendency plays out in the brawl between *sa'ayda* and *fellahin* in which Majd al-Din's brother, Bahi, is killed.

But, lest we assume from the bounding of the era of wanton self-destruction between the Roman and French Empires, that only foreign rule will curb the Alexandrian's instincts, we are reminded of acts of violence and oppression carried out by foreign powers, past and present. One morning after a night of heavy bombing, Dimitri, Majd al-Din's Coptic landlord, ruminates on the bloody history of the region—particularly the ancient martyrdom of Christians that had taken place on the same spot that had been destroyed by a German air raid.[17] Pompeii's pillar, he explains, was constructed by the people of Alexandria as a popular expression of support for the peace brought to the city by the Roman Emperor Diocletian (240–312 AD). However, as the narrator reminds the reader, Diocletian was infamous for his brutal persecution of Christians.[18] Thus, in the distorted reflection of the monolith's polished façade, repression in the form of eradication of difference comes to look like peace.

When on September 1, 1939 an anonymous train passenger expresses his view that "Alexandria itself will be the reason the war comes to it,"[19] he means that with the Italians in neighboring Libya, the key Mediterranean port of Alexandria under British rule would be an obvious military target. But, as the history of civil strife in Alexandria unfolds throughout the novel, we come to question if, perhaps, Alexandria in its divisiveness indeed brings war upon itself. The narrative makes a point of identifying Rudolf Hess, the Nazi leader who had risen to become the third most powerful man within the regime of the Third Reich, as a native of Alexandria.[20] The novel, thus, provides for the possibility that Alexandria, through its long history as a space of intercultural contact, functions as a breeding ground for intolerance. In a sense, the violent encroachment on the borders of the city by the Nazi war machine can thus be rendered effectively as an extension of Alexandria's internal civil strife.

So, on what basis then, are the amicable relations between Majd al-Din and Damyan forged? And in this vision, what hope can there be for a peaceable Cosmopolitan Alexandria? Perhaps the answer lies in the resolution to another conflict. In the opening pages we learn that a bloody vendetta, sparked by an illicit affair between Majd al-Din's brother, Bahi, and a married woman, had over a decade earlier nearly wiped out two families in a small delta village. The sole surviving male relatives of each family remaining in the village, Majd al-Din and his former classmate, Khalaf, make peace on the basis of mutual self-interest.[21]

This recognition of mutual interest through difference lies beyond the confines of the city, and perhaps, too, on the macro-level, the resolution to Alexandria's intercommunal strife lies beyond the city's boundaries in the national imaginary.

The text's characterization of national desires transcends the Alexandrian cosmopolitanism of intercommunal violence, and replaces it with a pluralist nationalism. For example, one character cites a pluralist slogan from the 1919 national movement: "Religion belongs to God, and the country (*al-watan*) belongs to everyone (*al-jamii'*)."[22] The term "*al-jamii'*," here rendered as "everyone," could also be translated as "the public at large," a term, simple in its ambiguity, that leaves open the question of the identities of those who call the homeland (*al-watan*) home.[23] The text also cites the words of Mustafa Kamil, an Egyptian nationalist at the turn of the twentieth century: "Free in our land, hospitable to our guests. My soul, forged from the shining light of patriotism, cannot live in the dark of oppression and despotism."[24]

While characters in the novel do struggle with their anti-colonial desires, torn between the relative evils of the foreign powers warring over them—in contrast to the prevailing Egyptian discourse, the articulations of nationalism in the text are uncoupled from anti-colonial sentiment. In this way, the novel re-figures the received knowledge of the relationships between cosmopolitanism, the polis, and the nation. Alexandrian cosmopolitanism is, on the one hand, figured through articulations of difference that frequently devolves into conflict; the imagined cosmopolitan nation, on the other hand, is figured through an acknowledgment of mutual interest through difference.

Circling the square[25]

While *No One Sleeps in Alexandria* focuses primarily on relations between Egyptian Alexandrians, *Ambergris Birds* explores the interrelationships between the city's Egyptian, European, and foreign minority residents. The novel opens with a description of disruption in circulation caused by the outbreak of hostilities in October 1956: "There is no one as far as the eye can see. The Mahmudiyya canal is empty of boats, both big and small. Not a single tram is moving along the opposite bank."[26] One character, 'Araby, whose name, not insignificantly means "Arab," is described crossing the empty expanse of the grounds used by the many companies owned by Constantine Salvagos, the Alexandrian Greek capitalist, to store industrial byproducts, the detritus of capitalism: "drums of oil and grease, bundles of thread, spools of wire, old leather and iron belts and a variety of other strange rusty, metal objects that shone in the sun."[27] The text goes to some length delineating the various companies in which Salvagos was a major investor—the companies that used this space as a dumping ground. 'Araby, a 30-year-old unskilled laborer, lives in a nearby working-class district between the Mahmudiyya Canal and the railway yard. In the context of the Suez conflict that frames the novel, one is tempted to read this scene as an articulation of the reach of "foreign" capitalists into the "native city."

Yet, what follows in the novel undermines this type of dualistic polemic. "Egyptian" characters, 'Araby among them, are also depicted as circulating within the "European" neighborhoods of the city. In other words, rather than privileging

a representation of the city as divided, the novel instead foregrounds the interrelationships between East and West. Further, the novel rejects the rhetoric of "native"
and "foreign," re-humanizing Alexandria's "foreign-minorities," and calling into
question their collective status as compradors. Throughout the novel the emigration of Jewish, Greek, and Italian Alexandrians is depicted as a loss broadly felt
across society. Furthermore, the novel represents interactions among members of
different cultures and nationalities along the socio-economic spectrum, and not
exclusively among the *bourgeoisie* and élite.

Ambergris Birds maps the physical, social, and demographic shifts the city
undergoes in the period between the 1956 Suez Conflict and the sweeping nationalizations of industries that began in 1961. In particular, it focuses on the impact
of these shifts on the lives of a variety of characters who, like 'Araby, inhabit the
cramped working-class neighborhood near Salvagos's warehouses.

The narrative of the city's transformation pivots on the transformations evident in Manshiyya Square. As one character, Sulayman, expresses: "The history
of Manshiyya is the history of Alexandria."[28] A number of the characters cross
Manshiyya throughout the novel and reflect upon what they see and experience.
Through these descriptions the narrative relates both the social history and monumental history of the square, while reflecting on the contrast between the grand
European architecture and the dislocations of the Egyptian economy.

Manshiyya Square, known at various points in its history as Place des Armes,
Place des Consuls, and Place Muhammad Ali, became the commercial center of
the city with the opening of the Bourse there in 1866. In 1868 Khedive Isma'il
commissioned the statue of Mehmed Ali to be erected in the center of square.
Many of the buildings bounding the square were destroyed by the British bombardment of the city in 1882. The surrounding area was quickly rebuilt in the
"conservatively eclectic" Italian style, with "pro-Renaissance forms and decorations" still in evidence today.[29] In 1909 the square was enhanced by the addition of
the French Gardens that ran perpendicular to Manshiyya Square, connecting it to
the sea. These gardens were graced with the statue of Khedive Isma'il in 1938, as
described in the previous chapter.

Following the 1952 Revolution, the square was renamed "*Tahrir*" or "Liberation" square. Egyptian President, Gamal Abdel Nasser used the balcony of the
former Bourse, transformed into the Socialist Union building, for public speeches.
Manshiyya was the site of an attempt on his life by members of the Muslim
Brotherhood in 1954. And, in 1956 Nasser delivered his speech announcing the
nationalization of the Suez Canal in the square as well.

In *Ambergris Birds*, for 'Araby, Manshiyya Square represents foreign wealth.
However, when he crosses the square following the Suez Conflict, its emptiness
reflects a projection of his own sense of loss. Throughout much of the novel 'Araby
worked doing odd jobs in the atelier of a Greek seamstress, Katina, who catered to
the tastes and styles of upper-class, European and Europeanized women. A Jewish
woman, Rachel, one of Katina's clients, had taken a liking to 'Araby, and gave him
some money when she decided to leave with her family following the war. On
the night Rachel simultaneously proclaims her love for 'Araby and announces her

intent to emigrate, 'Araby sets out on a long, reflective walk. His wanderings take him through Manshiyya Square:

> The wide square was as it always had been, with Mehmed 'Ali at its center on top of his horse. But, 'Araby had a sense of the place as if he were seeing it for the first time. Its stores were closed, and there were few lights shining through the windows of the buildings. There are no moneychangers or Bourse at night. The patrons of Café Alexandria were taking refuge indoors and not sitting in the narrow alley between two buildings. There was less light in the square. Perhaps.[30]

'Araby, in his way, acknowledges that the "square was always as it had been," that its abandoned feel was a function of the weather and time of day, and that the dimness he experiences may be imagined. But, what starts as bleak emptiness in the description of Manshiyya, ends with abandonment; continuing on his walk, he finds himself wandering in the Jewish quarter, now nearly empty.

The teenage Sulayman, a budding writer and the chronicler of the city's fortunes, also reflects at length on the transformations of Manshiyya Square. Like 'Araby, Sulayman's representation of the city is inflected with a sense of loss. Sulayman had developed a close friendship with Jean Bancroft, the daughter of a British diplomat. She, too, left Alexandria with her family in the days following the outbreak of the Suez Conflict, before Sulayman had a chance to say goodbye. Sulayman could no longer bear to visit Manshiyya. The reports he receives from friends about the changes in the square depress him. The stores once selling jasmine blossoms were instead offering fabric and cheap Egyptian-made shoes. The number of unemployed youths scrounging for cigarette butts had increased proportionately to the decrease in the number of foreign currency exchanges.[31]

In the spring of 1957, a group of characters, Karawan, Husna, Shawqiyya, and Hikmat, crossed the square together on their way to a wedding reception. Karawan is the son of Nirgis, a seamstress, who trains young women in her craft, while also offering them a place to congregate and socialize. Husna, Shawqiyya, and Hikmat were among the girls who spent their evenings in Nirgis's apartment. They were all on their way to attend the wedding of their compatriot Fatima, who had chosen to get married at the Shahrazade Theater in Ramla Station in the Westernized district of the city. Although Karawan and the young women were less directly affected by the mass emigrations from Alexandria, they too recognized the changes in Egyptian society through changes in the square:

> They got off [the tram] in Manshiyya Square and walked the rest of the way. […] In spacious Manshiyya Square bounded by grand buildings with tall, lofty windows and luxurious ornamentation, they stopped to look at the statue of Mehmed 'Ali. […]
> Karawan, whom they had just noticed was with them, said, 'Mehmed 'Ali is an ancestor of King Farouk.'
> Husna responded, 'King Farouk is enjoying himself abroad.'

'Enjoying himself?' retorted Shawqiyya. 'The revolution kicked him out, you idiot. For some time already he has been suffering from spells of Belgian dizziness.'

None of them knew what 'Belgian Dizziness' meant, but it was something someone witty had once said about the tram, owned by a Belgian company, which traverses Alexandria on a circular track with no beginning or end.

They ran a little after having gazed for a long time at the statue that appeared as if it were about to jump off its pedestal—a colossal man on top of a strong horse. Hikmat took them toward the Corniche where they encountered the sea breeze. The place of the statue of Isma'il was still empty. It was said that the Revolution would remove all the statues of Mehmed 'Ali's family from around the country. Others said that they had seen the statue of Isma'il in state of neglect in the Antonides gardens. The Revolution intends to erect a memorial to the Unknown Soldier in its place.[32]

The women's attention is drawn particularly to the statues—the imposing figure of Mehmed Ali on his horse and the notable absence of Isma'il. They note the signs of the change in regime signaled by the absence of the statue of Khedive Isma'il [*sic*], and the monument to be re-dedicated in the service of the structures of memory of the new regime.[33] From the perspective of these characters, regardless of the regime, the square represents state structures, power and order.

The square later becomes the scene of a demonstration against Belgian imperialism in the Congo in which Karawan, Nirgis's son, participates.[34] For Karawan the demonstration represents a political coming of age, but the reader also recognizes the parallels between its anti-colonial message, and that delivered by Nasser in the same square that set in motion the events described by the novel.

If the square for Karawan sits ambivalently between the finding of his political voice, and the coopting of that voice by state interest, for another character, Nawal, the relationship between voice and state is much less ambiguous. Nawal, who works as a nurse, frequents Nirgis's salon. She had become famous in the neighborhood and in the hospital for her beautiful voice.[35] She falls in love with a doctor involved with a group of artists and intellectuals who dabbled in Communism. The doctor invites her to sing at a private New Year's Eve celebration at the home of one of his friends on Manshiyya Square.[36] After she leaves that night, the party is raided, and the guests are arrested. The authorities later track her down, along with the other guests, and all are imprisoned. Her time in prison takes its toll on her voice, and upon her release and rehabilitation she discovers that her criminal record represents an obstacle to pursuing her dreams of singing for Egyptian radio.[37]

Nawal is the only character from the working-class district to enter one of the buildings bounding Manshiyya Square. Whereas she encounters the wealth of district, the capitalism it represents to the others is offset by the communism espoused by the inhabitants of the apartment. Through the dizzying experience of the encounter, the distinctions between Egyptians and foreigners become blurred. Stepping up to the entryway of the elegant building, Nawal imagines herself to be "an actress in a foreign film," a fantasy which does not shake her identity as a conservative Egyptian girl from a traditional family.[38]

As we have seen, in the novel Manshiyya Square is associated with wealth and state power, but not with foreign domination. For the adult male characters who had contact with Alexandria's European inhabitants, Manshiyya functions as a microcosm of the losses they experience. The departure of individuals reflects the loss of the larger communities they represent, and the loss of the contributions those communities made to Alexandrian society. The increasing economic depression of the square 'Araby and Sulayman witness also mirrors the economic hardships they both encounter during this period of transition.

For the women who were less connected to the foreign communities, and whose work in the informal economy protected them, to a certain extent, from the economic dislocations of the era, the square rather represents state power. Nawal in particular, is affected by abuses of that power. Her glimpse into the inner circle of communist-leaning artists and intellectuals distances some affluent members of the society from the colonial system under which they or their forebears had benefited.

Pluralist Arabism and a pre-colonial cosmopolitan

There is a historically significant gap between the first two volumes of Abdel Meguid's planned Alexandria trilogy. *No One Sleeps in Alexandria* ends in 1942, and *Ambergris Birds* picks up in 1956. As a result, the novels do not directly represent the intervening period of unrest, anti-colonialism, and the deterioration of intercommunal relations. Whereas the affection Sulayman and 'Araby feel towards Jean and Katina respectively reflects a romanticization of intercommunal relations, the novel's approach to the colonial system that fostered the cosmopolitan society and the regime that overturned it is nuanced and critical. The novel also offers two images that provide alternate possibilities to the rejection of cosmopolitanism that accompanied the ejection of the colonial power. First, the novel posits a vision of Arabized inclusiveness, an acknowledgment of the admixture and influence of other cultures on Egyptian society. Second, the novel also explores an alternative cosmopolitan idiom drawn from Egypt's past and separated from the Western colonial encounter.

The character 'Araby in a literal sense comes to enact the process of Arabizing the city. When at the end of the novel Katina leaves for Greece, the uneducated, and unskilled 'Araby is forced to look elsewhere for a job. He hears that there are openings in the municipality. He is placed in the city planning office, where he is assigned to the crew changing streetnames throughout the city to erase traces of the city's colonial-Western past. He is given a motorcycle and a quota of signs to replace in various neighborhoods throughout the city. In the process of changing signs he reflects wistfully on how he is erasing the memory of Katina's world. He pauses before replacing the signs for the street named after Cavafy and the ancient Greek figure, Helen. When confronted with Hercules Street, however, he refuses to make the change, instead Arabizing the name rather than replacing it altogether.

This small act of resistance signals that 'Araby's vision of "Arabization" includes within it a pluralist past.[39]

As a result of the bleak economic prospects, a handful of characters find opportunity outside of Alexandria and Egypt, like Mahmud the aspiring film director who seeks professional training in Italy.[40] The escape route of one character, "Ground Pepper," the spice merchant does not follow the anticipated trajectories. Pepper longs to retrace the routes traversed by his ancestor, a thirteenth century spice merchant who devoted his life to searching for the ambergris along the shores of Oman, Zanzibar, and in the depths of the Indian Ocean. Ambergris is a substance excreted by sperm whales that is prized for its fragrance and legendarily for its ability to make women swoon. Although medieval and early modern spice merchants knew that ambergris was harvested from the sea and that it was sometimes found inside whales, the source remained a mystery. One hypothesis held that ambergris originated in the droppings of birds. Pepper's ancestor was said to have traveled to the Maldives in search of mythical birds who were believed to be the source of ambergris.[41]

By the end of the novel, Pepper has discovered documents belonging to his ancestor, containing a map to a purported family treasure buried in India. He announces his intent to undertake the journey to search for the lost treasure.[42] Pepper's story ends on a note of uncertainty. One fears that Pepper's attempt to recuperate the past, amounts to none other than the search for mythical beings, the ambergris birds. However, Pepper's route represents an alternate trajectory— unlike Mahmud, he does not turn to Europe for his panacea. Pepper's story, rather, reflects a shift in the conception of cosmopolitanism represented in the text. The medieval and early modern spice trade, as Pepper articulates, represented another cosmopolitan moment in Alexandria's history, one that like its dissipating contemporary counterpart also flourished under an (Islamic) imperial order. His journey to India could represent an Islamic or third-worldist internationalism filtered through nostalgia for a different but equally inaccessible cosmopolitan moment in Alexandrian history.

Together 'Araby's refusal to change the sign and Pepper's mythic search offer opportunities to re-think the way one interprets the stories Alexandria tells of itself. 'Araby's gesture represents a small act of resistance to repressing the memory of Alexandria's cosmopolitan history. Pepper's journey rescues the notion of the cosmopolitan from its indebtedness to the European colonial experience.

Countervailing forces of circulatory motion

Embedded near the end of *Ambergris Birds* is a short story attributed to the character-writer, Sulayman. He is distraught at a friend's death, and the loss of his English friend Jean. Although he is intelligent and well-read, he is denied entrance into college for bureaucratic reasons, and considers leaving Egypt like his friend Mahmud, to pursue an education abroad. The embedded story reflects Sulayman's disillusionment, offering a bleak cityscape featuring destroyed infrastructure, disruption of markets, the over-running of nationalist icons by rampant consumerism, infestation, emigration, and ultimately the displacement of the entire city altogether. The story lives up to its title, "A Surrealistic Story," with its disturbing images of disembodied human sexual organs and anthropomorphic buildings.

The story opens recalling the 1937 film *Elephant Boy* based on a piece by Rudyard Kipling. The film starred the Indian actor Sabu who, in Sulayman's story, leads a line of elephants into the city where they wreak havoc on the fish market. They then proceed to the Mahmudiyya canal, which they drink dry. When Sabu leads the elephants away, the water in the canal begins to rise again. The women in the marketplace return their attention to buying fish as the workers load up carts to sell their wares throughout the city. Then people begin to flock to the Westernized commercial district of Alexandria after hearing that women's and men's undergarments replete with the appropriate genitalia are available for sale. Men rush to Sa'ad Zaghlul Street, named after the leader of the 1919 revolution, to buy the women's underwear, and women congregate on Safiyya Zaghlul Street, named after the wife of Sa'ad, and independently known as "the mother of the Egyptians," to buy the men's underwear. The men retreat with their purchases to the eastern districts of the city and the women to the west. The buildings of the city then begin to grow human features such as eyes, hair, and feet, and they wander around the city greeting one another and wailing before returning to their places. At night the four winds pick up the city and carry it away—people, buildings and all—dropping them in another galaxy, far away. The underwear, jettisoned by the men and women as they flew through the air, land on the ground where they become filled with mice. The mice then board boats whose impoverished passengers throw themselves into the water to escape the infestation.[43]

The "story" offers a circulation of truncated symbols existing outside of narrative, outside of history. Both the title, "A Surrealistic Story," and its mode of production, described as an unwilled outpouring of the unconscious, beg us to interpret its floating symbols as if reading a dream.[44] As such, the "story" represents repressed memories bubbling through to the surface of consciousness in fragmentary form. The "story," then, can be read as a recovery of the repressed postcolonial subject (Sabu acting out) and repressed sexuality (the acting out of sexual fantasies).

In the "story" the buildings circulate, not as commodities in a real estate market, but rather by propelling themselves through space. The buildings, it turns out, have feelings, too, although they are not given voice to articulate the nature of their laments; is it perhaps the loss of their inhabitants? Neglect? Recognition of their own mortality? We recognize through their personification—their development of human features—the interdependence of the built environment and its inhabitants. At the end of empire and at the limits of narrative, what remains is the city—its infrastructure and its inhabitants—in motion.

As in Sulayman's story of the divided city, the valences attached to circulation breakdown along gender lines. Let us return momentarily to the passage quoted above describing the group of women arriving in Manshiyya Square.[45] The women are suspicious that circulation breeds disorientation and disease—the "Belgian dizziness." In contrast, by the end of the novel, Sulayman is lifted from his deep despair when his neighbor, Saʻada, the object of his affections, declares her love for him. Sulayman expresses a renewed resolve to remain in Alexandria. To celebrate, he sets out on a tour, walking and riding through and around the neighborhoods of the city. He exclaims: "Alexandria is an easy city, truly long, but she gives herself over easily to walking and riding, to her inhabitants and immigrants from all over the world, and from the north and south of the country."[46] While the women suspect that despite its closed circular loop, circulation is centrifugal or tantamount to exile, for Sulayman, it is centripetal, encircling and embracing Alexandria's diversity, even if only in memory.[47]

In the novel, circulation becomes not only a trope for the movement of people and goods through the spaces of the city, but also for the repeating cycle of a closed circuit. As we have seen in Chapter 2, this is also true in the functioning of the city of Alexandria. In the years immediately preceding and following the turn of the twenty-first century, the governate of Alexandria concerned itself with improving transit through the city streets; it did so by tapping into recycled narratives and images. As in the novel, this cyclical aspect of circulation can be both centripetal and centrifugal—flinging away heavy symbols or drawing them in. In the aftermath of the colonial experience, the heavy matter of cosmopolitanism was flung away, and at the moment of the city's contemporary revitalization, it is being drawn in. As in Sulayman's vision in the novel, the governate and the marketers of the Alexandria's image have embraced an inclusive vision of the city, even if that inclusiveness exists only as memory.

Part II
Counterpoint New York

5 Why New York?

Youssef Chahine

Like his literary counterparts discussed in the previous two chapters, Youssef Chahine (1926–2008) also contributed significantly to the nostalgic memorialization of Alexandria's colonial cosmopolitan era within Egypt. Between 1978 and 2004, Youssef Chahine, already considered one of Egypt's premier filmmakers, directed a cycle of four autobiographical, or as he prefers to call them "self-critical," films:[1] *Alexandria..Why?* [*Iskadariyya..lih?*] (1978), *An Egyptian Story* [*Hadduta misriyya*] (1982), *Alexandria Again and Forever* [*Iskandariyya kaman wa-kaman*] (1989) and *Alexandria..New York* [*Iskadariyya..New York*] (2004). Released at uneven intervals over more than a quarter of a century, these films offer representations of Chahine's shifting vision of Alexandria in personal, national, literary, and cultural history. Together the four films of the autobiographical cycle offer a multi-faceted exploration of tolerance and intolerance in Alexandria and beyond Egypt's borders.

Although working in a different medium, Chahine shares a certain artistic vision with his contemporary, the writer Edwar al-Kharrat. For Chahine, like al-Kharrat, the autobiographical impulse reflects a desire to interrogate the self within the past, the individual within society, and the simultaneous coming of age of a subject and the nation. Both juxtapose fragments of autobiography with surrealistic flights of fancy.

Like al-Kharrat, Chahine was born to a Christian family in Alexandria in 1926.[2] Following the end of the Second World War, despite their interests in studying literature and drama respectively, both enrolled at the recently founded University of Alexandria: al-Kharrat to study law and Chahine to study engineering.[3] Both al-Kharrat and Chahine are equally comfortable in their native Arabic as they are in English and French. In their professional careers, both have served as mediators of Western culture within Egypt—al-Kharrat as a translator of literature, and Chahine in his frequent citations of Hollywood films. However, in contrast to al-Kharrat who, although highly respected within literary circles in Egypt and the Arab world and by a small group of international scholars, has a somewhat limited readership, Chahine's films reach a broad Egyptian, Arab, and international audience. In a 1996 poll of the Egyptian film industry, 13 of Chahine's films ranked among the top 100 Egyptian films, more than any other director.[4] In addition to his stature in Egypt and the Arab world, his films have also competed in prestigious international film festivals since 1952, when his second film, *Ibn al-nil* [*Nile Boy*] (1951), was entered into competition at Cannes. He won a Silver Bear at the Berlin International Festival in 1979 for *Alexandria ... Why?*, and in 1997 he was honored with a lifetime achievement award at Cannes.

My discussion of the writings of al-Kharrat and Abdel Meguid in the previous chapters began by posing the question, "What face does Alexandria present of Egypt?" Their work reformulates the characterizations of Alexandrian cosmopolitanism perpetuated by Lawerence Durrell, and to a lesser extent by E. M. Forster and other writers of European languages. Their response is a non-essentializing, local and particular re-formulation of the cosmopolitan myth. Their writing, although nostalgic for elements of coexistence and tolerance, is also critical of the colonial system in which cosmopolitanism thrived in Egypt. Abdel Meguid's novels in particular are situated in the materiality of the city and in the details of everyday life: birth and mortality rates, the cost of groceries, and local scandals. Abdel Meguid's and al-Kharrat's novels attempt to reclaim the cosmopolitan moment within the context of Egyptian cultural memory, and, as I argue, offer an "authentic" and locally specific alternative to parochial ethno-linguistic nationalism. My analysis of the novels situates them squarely within Egyptian Arabic literary and cultural history.

Chahine's films, like al-Kharrat's and Abdel Meguid's novels, project back at their Egyptian audience a reflection of themselves, a portrayal of their collective past, and a vision of the self within the nation. In content and aesthetics, Chahine's films are indeed very Egyptian. Chahine initially rose within the Egyptian film industry as a director of melodramas for the commercial market. With the release of his sixth film *The Blazing Sun* [*Sira'fi al-wadi*] (1954) that represents exploitation of the peasantry in the Egyptian countryside, Chahine began to make a name in Egypt and the Arab world as a politically engaged director with commercial appeal. Critic Ibrahim al-'Aris notes that several of Chahine's films preceding *Alexandria ... Why?* demonstrate commitment to class struggle, nationalism, and socially relevant psychological analysis.[5] His film *The Sparrow* [*al-'Usfur*] (1973), depicting corruption, the regime's manipulation of the media, and the people's response to the defeat of the 1967 Arab–Israeli war, captured the mood of the nation. Other films, explore either specific social issues Egypt faces, such as *The Earth* [*al-Ard*] (1969), or interrogate what it means to be Egyptian, like *The Other* [*al-Akhar*] (1999).

To Western viewers Chahine is perhaps best known for his engaging late-career Franco–Egyptian coproductions such as *Destiny* [*al-Masir*] (1997), a bio-pic of sorts of twelfth century Muslim philosopher Ibn Rushd (Averroes). *Destiny*, like Chahine's *Alexandria Quartet*, reflects on questions of tolerance and coexistence. The East–West divide in the perception of Chahine's work could perhaps be articulated as a disjuncture between the terms "engagé" and "engaging." However, these terms need not be perceived as mutually exclusive, as Chahine's films demonstrate again and again.

Chahine's notion of himself as a political actor is situated within, but not limited to, the confines of the nation. In an interview following the release of *An*

Egyptian Story, Chahine articulated a vision of the self as a social, historical, and cosmopolitan being: "The term 'my life' requires some clarification. My life is connected to others who constitute my society, my country, and the whole world."[6] This view is also evident in his films. Taken in aggregate, the purview of Chahine's autobiographical quartet, for example, extends well beyond the boundaries of the nation—the principles of tolerance and coexistence he explores in these films are not locally specific. Furthermore, although in the autobiographical cycle Alexandria functions as a point of departure and point of return—at least on the emotional and artistic level—the narrative is peripatetic. Yahia, Chahine's on-screen alter ego, travels to London, Moscow, Berlin, Cannes, Algiers, and New York, and spends as much time on screen in Cairo, the adult Chahine's home, as he does in Alexandria.[7]

Thus, unlike his literary counterparts, it is more difficult to situate Chahine's work in a single locality or nation—he sees himself, and has been received as both an Egyptian and an international artist. Indeed, the title of Chahine's fourth autobiographical film, *Alexandria ... New York* suggests that one needs to read the film, and the entire autobiographical cycle, in the context of its multiple points of reference.

We can also see this resistance to a single locality, to a single cultural tradition in the myriad of intertexts in Chahine's films. Critic David Kehr has described referentiality as a constant feature of Chahine's films: "You are never alone watching a Chahine film, but sharing his company with a third party—the phantom of whatever filmmaker he is invoking at the moment."[8] Sometimes the references take the form of emulation of directors or works that have influenced him. *An Egyptian Story* is a clear nod to Bob Fosse's *All That Jazz* (1979). Likewise, in *Alexandria Again and Forever* one can see the influence of Federico Fellini's *8½* (1963). References in Chahine films also take the form of direct citations. For example, in *Alexandria ... Why?* Yahia walks past a poster advertising *Ziegfeld Follies* (1946),[9] and is shown viewing the "Stairway to Paradise" scene from *An American in Paris* (1951),[10] followed by Eleanor Powell dancing to "Three Cheers for the Red, White, and Blue" from *Born to Dance* (1936).[11] Chahine's films in their citation and emulation of Hollywood musicals clearly serve as a tribute to the genre.

Yet, the relationship between Chahine's films and American cinema is not unidirectional; it is dialogic. For example, the scene from *An American in Paris* that Yahia views features the performance of Georges Guétary (né Lambros Worldou) a singer of Alexandrian Greek origin who settled in France. Some critics have noted the anachronism of the inclusion *An American in Paris* (1951), a decidedly postwar film, within a period piece set in 1942.[12] However, I would like to suggest that this inclusion is more a comment on place and identity than it is about time and history. Although Chahine is particularly fond of musical dance numbers that feature the star descending a staircase, his selection of this scene from this particular film draws attention to Guétary, destabilizing notions of identity and place. In *An American in Paris*, Guétary's character, Henri Baurel, represents the quintessential Parisian. The audience is informed by the title of the film and the opening voiceover that Jerry Mulligan, the "American," is out of place—it turns out that behind the scenes, the "Parisian" is, too. Guétary, an international star, emerged from the same milieu that Chahine is representing on film. Chahine's citation of this particular American film, in other words, is not merely a form of adulation for Hollywood musicals, but a reflection upon cosmopolitanism itself. Furthermore, Chahine is in effect writing Alexandria into American cinema, just as he is writing the minorities back into Alexandria from which their memory had been erased.

Chahine's references to Egyptian culture are similarly unstable. In *Alexandria ... New York* when the young Yahia first lays eyes on his beautiful classmate, Ginger Fox he experiences a flashback to an Egyptian cinema where he watched Layla Murad, the much beloved actress–singer of Jewish extraction, perform "*Ana qalbi dalili*" ["My heart is my guide"] the title song of a 1947 film directed by Anwar Wajdi. In *The Other* the protagonist, Adam, quotes Salah Jahin, a poet famous for composing verses in the colloquial dialect, as well for his work as a cartoonist and artist. One could read these references as situating Chahine's late-career films—films explicitly about American economic and political influence on Egypt and the Arab world—within an Egyptian cultural context, diffusing complaints by some Arab Nationalist and Islamist critics of the wholly Western orientation of his films. However, one could also read these citations as an oblique form of self-referentiality or personalized tribute to individuals with whom Chahine had worked on other projects: Murad starred in Chahine's *Lady on a Train* [*Sayyidat al-qitar*] (1952) and Jahin is credited with cowriting the script for *Return of the Prodigal Son* [*Awdat ibn al-dal*] (1976). This richness of unexpected juxtapositions, self-referentiality, and playful blurring of boundaries define Chahine's artistry, and destabilize rigid notions of identity and place in his work.

This fluidity of identity extends to Chahine's representation of the self on screen. Although Chahine's works can be grouped into loose categories, as critic Ibrahim Fawal has done—social dramas and melodramas, wartime and postwar films, auto-biographical films, and historical films[13]—they are perhaps best characterized by their mixing of genres. The quartet of films is identified by the predominance of its representation of the experiences of the character, Yahia. In other words, it privileges the autobiographical over other genres, even as it includes elements of social drama, melodrama, history, fantasy, and the musical.

There is no doubt that protagonist of the film cycle, Yahia, is intended to function as Chahine's dramatic projection of himself—a point Chahine himself has made in numerous interviews.[14] This identification between character and film-maker is perhaps most evident in the attribution of films that Chahine had directed to the character, Yahia. In *An Egyptian Story* Yahia is seen on the set of *Cairo Station* [*Bab al-hadid*] (1958) and *The Sparrow*—both films Chahine directed. Yahia is also depicted attending a number of international film festivals in which Chahine's films competed. In *Alexandria Again and Again*, Yahia is shown at the 1979 Berlin Film Festival receiving the Silver Bear for *Alexandria ... Why?*. And, in *Alexandria ... New York* Yahia is feted at a retrospective of his work at Lincoln Center that featured screenings of *Cairo Station* and *Alexandria ... Why?*, and is shown receiving a lifetime achievement award at the Cannes Film Festival.

However, the plots of the films diverge, to varying extents, from the facts of Chahine's life,[15] and details are sometimes inconsistent from film to film.[16] Chahine's quartet of films are also stylized self-portraits rendered into spectacle to distance them from an objectivist or realist aesthetic. What, then, does it mean to call them autobiographical?

The writings of John Paul Eakin, influenced by the work of Philippe Lejeune,[17] take as their premise that "the self that is the center of all autobiographical narrative is necessarily a fictive structure."[18] Eakin reads autobiography simultaneously as "both an art of memory and an art of the imagination."[19] In what follows, I rely upon a flexible definition of autobiography less concerned with issues of genre, factuality, and authenticity, than with the texts as constructed narratives of the self. As Rachel Gabara writes, "Autobiography is always a locus of contact among many genres, at once representation and invention, nonfiction and fiction, in the present and in the past and in the first and third persons."[20]

Some critics have cast doubt on whether it is accurate to apply the term "autobiography" to the medium of film at all. Such critics point to the inherently collaborative process of filmmaking and the presence of actors as indicators of the fundamental impossibility of autobiographical film. Gabara has refuted these views, charging that critics place "revert to a more restrictive generic classification" for film autobiography than they apply to text.[21] Gabara rather points to the ways in which the medium of film provides access to new modes of representation of the self. She writes, "Filmic autobiography with its material, visible split between director or filmer and actor or filmed self ... troubles our conventional notions of coherent identity and provides us with new forms in which to explore and represent fragmented subjectivity."[22] In my analyses of Chahine's quartet, I rely upon Gabara's inclusionary characterization of "autobiography" and "filmic autobiography" as concepts that transcend genre and other limiting classificatory boundaries.

To this end, it is also worth noting that by the time he began filming *Alexandria ... Why?*, Youssef Chahine already exerted substantial control over the creative process. Chahine wrote or coauthored, and, of course, directed all four autobiographical films, and had a hand in producing them as well. In the first two decades of his career, Chahine had worked within the private sector film industry and the public film sector established in 1962 under the Socialist Charter. When Anwar Sadat succeeded Gamal Abdel Nasser to the Egyptian presidency, he dismantled the apparatuses of the Socialist state put into place during his predecessor's regime, and opened the economy to foreign investment, a policy known as *infitah*.[23] In 1972, the year the public film sector was officially dismantled, Chahine established his own production company, Misr International Films [*aflam misr al-'alamiyya*]. The first three films he made after the establishment of Misr International Films, including *Alexandria ... Why?*, were coproductions with the Algerian state film company, Office National du Commerce et de l'Industre Cinématographiques (ONCIC). Chahine independently produced *An Egyptian Story*. In 1985 he secured an arrangement for French coproduction of his films, a situation that persisted through the completion of *Alexandria ... New York*.[24]

Over his career a number of Chahine films have been the source of controversy. In particular, he has been subjected to criticism from a variety of camps within Egypt for his work produced with French financing. Whereas some critics have charged that his films turned away from conventions of Egyptian popular cinema toward the tastes of European connoisseurs of art cinema, other more radical voices accused him of treason and blasphemy. The controversies surrounding specific films are detailed below. However, there is some irony in the criticism that has accompanied Chahine's increasing visibility in the West. As Joel Gordon notes in his study of films of the Nasser era, "scoring higher in international competitions and gaining larger foreign (non-Arab) audiences" was one of the goals of the socialized public sector film industry in the late 1960s.[25]

From Alexandria to New York

The thread that binds together the autobiographical films is Yahia's narrative: his development as an artist and political actor. Each of the films addresses a different set of issues, arising at different historical moments, and at various stages in the character / filmmaker's life. The trajectory of the filmic quartet is also shaped by its cyclical structure. The story begins in Alexandria with a boy in the thrall of American popular culture. By the end of the first film, the boy, full of hope and promise, arrives in New York to pursue his dreams of entering show business. The final film represents his triumphant return to New York as a respected and successful filmmaker after many years of struggle. A closer look at the opening and closing scenes of the quartet highlights this circular structure and elucidates the contrasts it sets up between the two locales, and the images with which each is associated on-screen.

The opening credits of *Alexandria ... Why?* roll over scenes of children splashing in the turquoise waters of the Mediterranean as adults watch from the shade of the tiered cabanas that embrace the beach in a horseshoe curve. The year is 1942 and the Afrika Corps under Rommel has begun its drive toward Alexandria, but in Chahine's representation, the city's inhabitants are as yet oblivious of or indifferent to the threat and the brutality of the raging war, and continue pursuing their daily pleasures. Over the beach scenes, we hear the romantic strains of an orchestra playing the 1940s Latin jazz hit, "Perfidia"—a song of treachery and betrayal, "And to the sea, mirror of my heart / The times it has seen me cry (because of) / The treacherousness of your love."[26]

When the music swells to a dramatic crescendo, the image cuts to black-and-white footage of Hitler reviewing his troops taken from Leni Riefenstahl's propaganda film, *Triumph of the Will* (1935), then to a clip from *Easy to Love* (1953)[27] featuring Esther Williams emerging out of the water at the end of a tow line, and back to Hitler, before returning to scenes of people going about their daily lives and enjoying themselves along the Alexandrian shore—an aerial shot of the coastline, people fishing off rocks and piers, and boats in the harbor. The montage sets up a contrast between the visual orderliness of the Nazi military-propaganda machine and the relaxed disorder of the Mediterranean beach community—a contrast that

bears out in the remainder of the film as a conflict between Alexandrian cosmopolitanism and militarized ethno-nationalisms that threaten its existence.[28] The
embedded Esther Williams clip represents a different kind of choreographed order,
one that shares with Alexandria the love of sea and sun, and offers a referent to the
visual iconography of classic Hollywood cinema that shaped Chahine's representation of Alexandria. These clips from a variety of visual media introduce a poly-
phonic film with historical, autobiographical, and fictional elements. Released in
1978, the film offers a nostalgic representation of a cosmopolitan Alexandria that
no longer existed.

The final scenes of *Alexandria … New York* are also comprised of a montage of
iconic images of an urban landscape, this time of New York at the beginning of
the new millennium. Yahia, looking forlorn, emerges from Lincoln Center where
he has seen, perhaps for the last time, his estranged American son, Alexander,
perform with the New York City Ballet. To indicate that he is wandering the
streets of midtown Manhattan, we see a montage of New York landmarks: the
Chrysler Building, St. Patrick's Cathedral, and Times Square, where the camera
zooms in to identify Yahia within the anonymous, teeming crowd. As night falls,
Yahia continues to walk alone in the dark and rainy streets. These scenes are offset
by images of Alexander sitting alone in an empty bar, and losing concentration
during rehearsal. Despite his arrogant, indifferent exterior, in these brief scenes
Alexander appears to show signs of internal emotional conflict in response to
learning that a stranger, an Arab filmmaker no less, is his father. The soundtrack
accompanying these scenes of alienation features a loose interpretation of another
American musical standard, "New York, New York," the title song of the 1977
film directed by Martin Scorsese.[29] The film—like Chahine's—recreates the atmosphere of 1940s Hollywood musicals; the title song was composed in the idiom
of period show tunes. But, rather than the romanticized tribute to the city of hope,
opportunity, and new beginnings offered by the original song, the words to the
Arabic version reflect deep-seated bitterness: "If you have a heart on the branches,
immigrant, don't come / If you have a voice as sweet as a nightingale, don't sing /
New York kills all nostalgia."[30] The song continues: "Like the end of the most
beautiful love story / I longed to live within the most beautiful embrace." These
lyrics represent disillusionment—not the absence of nostalgia, but rather its loss,
its murder. Released in 2004, Chahine's decidedly anti-nostalgic film, set prior to
September 11, 2001, offers a representation of a New York of the past, a New York
that no longer existed.

These two collages of lost cityscapes frame Chahine's autobiographical quartet
of films. The first is accompanied by a song to the sea (and metonymically the city
on its shores) by a lover spurned. The second acts out a cynical retort by a rejected
suitor. What is the nature of these urban love affairs? Where have they gone awry?
And why is the reaction to their memory so different?

The title of the first film poses a question: "Alexandria, Why?" The interroga-
tive affords the possibility of ambiguity, of irresolution. It also functions as a cry
of protest, objection, lament. Why did she have to go? Why did its inhabitants not
see the effects of their own decadence, and the signs of decay? Why did foreign

powers seek to control Alexandria—first the French, then the British, and then the unsuccessful Italians and Germans? Or, as critic Ibrahim Fawal has put it, "Why ... is Alexandria made a stage for their battling armies?"[31]

The parallel structure of the titles invites one to extend the question—as protest and lament—to the other city as well: New York, why? Why is she so cruel and heartless? The film also begs the question in its inverse: Why New York? Why is New York—a city to which the film's protagonist has traveled infrequently, although with which he clearly identifies—chosen as the location for the final installment of Chahine's autobiographical film cycle, and what is its relationship to the other city in the film's title, Alexandria? If Alexandria is so important to Chahine, what is the significance of the relocation of the narrative to New York?

As the title of Chahine's 1989 film *Alexandria Again and Forever* (literally translated, "Alexandria Again and Again") articulates, Alexandria lives on in memory and representation. It remains Chahine's point of departure and point of return. Alexandria is the repository of nostalgia, the lost, irrecoverable cosmopolitan space. New York represents desire, perpetually deferred, unattainable. The fulfillment of desire is its death, its disappearance. In the first three films of the cycle Yahia aspires, desires, to "make it" in New York. His desire fulfilled, in the final film, Yahia is left disillusioned. New York supplants the absent Alexandria. However, New York must repel all nostalgia for itself in order to be a repository of nostalgia for the lost cosmopolitan space, Alexandria.

In what follows, I analyze the film cycle with an aim at interpreting Chahine's representation of cosmopolitanism through the relationship to these two cities. Throughout, Chahine's autobiographical film cycle articulates a concern with tolerance and coexistence in modern societies.[32] Whereas the commitment to cosmopolitanism is consistent, the understanding of the term undergoes some transformation throughout the films. I trace the shifting significations of the notion, and its association with the cities of Alexandria and New York in each of the four films, with particular focus on the films most directly engaged with the issues: *Alexandria ... Why?* and *Alexandria ... New York*.

A denomination like any other

As already noted Chahine's films offer a pastiche of film references; however, *Alexandria ... Why?* does not have the same relationship to past visual representations of Alexandria that his Egyptian literary counterparts have to the existing body of literature by writers such as Forester, Cavafy, and Durrell.[33] With the exception of the 1969 film version of Durrell's *Alexandria Quartet, Justine* directed by George Cukor, Alexandrian cosmopolitanism has had scant representation on film outside of Egypt.[34] Within Egypt, the television series *Zizinia*, the first season of which aired in 1997 also represents cosmopolitan Alexandria.[35]

In the world of Egyptian commercial cinema, Alexandria and its "northern coast" rather signifies the lighthearted frivolity of a beach vacation in which pleasure-seeking easily slides into vice. Several musical films have immortalized this image of Alexandria such as Layla Murad's romantic encounter on the shores of

Marsa Matruh in *Shore of Love* [*Shati' al-gharam*] (1950),[36] and 'Abd al-Halim Hafiz's campy installation to the club of beach-goers in *My Father is Up a Tree* [*Abi fawq al-shajara*] (1969),[37] reminiscent of the Frankie Avalon and Annette Funicello "Beach Party" movies of the 1960s. A more recent heartthrob, 'Amr Diyab, appears to have followed in their footsteps in attempting to re-define the Alexandrian beach musical for a new generation in *Ice Cream in Glym* [*Ice Cream fi glim*] (1992).[38]

Two Nasser-era films based on novels by Naguib Mahfouz, *Autumn Quail* [*Al-Summan wa-al-kharif*] and *Miramar*, diverge from this representation of Alexandria as the site of melodramatic summer romance, conforming instead to the literary model discussed in Chapter 2. The novels, both set in Alexandria, were made into films in 1967 and 1968, respectively.[39] These films, like the literary texts upon which they are based, reflect narratives that domesticate Alexandria and incorporate the city and its inhabitants into the national narrative.

Chahine's nostalgic turn in *Alexandria ... Why?*, then, was out of step with existing Egyptian filmic images of Alexandria, and as the tepid public response reflected, out of step with the tastes of the day. Critics often refer to Egyptian realist films of the late 1970s as "new cinema," a term reflecting shifts in both the modes of production in the Egyptian film industry and in the content of the films. As Walter Armbrust writes, "as public sector production facilities decayed—and were never returned to the private sector nor replaced by comparable private-funded facilities—directors were forced to become less reliant on studios."[40] Armbrust continues by saying, "The city became a backdrop for many films."[41] The realism achieved by shooting on location reflected cityscapes in decay, images consistent with the anti-modernist ideology Armbrust identifies in the films of this era.[42] Chahine's nostalgic representation of the past ran counter to this prevailing cinematic trend, as did his glorification of Alexandria in *Alexandria ... Why?*; the "city" in Egyptian cinema in general and in Egyptian "new cinema" in particular is Cairo.

The plot of *Alexandria ... Why?* proceeds chronologically from 1942 through the late 1940s, interweaving several narrative strands. Yahia's coming of age and the development of his dramatic interests provide the arc of the plot. Yahia's parents, Christians of Lebanese origin, struggle to provide for their children in an age of decadence and conspicuous consumption. The film traces Yahia's first successful dramatic efforts in high school, the embarrassing failure of his first large-scale production, and ultimately his departure to study acting at the Pasadena Playhouse. The other narrative strands explore earnest but unsophisticated attempts by a group of nationalist revolutionaries to oust the British, a homosexual encounter between an aristocratic Egyptian vigilante and a British soldier whom he kidnapped, and a love affair between an aristocratic Jew and a poor Muslim student who are both involved in a underground Leftist, anti-colonial organization.

Alexandria ... Why? is widely read as a film about tolerance and coexistence. According to Hala Halim, the film "nostalgically salvage[es] an intercommunal tolerance from the Alexandrian experience." In Halim's view, Chahine "avoids the facile enshrining of cosmopolitanism by training a keen eye on the relationship between the city's diversity and issues of social class, nationalism and colonialism."[43] Ibrahim Fawal views Chahine's representation of Alexandria as an expression of a utopian desire, "more idealistic than realistic." Fawal explains that, "even in his idealized Alexandria, not all ethnic groups mingled with and tolerated each other to the extent that he suggests."[44]

In an interview following the release of the film Chahine described Alexandrian society during his childhood as follows:

> Alexandrians coexisted in a special way, because all of their lives they lived with people from different denominations and nationalities—Jews, Italians, Greeks and others. The Jews were just another denomination like any other. The Jews began to interest us because of the situation in Palestine. It took on a different hue. But that came later. The coexistence in the environment of Alexandria was complete.[45]

In this statement, Chahine defines Alexandrian diversity along two axes: "denominations" (*tawa'if*) and "nationalities" (*jinsiyyat*). By denominations, as he makes clear, he means members of different religions, particularly the religious minorities.

Alexandria ... Why? depicts the interfaith harmony Chahine describes. Characters are all clearly identified with their respective religious heritages, but it never serves as a source of conflict in the film.[46] Yahia's identification as Christian, for example, features prominently. After the failure of his dramatic production, Yahia goes to visit the grave of his older brother, Freddy, who had died from pneumonia as a child. In a flashback rife with Christian imagery, Yahia recalls accidentally setting fire to a crèche and blaming it on his brother. In his youthful mind, he sees the two events as linked. To him, Freddy, in effect, died for Yahia's sins. Yahia's Christianity is portrayed as a matter of personal concern without any bearing on his outward comportment. Yahia's friends, fellow students at the prestigious Victoria College, include Muhsin, a Muslim, and David, a Jew. None of the characters in the film, the boys chief among them, ever seems to pay particular attention to religious difference.

The boys also represent the fluid, religiously inclusive notion of Egyptianness that the film portrays. In *Alexandria ... Why?*, religious difference does not preclude Jews, Christians, and Muslims, all of whom are equally considered Egyptian, in terms of nationality and national identification.[47] Chahine emphasizes this point in the interview cited above by explicitly stating, "David the Jew is an Egyptian."[48]

Despite Chahine's reference in the interview to tolerance in Alexandria between "people from different ... nationalities," in *Alexandria ... Why?* national identity serves as a somewhat more problematic marker of difference than religion. For example, whereas Yahia's religious identification is unflinchingly represented on-screen, the family's Lebanese origin is mentioned only by implication, and in a single fleeting reference, when Qadry, Yahia's father, takes his sister, Nadia, to Beirut to meet a prospective suitor. Throughout the film, there is also scant reference to or representation of Greeks and Italians, prominent communities within Alexandria in the 1940s, and which Chahine specifically mentions in his comments. The film appears to reflect a certain implicit discomfort with national identifications as markers of difference.

Furthermore, despite the film's portrayal of religious tolerance and coexistence, nationality turns out to be a source of strife. Whereas Greek, Italian, and Syro–Lebanese nationalities are downplayed in the film, the "nationalities" that are foregrounded are those of combatants—Egyptians versus British, British versus Germans.

This distinction between religion and nationality turns out to be particularly important for the Jews in the film. As already stated, in Chahine's representation of 1940s Alexandria, there is no question that Jews, like their Muslim and Christian counterparts, are considered Egyptian. However, Zionism, the articulation of Jewish national desires, is portrayed, not surprisingly, as incompatible with Egyptian nationality.[49]

The notion that characters can only identify with one nationality is made apparent by the fates of the members of the Jewish family, the Sorels, through the course of the film. The Sorel family is comprised of the patriarch, a wealthy Jewish businessman, his daughter Sarah, a Communist activist, and his son David, Yahia's classmate and friend. Sarah falls in love with another young revolutionary, Ibrahim. Just as Sarah discovers she is pregnant with Ibrahim's baby, she is compelled to flee the approaching Nazi army with her family. While she is gone, Ibrahim is arrested and convicted of treason for engaging in revolutionary activities.

The Sorels wait out the war in South Africa before continuing on to Palestine where identity politics takes its toll on family unity. David is shown participating in a guerrilla attack on what appears to be a hotel or public building. David, the Jew who was Egyptian, forsakes his homeland and the ideals of his city of origin, for Zionism. For father and daughter, both shaped by Alexandrian tolerance and coexistence, the experience in Palestine is disillusioning. The father condemns the use of violence, subscribing rather to a vision of coexistence proclaiming, "I refuse to affirm one right at the expense of another." After confronting the realities of the conflict in Palestine, and the implications of Zionism on a Jew's identification with her country of origin, Sarah turns her back on parochial nationalism and returns to Alexandria, the paragon of cosmopolitan coexistence, and to the revolutionary ideology that landed her lover, Ibrahim, in an Egyptian prison. She describes her experiences to Ibrahim as follows:

> Father told me that in Palestine he would show me the seed of the society we dreamed about. Sadly, there I saw Judaism becoming a nationality through violence and blood. Imagine when every Jew in the world suddenly finds himself belonging to an illusory nationality different from that of his country of birth.

As the two siblings demonstrate, Jews could either assert their loyalty to Egypt and remain there, like Sarah, or assert their loyalty to Zionism and the establishment of a Jewish state, and settle in Palestine, like David.

This distinction between religion and nationality is important within the film, although it was lost on its detractors. Released in 1978 amidst the political re-alignments of the region marked by Egyptian President Anwar Sadat's visit to Jerusalem and the subsequent negotiations between Egypt and Israel brokered by the United States,[50] the film was received in the Arab world as an endorsement of Egypt's rapprochement with Israel. The film was banned in Syria, Iraq, and Algeria.[51] Critic Ibrahim Fawal has summarized the controversy as follows:

> Arab intellectuals, who were eager for a film which would give vent to their frustration and would fuel their anger at Sadat's defection, were stunned. What they saw, instead, was a film depicting Egypt of the 1940s, and speaking of forgiveness at a time when the Arabs felt surrounded by enemies. Some went so far as to accuse Chahine of complicity with the Jewish state.[52]

Chahine, however, has denied playing politics with the film.[53] Although he may not have intended to enter into the fray following Sadat's controversial overtures to Israel, he was acutely aware that in any portrayal of Jews in the Arab world, the Israeli–Palestinian conflict is not far from mind.

Rejected in the Arab world, *Alexandria … Why?* was the first of Chahine's films to win a prize at a major European film festival. Several of Chahine's films had previously been entered into international competition at prestigious European film festivals. *Cairo Station* was entered into the competition at the 1959 Berlin International Film Festival, and three other Chahine films, *Nile Boy* (1951), *The Blazing Sun* and *The Earth* had competed for the top prize at the Cannes Film Festival. At the 1979 Berlin Film Film Festival, *Alexandria … Why?* was awarded the Silver Bear Special Jury Prize. It would not be surprising if the depiction of coexistence set against the violence of the Second World War on the one hand and the Arab–Israeli conflict on the other appealed to the jury in much the same way it had offended the film's Arab detractors.[54]

Whether or not the film was intended as a timely political commentary, the presence of Jews is not merely incidental. In *Alexandria … Why?*, as well as the other films in the autobiographical cycle, Jews are not merely a *part* of cosmopolitan society—they represent its *primary, essential* component. Both off- and on-screen, Chahine's descriptions and portrayals of Alexandria's cosmopolitan past single out the former presence of Jews as exemplary. In the interview cited above, Chahine pauses after describing Alexandria's various denominations and nationalities to emphasize that, "the Jews were just another denomination like any other." As already mentioned, the Italians and Greeks are largely absent from Chahine's purview, and the presence of good Muslim–Christian relations persists in the later films, well past the demise of Alexandria's "cosmopolitan" society. For Chahine, the presence of Jews—above all others—serves as evidence of a society's cosmopolitan character.

This identification of Jews as cosmopolitan, although intended in Chahine's *oeuvre* as an expression of a desirable trait in a society, raises the uncomfortable history of the relationship between the terms. In anti-Semitic discourse through the nineteenth century and in Stalinist Soviet rhetoric, "cosmopolitan" was "a code word [...] for the Jew, where rootlessness was a condemnation and a proof of nonbelonging."[55] Such negative implications of the term "cosmopolitanism," according to critic Timothy Brennan, are not "local and idiosyncratic," but rather central to the development of the word's meaning and remain embedded in contemporary usages of the term.[56] Although the portrayal of Jews in *Alexandria ... Why?* functions as an attempt to dislodge misconceptions of the Jewish past in Egypt and to call into question prevalent anti-Semitic stereotypes of Jews held by the Egyptian and Arab public, the film's identification of Jews as figures of the cosmopolitan nevertheless retains an uneasy ambivalence.

The understanding of cosmopolitanism derived from Yahia's experience in Alexandria follows him to America, and shapes the experience of his arrival. The closing scene of *Alexandria ... Why?* shows Yahia aboard an ocean liner arriving in New York harbor. Glenn Miller's big band arrangement of "Moonlight Serenade" plays on the soundtrack as Yahia watches the approach to the Statue of Liberty from the upper deck. The music blends with the sound of chanting, and he notices a group of religious Jews in traditional Eastern European garb—presumably immigrants—praying on the lower deck.[57] When he looks back up at the Statue of Liberty, she has been transformed into a grotesque, cartoonish figure—a heavy-set woman with taunting eyes, missing teeth, and a green-painted face. She returns Yahia's gaze and laughs at him.

Why does Liberty laugh? Is she mocking Yahia's naïve vision of America forged through Hollywood imagery played against a big band soundtrack? Is she a jaded immigrant of an earlier generation mocking the new arrivals? Is she, as some critics suggest, a painted woman, and if so, to whom or what is she—as an analogue for America—prostituting herself?[58] Or, is it a commentary on the self-serving nature of American foreign policy in the Middle East, and the privileges granted to Jews and the Jewish state at the expense of the Arabs, as Chahine himself has expressed?[59] The film ends abruptly with this puzzling image, letting it stand in all its ambiguity.

The film leaves Yahia on board a ship in New York harbor, poised to enter the New World, his promised land. He hangs in the liminal space between his Alexandrian past and his future as a filmmaker, between childhood and adulthood, between Egypt and America, between Alexandria and New York. It is not until 26 years after the release of the film, in *Alexandria ... New York*, that Chahine explores on film what Yahia found in America.

A revolutionary demon

The second installment of the autobiographical film cycle, *An Egyptian Story*, narrates how Chahine came to make *Alexandria ... Why?*, although it contains no direct references to its predecessor. *An Egyptian Story* opens with a depiction of the event that Chahine attributes to leading him into the more introspective and self-reflexive mode of the autobiographical films, his heart attack during the filming of *The Sparrow* (1973). In *An Egyptian Story*, Yahia experiences chest pain on the set and his doctor sends him to London for tests followed by emergency bypass surgery. The film literalizes the notion of inner conflict by staging a trial of Yahia's character inside his chest cavity as he undergoes the surgery.[60]

An Egyptian Story proceeds as a series of flashbacks about his relationships with family and close associates spanning from his early childhood to the recent past, punctuated by "trial" scenes. In particular, the flashbacks function as a retrospective of the filmmaker's life and work. Yahia's struggle for recognition at international film festivals and by American studio executives is played out again and again throughout the film as he meets with one rejection, insult, or near miss after another. And in Egypt, Yahia is faced with the added pressure of censorship. He is forced to defend his film, *The Sparrow*, before the censorship board, which sends one of its members to monitor the filming.

In Yahia's struggle to reconcile with his past, he emerges as a political actor, in comparison to his portrayal in *Alexandria … Why?* as a character driven by art more than politics. Of note is a scene marking this transformation in *An Egyptian Story* in which Yahia, during the period between his completion of high school and his departure for the United States—the period depicted in *Alexandria … Why?*—participates in a demonstration against the British occupation.[61] When his friends come to the bank where he is working to tell him about ongoing mass demonstrations, Yahia displays his ignorance of Egyptian politics. Yet, he joins them in the demonstration outside a British outpost guarded by Egyptian officers and British cavalry. Yahia exacts his personal revenge on the occupying power and the collaborating Egyptian forces by striking two commanding officers in the head with rocks launched by a slingshot. Yahia is heroically injured in the melee that ensues as the cavalry break up the demonstration.

At other points in the film, the adult Yahia is portrayed as an activist filmmaker concerned with portraying those marginalized by society (*Cairo Station*), and the struggles of anti-colonial nationalist movements (*Jamila, the Algerian* [*Jamila al-jaza'iriyya*] (1958)). While Yahia is completing the filming of *Jamila*, his screenwriter Mahdi praises him for becoming "a revolutionary demon" through his actions. In this context, the film could also be read as a corrective to *Alexandria … Why?*; the foregrounding of Yahia's activism in *An Egyptian Story* could serve as a proof positive of both the character's and the director's Leftist and decidedly pro-Arab political allegiances.[62]

Ibrahim Fawal writes, "From the beginning Chahine insinuates that this is not merely an account of his life, but also a premonition of Egypt's future."[63] The title of the film—the only one of the autobiographical sequence not to contain the name of his beloved city—also signals a shift. The film's representation of Egyptianness is more normative than that of *Alexandria … Why?*. From Yahia's participation in the anti-colonial struggle to his attendance at a concert by Umm Kulthum in Cairo, and the inclusion of footage from Nasser's speech nationalizing the Suez Canal, the film is rife with iconography of Egyptian national pride. With the exception of flashbacks to his childhood already mentioned, the "Egyptian" scenes transpire in Cairo. Further, by contrast to the previous film, Egyptian diversity is defined regionally, embodied by the exoticism of Yahia's "Pharaonic Nubian," his collaborator, Mahdi.

The film's depiction of Egyptianness, though, is also deterritorialized, portable and transnational. In contrast to *Alexandria ... Why?*, which expands notions of Egyptianness to include resident minorities, *An Egyptian Story* expands national identity beyond the physical boundaries of the nation. Throughout the film Yahia travels. At the Cannes and Moscow film festivals (and Berlin in absentia) Yahia literally represents his country. Yahia also meets with studio executives in New York, travels to Algeria to witness the revolution first-hand, and seeks medical attention in London, where he visits with expatriate Egyptian friends and family. In contrast to the more typical narratives of *abna' al-balad*—be they of *fellahin* working the land or the struggling urban working-classes[64]—the film posits both Yahia's sensitivity to Egyptians and their concerns, and his struggle for international recognition as equally significant parts of his "Egyptian story."

In other words, the urban culture of tolerance and coexistence of *Alexandria ... Why?* is replaced by transnational individualism in *An Egyptian Story*. Despite Yahia's globetrotting, the purview of political action in the film is as a citizen of a country, Egypt, and a nation, Arab, not as a citizen of the world. His travels are for individual gain on a global scale, in the name of Egypt or pan-Arab solidarity.

However, Alexandria, and the society of tolerance it represents, remains a point of reference for Yahia. In particular, Yahia invokes the cosmopolitan experience of his youth in a series of scenes set in the mid-1950s. Yahia, flush from the filming of his masterpiece *Cairo Station*, prepares to go to a New York studio to appeal for a studio contract.[65] His skeptical wife, Amal, rebukes him, "For the twentieth time you will hear an American Jew say, 'Very good, but no deal.' Why would they take an Egyptian director? There are no directors left but an Arab one?" Yahia responds to his wife's prejudice and the projected prejudice of the studio executives by evoking his beloved city: "In Alexandria we were a hundred religions and a hundred nationalities. It never happened that any one asked why." (No one, that is, except Chahine, and then only with the hindsight of two decades.) Exasperated, his wife retorts: "Everything's changed. It's all gone. Alexandria, forget it ... New York, never!" (*iskandariyya khalas ... New York, never.*)

Yahia's retort to Amal is oblique. One could read his response as implying that as a product of a culture of tolerance, he harbors no such prejudice. His reference to Alexandria's "hundred religions" and "hundred nationalities" in response to Amal's characterization of American Jewish studio executives makes somewhat more sense if we read it as an expression of the notion discussed earlier that Jews in Chahine's films are the essential marker of a cosmopolitan society. As signaled by the closing scene ending of *Alexandria ... Why?* the visible presence of Jews has shifted from Alexandria to New York. The presence of Jews in New York, according to Yahia's logic, would preclude the prejudice Amal anticipates.

Yahia arrives in New York where the studio executive enthusiastically responds to *Cairo Station*, and instructs his assistant to give Yahia a chance. The film then crosses over into fantasy as Yahia leaps in slow motion through a window, and soars through the night sky over skyscrapers to the strains of George Gershwin's "Rhapsody in Blue." As with everything in Chahine's films, his "New York" is citational of preceding film referents. As already long established in a myriad of backstage plays and films, the dream of "showbiz" is always already circumscribed by preexisting expressions of the medium. In this case, the referent is not a 1940s musical, but a contemporaneous vision of the city, Woody Allen's *Manhattan* (1979).[66] In other words, in this scene, Chahine's vision of New York City is circumscribed by the artistic works of two prominent American Jews, both doyens of the entertainment business of their time: George Gershwin and Woody Allen. New York, then, is coded as a Jewish city, not through an encounter with Jews per se, as at the end of *Alexandria ... Why?* but rather through citation.

This fantasy homage to Jewish New York ends abruptly. Amal, it turns out, accurately predicted the outcome of his meeting. Upon his return, Yahia narrates his New York experience to Amal and his associate Mahdi. After days of substantive discussions about scripts and actors, Yahia was inexplicably sent home. In his frustration, like Amal before him, he attributes the studio's motives to prejudice. Mahdi advises him to give up on his American dreams and rebukes him for his own intolerance, just as Yahia had done to Amal in the earlier scene:

MAHDI: Man, your movies are sold throughout the East. Millions see them. All shapes and colors, Druze and Russian, Yellow and White ...

YAHIA: Even the Pharonic Nubian ...

MAHDI: Enough with the Pharoahs. I prefer that the poor people in Nubia and those walking in the streets who love your movies. Why is the world for you only England and America?

AMAL: They are the ones who make movies.

MAHDI: Those are the ones whose films we see. There are many others who make better films.

YAHIA: In any case, we won't win over the Jews. They control everything.

MAHDI: Aha! Weren't you upset when they left Alexandria? Have you become racist?

YAHIA: I mean the Zionists. Do you deny that they control all of the world media?

Yahia's final remark is left to stand without comment. Whereas Jews function as an emblem of a society's tolerance—in New York as in Alexandria—Zionism in the film cycle plays the opposite role. As already articulated, in *Alexandria ... Why?* the distinctions between Judaism and Zionism are clearly demarcated, and geographically delimited—"Jews" embraced the national identity of their home countries, and "Zionists" embraced Jewish nationality and migrated to Palestine. In the remaining films, the geographic boundaries become blurred, and "Zionism" shifts from a marker of nationality to a designation attributed to supporters of the State of Israel and its military. The term "Zionism," then, in *An Egyptian Story* and the later films, functions as a shorthand for intolerance, particularly prejudice against Arabs.

Ultimately, as Mahdi points out, Yahia's frustration and bitterness stems from his repeated slights by the Western, particularly Anglo–American, film industries—studios, critics, and film festival juries alike. The above dialogue unfolds as Yahia is awaiting word from the Berlin film festival, where he has been nominated for best actor for his role in *Cairo Station*. Initially considered a favorite for the award, he was reportedly passed over in his absence because the jury could not determine if the actor shared the character's physical handicap—evidence of prejudice, but certainly not of Zionist conspiracy.

An Egyptian Story is a narrative of an artist's frustration; however, it is not one of utter failure. Although Yahia, like Chahine, is not depicted winning awards at major film festivals in Europe prior to *Alexandria ... Why?*, his films were repeatedly nominated for prizes at Cannes and Berlin. And, although Yahia did not succeed in signing a contract with an American studio, the film does not offer evidence that his dismissal was discriminatory. Indeed, the talent scout speaks to him in broken Arabic that he picked up while working in Cairo, indicating that the studio, on the contrary, actively sought out Arab talent.[67] However, these three scenes that revisit the issue of Jews as figures of the cosmopolitan are somewhat anomalous in this film, and serve only to mark a shift of the cosmopolitan imaginary from Alexandria to New York. These scenes also suggest a blurring of the distinctions between Jews and Zionism that were so carefully maintained in *Alexandria ... Why?*.

The conclusion of the film returns to the major theme discussed above—the depiction of Yahia as an activist director who represents the voice of the nation. Yahia stands up to the censorship board that demands he cease shooting, and returns to complete filming *The Sparrow*. Yahia is shown on the set of the film while we hear a voiceover of Nasser's speech announcing his resignation in 1967 following Egypt's military defeat. The scene then cuts to the closing images of *The Sparrow* that depict the popular response to Nasser's resignation. Crowds of Egyptians take to the streets, and we hear the main character, Bahia screaming, "No, we'll fight." This image of the handiwork of the character/director Yahia secures his credentials both as an independent artist who won't bow to censorship, and as an Egyptian filmmaker with his finger on the pulse of the nation.

It is Yahia's commitment to "struggle" that saves him. The film returns to the conclusion of the trial taking place in his chest as he undergoes heart surgery. Both his family and the magistrate finally take his side in the trial on account of his life-long "struggle" [*kifah*]. Yahia, the fighter, thus, survives the surgery. The final scene in the recovery room represents Yahia's reconciliation with his past, effectively setting the stage for undertaking the autobiographical cycle.

Hamlet and Antony

As already described in the context of the release of *Alexandria ... Why?*, Chahine's cosmopolitanism raised suspicions and criticisms from various nationalist and pan-Arab elements in Egypt and the Arab world. In the years following the release of *An Egyptian Story*, Chahine was subjected to further criticism for agreeing to French coproduction of his films. Some of Chahine's detractors disparaged the French financing as a sell-out to foreign interests—the interests of a former colonial power. The first film to emerge from this coproduction arrangement, *Adieu Bonaparte* [*Wada'ya Bonaparte*] (1985), fanned the flames of criticism. One of the outcomes of an accord of cultural exchange between Egypt and France in 1984 was the commitment to cosponsor a film about the French Expedition to Egypt under Napoleon Bonaparte from 1798–1801.[68] Representatives from both countries independently selected Chahine to undertake the project. The film—a creative interpretation of intercultural contact under military occupation—did not satisfy adherents to Egyptian nationalist, anti-colonial representation of history.[69]

Chahine does not give credence to his detractors by representing the controversies on-screen, but obliquely uses his films to undermine their criticisms. In response to the criticisms of *Alexandria … Why?*, *An Egyptian Story* relates the filmmaker's political coming of age, reviewing the films that had established his credentials as an activist filmmaker. Following *Adieu Bonaparte*, Chahine directed, *The Sixth Day* [*al-Yawm al-sadis*] (1986), based on the novel of the same title by the Egyptian-born, Francophone author, Andrée Chedid.[70] Set during a cholera outbreak in 1947, the film is a family drama against the backdrop of continued British presence in Egypt. Chahine's following film, *Alexandria Again and Forever* (1989), abandons the historical, postcolonial explorations of the previous two films to engage with issues of pressing domestic concern—democracy, solidarity, and freedom of expression. In doing so, Chahine also punctures the criticisms that his foreign funding was driving the agenda of his filmmaking, and once again positions him as an activist filmmaker concerned with contemporary Egyptian affairs.

Alexandria Again and Forever, the third installment of Chahine's autobiographical cycle, is framed by a 1987 hunger strike by Egyptian actors against a change in government laws regulating their union. In the film, Yahia, along with other directors, offers his solidarity with the striking actors by camping out with them in the union building until their demands are met. The film features cameo appearances by a number of luminaries of Egyptian cinema who are shown participating in the strike. The narrative of the strike is interspersed with flashbacks as well as clips from imagined or incomplete films. Unlike the films cited within *An Egyptian Story*, which were all films that Chahine had made, in *Alexandria Again and Forever* the film projects with which Yahia is engaged do not come to fruition—neither within the context of the film, nor in Chahine's *oeuvre*.[71]

The other significant narrative thread in *Alexandria Again and Forever* is more personal than political. The four films that Chahine had directed between 1978 and 1986 featured a young actor, Muhsin Muhyi al-Din, who had played the teenage Yahia in both *Alexandria … Why?* and *An Egyptian Story*. *The Sixth Day* was their last film together. The young actor turned his attention to more lucrative and less demanding roles in television series financed by oil-rich investors from the Gulf States. *Alexandria Again and Forever* also represents an act of mourning for the loss of his protégé, the actor who had played his alter-ego on-screen.

In what could only be described as a doubly narcissistic twist, Yahia (played by Chahine) sees in the actor a young version of himself. In the film, the young actor is named 'Amr. In addition to playing Yahia on-screen in his autobiographical films, 'Amr had been cast to play Hamlet, a role that Yahia had always imagined himself playing. 'Amr, oppressed by Yahia's demanding shooting schedule, and by the director's over-identification with himself and with the role he was cast to play, storms off the set.

To complicate matters further, the visual representation of Yahia and 'Amr implies a romantic connection between them.[72] In one scene, for example, the two soft-shoe together on the snowy streets of Berlin following Yahia's acceptance of the Silver Bear for *Alexandria ... Why?* at the Film Festival. As the scene features both synchronized and competitive dance sequences between the two, it is not clear whether 'Amr is playing Ginger Rogers or Gene Kelly to Yahia's Fred Astaire.[73]

Yahia is devastated when 'Amr walks off the set of *Hamlet*. He keeps hoping that 'Amr will join the strikers, and continues to imagine casting him in the role of Alexander the Great in a historical musical he hopes to direct. In Yahia's imagined film-within-the-film, 'Amr's Alexander is a disengaged despot whose military leaders and clergy terrorize the populace. Yahia appears in the role of a love-struck apologist for the god-king, trying to convince others of his good intentions, despite the atrocities carried out before their eyes. The scene is both a representation of blindness in love—particularly Yahia's blindness to 'Amr's indifference—as well as a biting critique of abuses of power in a police state carried out in the name of the leader's cult of personality.[74]

Alexandria Again and Forever also gives full articulation to Chahine's obsession with *Hamlet*. *Hamlet* features prominently throughout the autobiographical quartet; all three other films contain scenes of Yahia reciting long passages from the play.[75] *Alexandria Again and Forever* features brief clips from Yahia's incomplete film version of Hamlet set in a present-day fishing community in Alexandria, as well as scenes on set during filming. Chahine's affinity for Hamlet's soliloquies represent a nostalgia in their own right to his first love, the theater; Chahine began his career as an actor. But the prince's introspective musings on life, love, and betrayal are also particularly apt within the context of the inherent self-indulgence of a multi-part autobiographical film cycle.

Within *Alexandria Again and Forever* the characters close to Yahia urge him to give up on *Hamlet*. During the strike, a young actress, Nadia, a fierce individualist, challenges Yahia—in his assumptions about gender roles and the concept of the individual within the collective—and appears to pique his romantic interest as well. Nadia implores Yahia to drop his dreams of *Hamlet* in favor of another Shakespeare tragedy, *Antony and Cleopatra*, casting her in the lead. Nadia views Yahia's fascination with *Hamlet* as a solipsistic endeavor—one that inhibits action: "You are one of those who wasn't here with us. Where were you when [Egypt] got to this point? Where were you when it was destroyed? Were you dreaming of Hamlet, or a leader you wanted to bring back to life? Could that leader have been you?"[76] In other words, was he, like Hamlet, paralyzed by indecision, or had his own self-involved musings on this film version of the play prevented him from taking action.[77] Following these remarks, Yahia gives lie to these criticisms. He is thrust into a leadership role in the strike, when the President's office explicitly requests that he join the delegation in negotiations over their demands. Yahia rises to the occasion.

For Nadia, *Antony and Cleopatra*, by contrast to *Hamlet*, represents not just a love story, but a model of heroic leadership, albeit one brought to a tragic end. The play is also a representation of the fall of Ptolemaic rule in the face of consolidation of Imperial power in Rome, and can be read in the context of Chahine's film as an analogue for Egypt's political subjugation to colonial rule (and neo-colonialism) in the modern period. In other words, for Nadia, *Antony and Cleopatra* is a play that gives voice to Egyptian resistance to foreign domination.[78] Yahia ultimately lets go of *Hamlet* and 'Amr. He returns his energies to the literature and lore of his imagined Alexandria, and he turns his attention toward Nadia, the actress aspiring to play Cleopatra.

The various imagined films, flashbacks, and musical sequences embedded in the frame story of the strike make *Alexandria Again and Forever* a rich, textured film. Chahine has identified it as his favorite within his *oeuvre*. Like *An Egyptian Story*, this film establishes the filmmaker's political credentials, although in a somewhat more nuanced and symbolic way. Chahine plants himself firmly within the culture wars of contemporary Egypt, but his references to literature, myth, and history, although they transpire on Egyptian soil, are not Egyptian in the narrow, parochial sense of the term. As such, *Alexandria Again and Forever* stands out in the autobiographical quartet as the film most steeped in Alexandria's long literary history, and the one least engaged with the modern cosmopolitan myth.

A divided self

Following *Alexandria Again and Forever*, Chahine continued his introspective reflection on contemporary Egyptian society in the semi-documentary short film, *Cairo ... As Seen By Chahine*, made at the behest of French television. The controversy that had plagued Chahine in the 1980s continued to follow him. *Cairo*, a lovingly rendered tribute to the Egyptian capital and its inhabitants, also offered an unflinching representation of the city's hardships: unemployment, overcrowding, economic disparity, and pollution. Chahine's detractors criticized him for airing Egypt's dirty laundry on foreign television, and once again called his loyalties into question.[79]

However, the most visible and disruptive opposition to Chahine's work was directed against his film *The Emigrant* [*al-Muhajir*] (1994), a re-telling of the Biblical story of Joseph. The tenor of the criticism directed against this film differed from what had come before. Although, like several of Chahine's films since the mid-1980s, *The Emigrant* had raised questions about the filmmaker's national loyalties and political sympathies, the primary challenge to the film issued from Islamists who were gaining increasing power and visibility in Egyptian society in the 1990s. Upon release of the film, a suit was brought against Chahine accusing him of blasphemy for depicting a holy prophet of Islam. Whereas in the past Chahine had run afoul of Egyptian government censors on a number of occasions, in this case, the Egyptian Board of Censors, which had approved the film, testified on Chahine's behalf. The film was pulled from circulation during the trial, but upon Chahine's acquittal it was returned to theaters.[80]

The campaign against *The Emigrant* was part of an onslaught of aggressive tactics employed by Islamists—both in the legal system, as with the case against

Chahine, and outside of it in the use of violence. As already noted in the previous chapter, the 1990s saw a significant rise in intersectarian strife in Egypt. The attempt to silence him coupled with the raging armed conflict appears to have renewed Chahine's interest in revisiting the issue of coexistence on-screen. His following two films take on the intolerant teachings of radical sheiks. The masterful, and critically acclaimed *Destiny* (1997) represents an appeal for Muslim–Christian understanding. In his 1999 film, *The Other*, Chahine exposes the devastating effects on contemporary Egyptian society of the spread of militant Islam. Chahine's only full length feature to appear between *The Other* and *Alexandria ... New York, Silence ... We're Rolling* [*Skut ... hansawar*] (2001), is a light melodramatic-musical confection starring Latifa, but Ibrahim Fawal suggests that the title reflects a desire on Chahine's part to silence his critics, and represents an appeal to be left alone to make his films.[81]

In addition to its anti-clerical and anti-fundamentalist posture, *The Other* also offers a biting critique of American, capitalist-driven globalization depicted as hiding behind a chimerical façade of tolerance and coexistence. The cynical definition of tolerance offered by this film is consistent with Wendy Brown's insight that tolerance is "an international discourse of Western supremacy and imperialism."[82] Chahine's next films shot in the aftermath of the re-escalation of violence between Israelis and Palestinians of September 2000 known as the al-Aqsa Intifada and the terrorist attacks against the United States on September 11, 2001, continue his investigation of the American political and cultural legacy. Chahine's films in this period express particular distaste for the close relationship between the United States and Israel, and America's complicity in Israel's repression of Palestinians in the occupied territories.

In order to explore his ambivalent relationship with the United States, Chahine once again returned to the self-reflexive idiom of the autobiographical film. Prior to filming *Alexandria ... New York* in 2004, Chahine directed a short autobiographical film that depicts in condensed form some of the issues explored at greater length in the feature. Chahine was invited to contribute to *11'9" 01* (2002), a compilation of short film responses to the attacks on the U.S. on September 11, 2001. In Chahine's piece Nur al-Sharif, who played the adult Yahia in *An Egyptian Story*, reprises his role as the filmmaker's alter-ego, although in the short film, the character's name is identical to that of the filmmaker.

Chahine's following feature, *Alexandria ... New York* (2004), also takes issue with American foreign policy, while engaging with the lasting legacy of American popular culture. After the years of struggle depicted in *An Egyptian Story*, Yahia, at the age of 70,[83] finally receives bittersweet recognition in the United States—a retrospective of his work by the New York Film Forum. Although the present time of the film is not specifically established, it is clear that the narrative unfolds sometime between the outbreak of the al-Aqsa Intifada in October 2000 and the terrorist attacks on the United States of September 11, 2001.[84]

During his stay in New York, Yahia is reunited with his girlfriend from his years at the Pasadena Playhouse, Ginger Fox—her name is an obvious composite reference to the dance icon Ginger Rogers and the movie studio 20th Century Fox.

Upon their reunion, Ginger reveals to Yahia that during his last visit to New York 25 years earlier he had fathered a son whom she named Alexander.[85] Only after she tells Yahia does Ginger reveal to Alexander the identity of his father. Alexander, a principal dancer with the New York City Ballet, angrily refuses to accept the news, and haughtily rejects overtures by Yahia to get acquainted. Ginger's reunion with Yahia and her conversations with Alexander occasion long flashback sequences— mostly of the young lovers' time together in Pasadena—that comprise approximately half of the film. Throughout the film, the adult Yahia adopts a public posture as a critic of American foreign policy whereas Alexander functions as a mouthpiece for American exceptionalism. Ultimately, their conflicting views stand as a barrier to building a relationship.

Yahia's conflicting feelings about America are established from the start. The film's opening sequence of four brief scenes enmeshes Yahia's repeatedly thwarted attempts to gain recognition in the United States with American policies that elicit from him a range of emotions from disappointment to outrage. Collectively, these scenes establish the centrality of the protagonist's internal conflicts over "America"—its image and its policies. These scenes trace not so much an evolution of Yahia's political views as a series of non-linear episodes that map his complicated and conflicted relationship with America.

The film opens with Yahia and a friend sitting in the Cairo train station in July 1956, following the announcement by the U.S. Secretary of State, John Foster Dulles, of the withdrawal of American financing for the Aswan High Dam. In their conversation, Yahia offhandedly likens the American administration's reversal of policy with Fox Studio's reneging on his contract that same year, as depicted in *An Egyptian Story*. His friend rebukes him for belittling the impact the dam would have on the lives of thousands of Egyptians. After his friend enumerates the benefits of the dam, Yahia responds, "If I were able to hate, I'd say that I had started to hate them." The friend then asserts, "America is done, finished. It is a myth created by Hollywood that we once believed." Agreeing, Yahia concludes, "It was a beautiful dream. It used to make us forget poverty and frustration."

The final scene of the sequence, set off from the previous three by the title screen, brings us to the present time of the film. Yahia sits at home watching the broadcast of a Palestinian funeral on television. Incensed by Israeli violence against Palestinians with American support and acquiescence, Yahia calls his assistant, May, and instructs her to cancel his ticket to New York. His rash decision prompts May and two other assistants to rush over to change his mind. May convinces him to go to New York by encouraging him to use his press conference at the film festival as an opportunity to air his political views.

The most pointed critiques expressed in the opening sequence and in Yahia's press conference are targeted at American support for, and arming of, the Israeli military. In this film, Zionism, already established in Chahine's lexicon as the quintessential parochial nationalism, continues in its shift away from its representation as a personal or communal struggle of self-definition pitting *ethnos* against *demos* as evidenced in *Alexandria ... Why?*, towards a political commitment backed by state power, the chief supporter of which is the United States government and the electorate that put it into power.

The primary tension in the film, played out through Yahia's internal conflict, is between nostalgia for the "myth," the "beautiful dream" of America, and contemporary political realities. Although Yahia is given the opportunity to speak his piece to the press both before and during his public appearance at the film festival near the beginning of the film, this conflict also plays out in a more sustained way in the private sphere between Yahia and Alexander.

There are all sorts of reasons why a 25-year-old might bristle at the sudden confrontation with a father he never knew. But, Alexander's reaction to the identity of his biological father focuses on his discomfort with his previously unknown Arab heritage. In the scene when Ginger reveals the information, Alexander bitterly refuses to accept her word as truth. In response he disparages Yahia, and heaps derision on Arabs as "backward and ignorant" people who "ride camels."

Alexander's rejection of his patrimony occurs on a symbolic level as well. Alexander bears the last name of the man he had viewed as his father, Ginger's former, long-time companion, Eric Penn. The terms he employs in rejecting Yahia and the cultural heritage he represents also constitutes a rejection of a greater symbolic American patrimony—the heritage embodied by the seventeenth century figure, William Penn, who founded the Quaker colony of Pennsylvania based on the principles of religious tolerance, inclusiveness, and pacifism. In the film, Alexander represents a decay of precisely these foundational values of the state.[86]

For Alexander, Yahia's visit and the surprising news of his parentage occasions an inquiry into his mother's past. In a sense, it is through his search for the truth about his mother that the film unfolds. Most of the long flashback sequences are framed by characters reminiscing to him about the past. By the end of the movie, Alexander agrees to see Yahia on the premise that it will permit him to understand his mother better. The meeting is disastrous and quickly devolves into an argument that clearly articulates the disparity between their world views. Through his repeated expression of intolerant American chauvinism, Alexander is meant to represent the antithesis of the characteristics that define Alexandria in Chahine's lexicon. He instead functions as an American Alexander, a figure of American conquest and imperialism, and a harbinger of the spread of American cultural hegemony and the subsuming of local cultural difference.

In their final confrontation, Yahia addresses Alexander's heartless arrogance:

> Do you know what the difference between you and Ginger is? It is the difference between Hollywood films of the 1940s and those of today: the difference between the elegance of Fred Astaire and his generation, and the vulgarity of [Sylvester] Stallone; the difference between the white stairs on which the star descends from the heavens to the strains of an orchestra, music, making you feel as if you're in paradise, and the animalism of action films, like the American superman who is invincible.

Alexander retorts: "We are the biggest power in the world. We are invincible." Taken aback, Yahia angrily responds, "If you read history carefully, you would know that what remains from the great empires are the philosophers, thinkers, poets, and artists—not soldiers, armies, and death." At the end of the argument Yahia, infuriated, dismisses Alexander, "The time to make a human being out of you has passed. This arrogance is what will lead you and your country into disaster. A chain of monstrous acts begins with Hiroshima and ends here with you."

The piquant criticism of American foreign policy and disdain for the violence of Hollywood action films reflected in Yahia's self-righteous speech drew the attention of the American media, to the extent that it noticed the film. A front-page article in the *Washington Post* on Egyptian anti-Americanism includes a description of *Alexandria ... New York*. The reporter, Daniel Williams, reads Chahine's film as "a cinematic divorce paper" that offers "a melodramatic metaphor for relations between the United States and Arabs."[87] Williams locates *Alexandria ... New York* within a larger trend of Egyptian films, music, and theatrical performances that lambast or lampoon the United States, its leaders, and its foreign policy.

Williams' interpretation, though accurate, is limited, reducing the film to binary oppositions by overlooking its nuances. Chahine complicates the relationship between father and son by employing the same actor, Ahmad Yahia, to play both the young Yahia in mid-century Pasadena, and Alexander in New York of the new millennium. This conscious doubling reflects a divided self—not a divorce, as Williams would have it. This casting decision underscores not only the biological link between father and son laid out by the plot, but also suggests a deep unstated interconnection between the characters that adds ambiguity to their adversarial relationship. An off-handed dismissal of Yahia's response and the unflattering portrayal of Alexander as unmitigated anti-Americanism misses the painful nuance of internal conflict.

Williams' critique also assumes that the audience is intended to take Yahia's remarks at face value. In the scene following Yahia's final confrontation with Alexander, his wife, Jane, rebukes him for unfairly laying at his son's feet the responsibility of the American history of violence. Like Jane, the viewer recognizes that Alexander is, after all, a ballet dancer, not a callous maker of foreign policy nor an actor in the violent Hollywood action films that Yahia disdains, and which he blames for Alexander's narrow vision of history. Rather, Alexander is a dancer deeply anchored in the high arts of Western culture, a means of artistic expression invested with at least as much nostalgia for the loss of its primacy among the performing arts and its dwindling audience as Yahia feels for the decline of the aesthetic of 1940s musical films. Further, the ballet in which Alexander features is Mikis Theodorakis's *Zorba*. Alexander's dancing brings to life a celebration of Greek and Mediterranean culture shared by his father's beloved Alexandria.[88]

Williams' reading of *Alexandria ... New York* also overlooks more than half of the film—the fondly rendered depiction of Yahia's experiences in 1940s Los Angeles. The flashback scenes serve to establish that although Hollywood—and film in general—does create myths as Yahia's friend states in the opening scene, for Yahia it also represents memory, not merely "a beautiful dream." These scenes also nostalgically depict Yahia's past love affair not only with Ginger Fox (and the Hollywood films of the era she represents), but also with America, capped off by an emotional graduation ceremony in which Yahia joins his classmates in singing "God Bless America."

Nevertheless, the criticism of American foreign policy evident in *Alexandria ... New York* and in the other contemporaneous works identified in Daniel Williams' *Washington Post* review is not new. In particular anti-Imperialist critique has been a common trope in Arab representations of the United States since the 1970s. According to Michelle Hartman, New York is a particular focal point for Arab literary works about America, with the city often functioning as synecdoche for the nation. Hartman writes, for example, that Yusuf Idris's *New York 80*, Adunis's "A Grave for New York" ["*Qabr min ajl New York*"], and Radwa 'Ashur's *The Journey* [*al-Rihla*]:

> all offer a critique and reaction to New York and the United States against the backdrop of the late 1970s and early 1980s, within an Arab nationalist, Third World solidarity framework. They all explicitly or implicitly condemn US actions in the Third World, specifically the war in Vietnam, complicity in the destruction of Palestine, and more generally the capitalist and materialistic greed that the US is taken to symbolize.[89]

In these works New York, as a symbol of America, signifies power—economic, cultural, and military—and self-absorption. But, Hartman also notes that within these same Arabic works, particularly Radwa 'Ashur's memoir, New York also functions in the inverse as a vibrant, diverse anomaly within the homogenizing American economy and suburban landscape.[90]

Chahine's New York, too, has many faces; among them it is both the American city par excellence and the cosmopolitan city par excellence, with all of the symbolic weight these two designations bear. The tension between these two countervailing significations of the city is evident in Chahine's use of the Statue of Liberty—an icon of both the city and the nation.

In the closing scene of Chahine's first autobiographical film, *Alexandria ... Why?* Yahia arrives on American shores to be greeted by a puzzling sight: the Statue of Liberty is transformed into a grotesque caricature of herself, and laughs at the boy's starry-eyed arrival. *Alexandria ... New York* effectively supplants the ambiguity of the closing scene of *Alexandria ... Why?* by providing a representation of what Yahia found upon his arrival (and return) to the United States. This replacement also occurs on another level as well. In *Alexandria ... New York*, when a contrite Alexander attends a screening of *Alexandria ... Why?* at the Walter Reade Theater, the scene of the Statue of Liberty is omitted. We see Alexander wiping away tears as he watches the child Yahia depart from Alexandria, and then the scene cuts away to the adult Yahia watching Alexander perform across the plaza in the New York State Theater, where his eyes well up with tears of his own.

Although she is absent from this clip of the film within the film, the Statue of Liberty does make an appearance in *Alexandria ... New York*. Her image, however, is stripped of the irony, caricature, and ambiguity evident the earlier film. The adult Yahia's reluctant arrival in New York is signaled by a close up, aerial shot circling around the statue's head, followed by shots of New York harbor and Lower Manhattan (including the World Trade Center towers). These images are accompanied by a brass band playing "The Star Spangled Banner," giving the footage a martial air.

Whereas in the earlier film Liberty greets a ship of immigrants as they enter New York harbor, evoking the statue's symbolism as the "Mother of Exiles" issuing a "world-wide welcome,"[91] in the later film, her iconography is static, and she is linked to American militarism carried out in her name. In this context, the title of Emma Lazarus's poem about the statue, "The New Colossus," reverts rather to its antithesis, the ancient Colossus of Rhodes which she describes as a "brazen giant ... / With conquering limbs astride from land to land." In other words, rather than a symbol of American cosmopolitanism, Liberty functions as a symbol of American imperialism.[92]

Between the contrasting representations of the Statue of Liberty as "New Colossus" and "Mother of Exiles" in Chahine's two films lies an important tension. As I argued in the previous two chapters, Egyptian Arab representations of the country's cosmopolitan past—images that have proliferated since the 1990s—are particularly attentive to the intertwining of colonialism and cosmopolitanism. Unlike earlier such representations that portrayed Egypt's foreign minority population as compradors, works in this period, such as the novels by Idwar al-Kharrat and Ibrahim Abdel Meguid discussed above, tease apart the two strains, providing a glimpse at a path not taken—a postcolonial Egyptian pluralism to supplant colonial cosmopolitanism, rather than the ethno-linguistic nationalism that prevailed.

Although the point of entry into the city in *Alexandria ... New York* is marked by the Statue of Liberty depicted as a patriotic symbol, like al-Kharrat's and Abdel Meguid's Alexandria, Chahine's New York nevertheless develops into a locus of ambivalence throughout the film recuperating its identification with cosmopolitanism. In the film New York clearly functions as a symbol of the nation and its imperial designs; however, I maintain, it also comes to stand in for the lost cosmopolitan Alexandria.

As already noted, despite its title, the fourth film of the autobiographical cycle does not move between Alexandria and New York, but rather between Pasadena of 1948–50 and New York 50 years later. If the title referred to the film's content it should, in effect, be called "Pasadena ... New York" or "Hollywood ... New York"—establishing a contrast between the lovingly rendered romanticism of Hollywood dance numbers, and the harsh coldness of the New York street scenes. Alexandria features in the film as a point of reference, but not as a location. Except for clips within the film from *Alexandria ... Why?* there is not a single shot in the movie that represents Alexandria. The majority of the action takes place in the United States, and the few scenes from Egypt that feature in the movie

are all set in Cairo, not Alexandria. The title maps the trajectory of the entire
film cycle from Yahia's childhood home to his belated recognition in New York;
however, it also invites the viewer to consider the relationship between the two
cities. Although it is easy to read the title as establishing a contrast between
the images of the two cities—cosmopolitan Alexandria versus parochial, patriotic New York—a closer examination of New York in the film suggests greater
ambivalence, and points to a more generous comparison that articulates the limit
points of cosmopolitanism.

In an interview published in 1999, Chahine articulates a great fondness for
New York even as his insists on a realistic vision of the contrasts it encompasses:

> You come to New York. There's the fabulous about it—if you don't see it,
> there's something wrong with you. But at the same time there's a lot of filth,
> a lot of dirt, a lot of poverty. It depends on what you're looking at and why
> you're looking at it. I am not being realistic if I look only in the garbage can—
> the garbage can is there, but the wonderful things are also there. If you say
> there's only poverty in New York, it's not true; that there's only wealth, only
> beauty in New York, it's not true; It's an amalgam of a lot of things.[93]

This realism of contrasting images—between Alexander's wealth and his mother's
one-time poverty, for example—is evident in Chahine's representation of the city
on film. The viewer recognizes the respect Chahine holds for New York, even as he
is critical of the city as metaphor for liberty, the city as metonymy for the nation.
In this, Chahine's portrayal of New York could perhaps best be summed up by
Isaac Davis in Woody Allen's *Manhattan* (1979), a film referenced in *An Egyptian
Story* and *The Other:* "He adored New York City. For him it was a metaphor for the
decay of contemporary culture." This comment is rendered by Isaac's voiceover
in the opening montage of black-and-white, fixed-camera images of the city as
he frustratedly attempts over and over to begin writing his great urban novel.
New York for Isaac, as for Chahine, is defined by its contrasts. Both understand
that great love also inevitably leads to loss or disillusionment.

Early in the film, at Yahia's press conference, New York is identified as a cosmopolitan space. In addition to responding to a Jewish journalist's sharp questions
about his views on the U.S. and Israel, Yahia also takes the opportunity to remi-
nisce about his past. In doing so, he introduces to the assembled crowd three
special guests—old friends from his school days, displaced Alexandrians living
in New York:

> I present to you three of my friends who were students with me at Victoria
> College in Alexandria when we were little. We haven't seen each other for
> 50 years and they came tonight like all of you to see me: Dicky Izmirlian,
> Armenian Orthodox Christian; Mohammad 'Ali Niyazi, Muslim, of course;
> and my friend Freddy Nadler. By the way, Freddy's sister was my first love—of
> course she was Jewish, just like him. I wanted to marry her but my family
> objected—not because she was Jewish, but because I was only 12 years old.

New York is the city where these old friends of diverse religious backgrounds can find refuge and meet again. It is through the displacement of these three men from Alexandria and their relocation to New York that we first see the latter's possibilities of supplanting the lost cosmopolitan space.

In addition to his offhand comments about his crush on Freddy Nadler's sister, in asserting his beloved city's former cosmopolitan character, Yahia makes particular note of the prominence of the Alexandrian Jewish community, overstating estimates of its size: "We had 300,000 [sic.] Jews in Alexandria, and people of more than 12 nationalities. We all lived together. When we met a pretty girl, we wouldn't ask her how she prayed."[94] This privileging of Jews extends to his representation of New York. Like Alexandria as portrayed in *Alexandria ... Why?*, New York's diversity in Chahine's fourth autobiographical film is telescoped onto the presence of Jews: a journalist of Egyptian origin; Ginger's long-time friend, Bonnie; and Alexander's teacher, Paddy, to name the most prominent ones. The ethnic diversity that characterizes New York in the works of Arab writers discussed by Michelle Hartman, is limited in Chahine's film to representations of former Alexandrians and Jews (including an Alexandrian Jew and an Ashkenazi Jew with ties to Alexandria). Excluded from this vision are New York's broader Arab and Arab American population, as well as individuals and communities that hail from Latin America, the Caribbean, Africa, South Asia, East Asia, Eastern Europe, and elsewhere that inhabit the city.

We see this focus on Jewish New York through the words and actions of Yahia's son Alexander. A rising star, Alexander assumes that Jews in show business would discriminate against him if his father's identity were publicly revealed. In particular, he worries how the news might affect his relationship with his Jewish teacher, Paddy.

But, like Sarah Sorel in *Alexandria ... Why?*, Paddy embodies the cosmopolitan ideal. Paddy's reaction to news of the identity of Alexander's biological father takes his pupil by surprise. Paddy's brother, it turns out, had found refuge in Alexandria during the Second World War, and he holds the city, its inhabitants, and its reputation as a cosmopolitan center in high regard. Paddy speaks wistfully of the cosmopolitanism that Alexandria once represented, as he berates Alexander for his chauvinism:

> You are civilized person? You are the son of an Alexandrian? Impossible! Alexandria was Cavafy, Durrell, and Curiel.[95] New York itself could only aspire to be on the same level as Alexandria in culture, love, and tolerance. You know I am a Jew who lived in Poland. When the Jews of Europe were being persecuted, the Jews of Egypt, and Alexandria in particular, lived in utmost security. Yes, my brother lived there. He died and was buried there as well. Hundreds of his Egyptian friends marched in his cortège.

This scene drips with nostalgia, even more so than Yahia's somewhat polemical evocations of his beloved city's cosmopolitan character at the press conference. As Paddy delivers his emotional speech, he is seated at the keyboard of a piano, unmindfully plucking out the melody to the wistful, sentimental Arabic song of parting and longing, "Visit Me Once a Year" ["*Zuruni kul sana mara*"], written by the great early twentieth century musician and composer born in Alexandria, Sayyid Darwish.

Paddy found refuge from persecution in New York in the same way that his brother had found refuge in Alexandria. The brothers both represent and embrace their respective city's cosmopolitan character. Although Paddy's image of Alexandria in this statement is shaped by his brother's experience, it is also, and equally importantly, shaped by the representation of the city in literature—via the works of Cavafy and Durrell.

But what do we make of his hyperbolic assertion that, "New York itself could only aspire to be on the same level as Alexandria in culture, love and tolerance"? There is, of course, the irony of the neo-colonial metropole becoming the locus of the "almost the same, but not quite"—an attribute ascribed to postcoloniality—in contrast to the authenticity of the colonial-cosmopolitan "original." Nevertheless, Alexandria's association with cosmopolitanism, of course dates to ancient representations of the city's founding—its renown as a cultural and intellectual center of the ancient world is legendary. New York, the young upstart of a city, pales in comparison to Alexandria's long history.

Yet, one could also read in Paddy's words a sense of dissatisfaction, if not disillusionment. He is visibly upset by Alexander's chauvinism, and sends him off to the theater to watch *Alexandria ... Why?* so he might learn something about tolerance and coexistence, and the culture that his biological father represents. Paddy's words suggest that he perceives a failure of the culture to transmit cosmopolitan values to Alexander and his generation.

As such, New York's failure to achieve the same level of "love and tolerance" resonates with sentiment of disillusionment evident in the words of the song, "New York kills all nostalgia" even as Paddy's own acceptance as an immigrant into American culture and his professional success speaks to just the opposite. The song warns hopeful new arrivals of the hardships and disappointments the city holds in store: "If you have a heart on the branches, immigrant, don't come / If you have a voice as sweet as a nightingale, don't sing."

The disenchantment evident in Paddy's comparison between the two cities is apparent elsewhere as well, suggesting that in New York coexistence is reduced from tolerance and interaction between people, to atomized subjects and communities merely existing side-by-side, not unlike Robert Ilbert's parochial definition of Alexandrian cosmopolitanism discussed in Chapter 1. The former Alexandrians reunited at Yahia's press conference appear alienated from one another. Dicky Izmirlian, Mohammad 'Ali Niyazi, and Freddy Nadler had all presumably been living in New York, perhaps since their departure from Alexandria, yet if we are to trust Yahia's words, his visit is the first time that they, too, have seen one another, and based on the distribution of their seats in the room, they seem not to have sought one another out on this occasion as well.

Nevertheless, in contrast to Alexandria which is perceived to have lost its cosmopolitan character,[96] New York is depicted as a thriving metropolis. For the exiled Alexandrians and the Polish Jew, New York supplants Alexandria, even if it can never replace or replicate it. Yahia's disillusionment with New York—the city to which he aspires to arrive, as opposed to the city he left behind—likewise, reflects his frustration with the limitations of the "copy" relative to his memories of the "original." Returning to the words of the song that plays over the closing montage of the film, one suspects that New York must repel, or kill, nostalgia for itself in order to become a repository of nostalgia for that other lost cosmopolitan space.

Part III
A mobile Levant

6   Gazing across Sinai

Ghosts of a Jewish past

In 1989 Israeli author Orly Castel-Bloom published a short story in Hebrew entitled "Cairo Joe" ["*Joe, ish qahir*"].[1] The narrative opens with a flashback, a ghost story told by a father to his children. The father had been the caretaker of the synagogue in the Cairo suburb of Maʿadi. One day, on his way to open the synagogue for the morning prayers he saw an apparition of a woman in white by the side of the road. Studiously ignoring her, the caretaker continued on his way. When he arrived at the synagogue at the usual time, he was surprised to find the door open as he possessed the only key. Inside, he found the chapel filled with people praying. They invited him to join them, and inquired why he had arrived late. Then, one of them extinguished the lights by sticking out his tongue. The father tells his children, "It was then that I realized they were demons."[2]

In 1989 when Castel-Bloom published this story, only a handful of Egyptian Jews remained in Cairo and Alexandria. With this hindsight, common knowledge among her Israeli readership, the story representing Jews in Egypt sets itself up to be read as a narrative about the ghosts of a Jewish past. The population of Jews in Egypt numbered between 75,000 and 80,000 at its peak in the 1940s.[3] Like other foreign minority communities in Egypt, Jews with foreign citizenship were affected by the provisions of the Montreux Convention in 1937 that abolished the Capitulations and by the 1947 Company Law that set a quota on the percentage of foreigners that companies could employ. In addition the loyalties of Egyptian Jews were challenged by the Egyptian participation in the first Arab–Israeli war in 1948.[4] Following the cessation of hostilities in 1949, stateless Jews—those who did not seek foreign nationality, and who were denied Egyptian citizenship—began leaving Egypt in large numbers. In 1954 several Egyptian Jews were charged with and ultimately convicted of espionage for Israel; two of the accused were executed, another two received life sentences and four others received sentences between seven and fifteen years in length. The trial, convictions, and executions undermined Egyptian Jews' sense of security. In the years following the 1956 Suez Conflict, the majority of the remaining Jewish community, comprised predominantly of the middle- and upper-classes who held European passports, emigrated as well. Before the outbreak of the 1967 Arab–Israeli war, the Egyptian Jewish population numbered approximately 7000.[5]

The tense atmosphere for Egyptian Jews produced by the outbreak of war between Egypt and Israel in 1948 underpins the narrative of "Cairo Joe." Jacqueline, the caretaker's daughter, who listened intently to her father's tales, retains a life-long fear of the spirit world. As an adult, Jacqueline, uneducated, religious, and deeply superstitious, tries to protect her own children from the unseen threats of spirits and demons. One afternoon, Jacqueline hears the sounds of rhythmic drumming coming from the upstairs apartment inhabited by a Muslim family. Recognizing the drumming as a mystical ritual, Jacqueline rounds up her children for their protection. The ritual, an exorcism, was being conducted for the benefit of Nafisa, the daughter of the upstairs neighbors for whom, despite her beauty, no suitors had come to call because she walked with a limp. Doctors failed to diagnose and cure Nafisa's ailment. So, Nafisa and her mother had concluded that she must be possessed by a *jinn*. Dozens of people come to participate in and observe the exorcism. Jacqueline's daughter, Arlette, fascinated by the exotic ritual, sneaks upstairs, only to be dragged out soon after by her superstitious mother. For weeks, Jacqueline watches her daughter closely for any sign that the *jinn* that left Nafisa's body—the exorcism successfully cured her of the symptom—might have possessed Arlette. To Jacqueline's relief, Arlette seems unaffected, but within weeks the war to the north encroaches on their daily life—Israeli aircraft begin dropping bombs on Cairo, letting another the genie out of the bottle, as it were. During one air raid on a Friday night, the family neglects to extinguish the Sabbath candles, drawing an angry crowd accusing them of sending signals to the Israeli jets circling above.[6]

In the context of the war swirling around the characters in the story, Nafisa's spirit possession and the subsequent exorcism rites can also be read figuratively. An exorcism is, in effect, the process of expelling a foreign presence living in one's midst. A demon possesses a person by stealthily infiltrating the body. The spirit can reside imperceptibly in the body it inhabits indefinitely, coexisting with its host. However, the spirit can also manifest itself at odds with the body, producing undesirable symptoms. Exorcism, read thus, represents a process of identifying and expelling an "other" within. Interpreted metaphorically, the expulsion of the *jinn* from Nafisa's body in "Cairo Joe" foreshadows the expulsion of Jews from the body politic of the Egyptian nation.

As discussed above in Chapter 1, in the middle decades of the twentieth century, the status of foreign minorities who had been living in Egypt shifted. Although some members of these communities had lived in Egypt for generations, most would not be considered Egyptian in cultural or legal terms. Indeed, the title character, Joe, Jacqueline's son, considers himself to be cosmopolitan (*ish ha-olam ha-gadol*).[7] "Cairo Joe," interpreted as a metaphor for the expulsion of Jews from Egypt, offers a skewed, but popularly accepted understanding of the dissolution of the Jewish community there.

In order to present a more nuanced representation of Egyptian Jewish history and culture, I begin this chapter by briefly outlining the demographics, cultural contributions, and decline of the Jewish community in Egypt.[8] The second section of the chapter explores the social and cultural positioning of Egyptian Jews who immigrated to Israel in the context of postcolonial analyses of Israeli society. In the third section I turn to literary representations of Egypt and Egyptian Jews in Modern Hebrew literature. Egypt, I argue, initially appears in Modern Hebrew literary works as a way-station. In works by Ashkenazim, Egypt functions as a port of call or temporary refuge in a trajectory bound for Palestine. These works tend to ignore, or disparagingly represent Jews residing in Egypt. Works representing Egyptian Jews only enter Hebrew literature in the 1950s following the dispersion of the community, and the arrival of some in Israel. Historian Joel Beinin notes that a significant shift occurs in the tenor of Egyptian Jewish representations of their past in the late 1970s as more Jews from the Arab–Islamic world found their voices in the Israeli literary and public spheres.[9]

Jewish life and cultural production in Egypt

In the late nineteenth and early twentieth centuries, Jews immigrated from around the Mediterranean basin and throughout the Arab world to settle in Egypt. Initially, Jewish immigrants, like their Muslim and Christian counterparts, hailed from Arab countries, Italy, and Greece. Jews from Eastern Europe and Morocco fleeing religious persecution in their countries of origin sought refuge in Egypt as well. Between 1897 and 1920, the number of Jews increased from an estimated 25,000 to over 60,000, making Jews, according to historian Jacob Landau's estimates, the fastest growing demographic group in Egypt.[10] By 1948, indigenous, Arabic-speaking Jews accounted for only about one-quarter of the Jewish population in Egypt.[11] Immigration continued through the 1940s when the Jewish population in Egypt peaked.[12]

Because of its heterogeneity, one cannot speak of a single Jewish community in Egypt. Egyptian Jews whose ancestors had lived in Egypt prior to the nineteenth century spoke Arabic and were integrated into Egyptian society. Among the indigenous Jewish population was a small but significant community of Karaites, a sect that rejects Talmudic law. Ladino-speaking Sephardi Jews from Greece and Turkey immigrated to Egypt seeking economic opportunity in the modern era, as did Judeo Arabic-speaking Jews from North Africa, Yemen, the Levant, and Iraq. Italian Jews who settled primarily in Alexandria maintained their own distinct ethno-linguistic identity. The small Ashkenazi community that had existed in Egypt since the sixteenth century increased in the late nineteenth century as Jews fled the pogroms in Eastern Europe. These various communities maintained their distinct linguistic-geographic cultural identities.[13]

Jewish political commitments were as diverse as the community's cultural make-up. Jews were to be found in the service of the royal court, on the rolls of the independence-minded Wafd party, and in Communist groups.[14] By most accounts, few Egyptian Jews became actively involved in Zionist movements, although many were sympathetic to the cause and some provided financial support to Jewish efforts in Palestine.[15] In contrast to the large waves of Jewish immigration to Palestine from Eastern Europe in the first decades of the twentieth century, immigration from Egypt constituted a mere trickle. Just over 4000 Jews immigrated to Palestine from Egypt between 1917 and 1947—a significant proportion of which were short-term residents of Egypt from Eastern Europe, Yemen, and Morocco.[16]

Jews inhabited the full range of the socio-economic spectrum in Egypt. Although Jews, like other foreign minorities, came to be judged on the actions of their Westernized economic élites—notably, the Cattaoui, Mosseri, de Measce, Suarès, Rolo, and Aghion families—the majority of the community occupied the middle- and lower-middle-classes, working as merchants, shop-owners, clerks, and craftspeople. Not all of the Jews in Egypt benefited from the economic expansion of the colonial-cosmopolitan era; there were a substantial number of Jews particularly among the residents of Cairo's Jewish quarter, *harat al-yahud*, who were unemployed or otherwise unable to support themselves.[17]

Although the Jewish community was perhaps best known for the commercial and financial endeavors of its economic élite, some Jews also contributed to cultural production in Egypt. The Arabic and Francophone Jewish press in Egypt offered one outlet for the circulation of Jewish letters; however, cultural production by a handful of Jews also reached beyond the limits of the Jewish community.[18] Ya'qub Sannu' (1839–1912) was an influential playwright and political satirist active in the late nineteenth century. Appointed early in his career to various posts under the reign of Viceroy Sa'id and Khedive Isma'il, Sannu' fell out of favor with the Egyptian government as a result of his public criticism and in 1878 he was exiled.[19] From Paris where he settled, Sannu' continued publishing his popular journal of political satire, *Abu Nazzara Zarqa'*, which enjoyed broad readership in Egypt. "An outspoken advocate of the liberal and humanitarian strain" of Egyptian nationalism,[20] Sannu' was also known to support a variety of groups aiming to overthrow foreign rule, including the right-wing *Misr al-Fatat*.[21]

Another visible Jewish advocate of pluralist Egyptian nationalism was Murad Faraj (1866–1956), a Kara'ite lawyer, poet, and essayist. Although Faraj's essays and poetry tended to avoid the contentiousness of nationalist rhetoric, his writings found a place within the journal *al-Jarida*, edited by Lutfi al-Sayyid, whose vision was to promote "national unity and encourage interreligious dialogue."[22] In the liberal nationalist idiom of their day, Sannu' and Faraj both contributed to the creation of a broad, inclusive vision of the Egyptian nation.

Jews were also active in the development of music and cinema in Egypt during a critical era in the consolidation of Egyptian national identity. Da'ud Husni (1870–1937) composed the music for the first full-length Egyptian opera sung in Arabic, "Samson and Dalilah." Over the course of his career, Husni collaborated with several prominent Egyptian figures of his era including, Badi' Khairy and Husayn Fawzi whose verses he set to music, and Sayyid Darwish whose death in 1923 cut short their collaboration on an operetta.[23] Jews were also involved in the Egyptian film industry from the early 1930s through the 1950s. Togo Mizrahi, for example, was a prominent director in the early years of Egyptian cinema. His innovations, particularly his use of photomontage, earned him great respect from his colleagues.[24] Mizrahi is also credited with discovering popular Jewish actress and singer Layla Murad who starred in 27 films between 1938 and 1955.

Jews participated in Surrealist Francophone literary circles in Cairo and Alexandria as well. Most notable of the Francophone Jewish writers was poet Edmond Jabès (1912–91) who immigrated to France in 1957.[25] His mature writings, published after his arrival in Paris, particularly his multi-volume poetry cycle, *Le Livre des Questions*, have received much critical attention. This monumental, multi-vocal work evokes a wide range of places and historical events while simultaneously evacuating them of meaning. Among the places that reappear periodically through the texts are what Ammiel Alcalay refers to as the principal way-stations of a nomadic Levantine Jewish trajectory, reflecting his years in Cairo.[26]

The production of *belles lettres* by Jews in Egypt, however, was somewhat limited. Jacqueline Kahanoff (1917–79), an Egyptian Jew whose literary production began in earnest after she left Egypt, laments this fact. In an essay published in the literary supplement of the Israeli newspaper *Davar* in 1973, she writes:

> The potential writers from the minorities did not know how to say anything meaningful or interesting to upper-middle class Arabs. Potential writers—and there were many among the minorities in Egypt—had to write to people, even if to a very few. To whom could they write in Egypt? Jews to Jews, Greeks to Greeks, Armenians to Armenians? And in which language?[27]

The lack of social cohesion amongst the Jews of Egypt, and between the Francophone and Anglophone minorities, may have contributed to the absence of an audience, and thus the limited literary production, as Kahanoff suggests. However, nostalgia literature representing the lost cosmopolitan Egypt abounds.

From colonial subjects to postcolonial subjectivity

After the majority of the Jewish population left Egypt, their nationality, or lack of nationality, often influenced the trajectory of their immigration. The majority of Egyptian Jews who immigrated to Israel were "stateless"—denied Egyptian citizenship and unable to obtain foreign citizenship.[28] According to Israel's 1961 census, 35,580 Jews living in Israel had been born in Egypt or the Sudan.[29] Jews who in Egypt had held foreign nationality generally settled in the Americas or Europe, particularly France.[30]

When Egyptian Jews began arriving in Israel in the early 1950s, they represented a small proportion of the more than 1,000,000 Jewish refugees flooding into the country from Eastern Europe and the Middle East. Because of the small number, their urban origins, their lack of a unitary communal structure, and their professional training, Egyptian Jews "assimilated successfully into relatively anonymous roles in urban Israeli life."[31] However, as Joel Benin expresses, this successful "anonymous assimilation" also meant that "among the Mizrahi communities in Israel, Egyptian Jews were often particularly invisible."[32]

For immigrants from the Arab–Islamic world, the transition into life in Israel was often difficult. Upon their arrival, immigrants from the countries of North Africa, the Levant, and Central Asia—among them Egyptian Jews—faced the cultural chauvinism of the Ashkenazi-dominated establishment. Their bodies were viewed as dirty, their culture backward, their language, that of the enemy. The state's effort to "absorb" the new immigrants amounted to dispossessing them of their languages and cultural heritage.[33] Many Jewish immigrants from the Arab–Islamic world languished in transit camps known as *ma'abarot*, before being transferred to housing projects in the development towns located along critical border regions or in under-developed areas, away from the cultural and economic center of the coastal plain. The Israeli establishment viewed these immigrants from the Arab–Islamic world as cheap labor on whose backs they intended to industrialize the economy.[34] As Ella Shohat argues the education and acculturation of immigrants from the Arab–Islamic world became inscribed in the Zionist master narrative as a success story:

> According to that discourse, European Zionism 'saved' Sephardi Jews from the harsh rule of their Arab 'captors.' It took them out of 'primitive conditions' of poverty and superstition and ushered them gently into a modern Western society characterized by 'humane values,' values with which they were but vaguely and erratically familiar due to the 'Levantine environments' from which they came.[35]

Collectively, the Jews whose families originated in the Arab–Islamic world came to be known as Mizrahi or "Oriental" Jews. Their communal identity was formed as much by the establishment that viewed them as an undifferentiated collective, as through their shared cultural identifications and shared experiences of discrimination.

There is some dissent over how best to refer to these communities in scholarly literature. Ella Shohat uses "Sephardi" in its broadest sense, as it is commonly understood in the Anglophone world, i.e. non-Ashkenazi Jews.[36] Ammiel Alcalay prefers the term "Levantine" to stress the cultural fluidity that characterized the region, and removes their identity from the over-determined categories "Arab" and "Jew."[37] Yehouda Shenhav, by contrast, prefers "Arab Jew," precisely because it "challenges the binary opposition between Arabs and Jews in Zionist discourse, a dichotomy that renders the linking of Arabs and Jews in this way inconceivable."[38] Each of these terms is politically freighted.

I opt for a somewhat more functional application of the terms "Sephardi," "Arab Jew," and "Mizrahi" for the sake of clarity, while remaining aware of the baggage attached to each term. I employ the term "Sephardi" in a somewhat narrower sense than Shohat, using it to refer to the Jews who trace their culture, religious tradition, and language to the Iberian Peninsula prior to the expulsion of Jews around the turn of the sixteenth century.

The term Arab Jew, as Shenhav and Alcalay note, subverts essentialized constructions of identity. Some in Israel, including Iraqi–Jewish writers Shimon Ballas and Sami Michael, have embraced the identity "Arab Jew." However, the term Arab Jew does not accurately represent all of the Jews from Egypt. A significant proportion of Jews who lived in Egypt were Sephardim who emigrated from Greek- and Turkish-speaking regions of the Ottoman Empire, and were, thus, not ethnically Arab. Some Sephardi families lived in Egypt for several generations, but many did not integrate into Egyptian–Arabic culture, and spoke only enough Arabic to communicate with servants or merchants. Indeed, Sephardim in Egypt cultivated their own highly developed sense of cultural superiority over Arabs, as Gormezano Goren details with relish in his novels, discussed in the following chapter.[39]

The term "Mizrahi," by contrast, encompasses all Jews from the Arab–Islamic world who settled in Israel. The term refers to the communities' collective status within Israeli society, and serves as a reminder of the culturally superior, Orientalist attitude they all face. It is precisely because of the term's flattening of distinctions—geographic, linguistic, cultural, and socio-economic—between and among communities, that I prefer to use "Mizrahi" over "Sephardi" or "Arab Jew" when I refer to this collective.

These scholars, Shohat, Alcalay, and Shenhav, all examine representations by and of Jews from the Arab–Islamic world through the framework of postcolonial theory. Shenhav divides the existing scholarship on Arab Jewish identity in Israel into three groups: "essentialist," "social constructivist," and "postcolonial." Works that characterize Mizrahi identity as rooted in the past, "the outcome of their lengthy sojourn in the Islamic world and of the colonial encounter there," tend to "attribute to Mizrahim essentialist, ahistorical traits."[40] Works in the second group, critical of essentialism, assert that "Israel did not receive Ashkenazim and Mizrahim, but created them."[41] However, Shenhav argues that, "even though the perspective that views the Mizrahim as a constructed cultural and economic category generates sharp criticism of the class society in Israel and its creation of a Mizrahi ethno-class, it fails to address Arab and Jewish pre-state histories."[42] Shenhav sums up his assessement of the "essentialist" and "social constructivist" approaches to Mizrahi identity as follows, "the first misses out on the contemporary colonial reality, the second on the colonial history."[43]

Shenhav credits Ella Shohat with "introduce[ing] the framework of orientalism into the study of the Arab Jews in Israel, thus paving the way to the adoption of colonialism and postcolonialism as relevant perspectives for analysis of Israeli culture in general and the Arab Jews in particular."[44] In her 1988 essay provocatively titled, "Sephardim in Israel: Zionism from the Standpoint of its Jewish victims," Ella Shohat writes, "within Israel, European Jews constitute a First World élite dominating not only the Palestinians but also the Oriental Jews. The Sephardim, as a Jewish Third World people, form a semi-colonized nation-within-a-nation."[45] In this article, as in her 1989 book *Israeli Cinema: East/West and the Politics of Representation*, Shohat draws upon the writings of anti-colonial critics such as Franz Fanon and Aimé Césaire, as well as Edward Said's *Orientalism*. This scholarship ushered in a postcolonial critique of Israeli society that explores parallels between the experiences of Palestinians and Jews from the Arab–Islamic world.

Ammiel Alcalay expanded on this work in *After Jews and Arabs* (1993), tracing the lines of shared culture between Jews and Arabs in Medieval and Modern times, as well as mapping its decline, and the impact on Palestinian and Arab–Jewish populations after the establishment of the state of Israel. Another critic, Yerach Gover, also explores Zionist representations of Arabs and Arab–Jews in *Zionism: The Limits of Moral Discourse in Israeli Hebrew Fiction* (1994). In Israel, as Laurence Silberstein notes, postcolonial critique of Israeli culture initially finds a voice in the pages of *Theory and Criticism* [*Te'oryah u-viqoret*] a journal founded by Hanan Hever and Adi Ofir in 1991.[46]

In the textual analyses that follow in this chapter and the next two I take as my point of departure this scholarship that views the Arab–Israeli conflict and the treatment of Mizrahi Jews in Israel as interrelated articulations of colonial power relations. As in my discussions about Egyptian literature in the previous chapters, my readings of texts by Egyptian Jews in Israel grow out of and respond to postcolonial critique. In the case of the works of Hebrew literature under consideration in the following pages, the tension between empire and the cosmopolitan bears different valences than the Egyptian texts previously discussed. The Egyptian anti-colonial nationalist master narrative did not distinguish between the foreign minorities and foreign powers. By contrast, the texts by Yitzhaq Gormezano Goren and Ronit Matalon I discuss in the chapters that follow, struggle with the place of Jews in society—Egyptian and Israeli—mobilizing cosmopolitan discourses to disrupt the binaries posited by the postcolonial conditions experienced in both locales.

Out, and out again—Egypt in Israeli literature

Egypt—*mitzrayim*—holds a privileged place in the Jewish imagination. The Exodus represents the first step in constituting the Israelite nation. Mirroring the Biblical model, Zionism, too, constructs a teleological narrative whose conclusion is defined by the triumphant arrival in the Promised Land. Through the journey, the disparate tribes or *tfutzot* are transformed into a nation. The modern Zionist narrative tactically removes Divine deliverance from its privileged place in its re-casting of the people's redemption. What also gets erased in the modern re-telling is the uniqueness of the point of departure. In the Zionist narrative of the ingathering of the exiles, destination bears greater significance than origin. As Sidra Ezrahi writes, "In reclaiming sacred space as habitable territory, a people who were on the road for two thousand years had to renegotiate in the twentieth century what had been an epic Jewish journey and a portable Jewish geography."[47]

In the modern era, some writers in Israel attempting to give voice to the unique experiences of Egyptian Jews rely on the powerful symbolism of "*mitzrayim*" in Jewish thought. Poet Ada Aharoni dubs the modern-day departure of Egyptian Jews a "second Exodus."[48] Jacqueline Shohet Kahanoff mines for its literary potential the irony of performing a Passover *seder* in Egypt.[49] However, for much of the twentieth century, the plot of Egyptian Jewish migration as represented in Hebrew literature is circumscribed—if not supplanted—by the Zionist narrative.

Egypt first appears in Modern Hebrew narrative as a place of a temporary sojourn. Travelers between Europe and Ottoman Palestine commonly passed through Alexandria and/or Port Said along their journey. As a result, the names of these ports and occasionally descriptions of the travelers' experiences appear in Hebrew narratives of travel and Zionist immigration of the period. In these narratives Egypt forms one point on a larger trajectory—be it from Europe to Palestine, or from one Levantine locale to another. Jewish residents of Egypt generally play a minor role in these Hebrew narratives of which interest lies in the fates of the characters who pass through or briefly alight there.

In Yosef Hayyim Brenner's novella "Nerves" ["*Atzabim*"] (1910), Egypt functions on many levels: it is a modern space through which the protagonist passes en route to Palestine, it is also the site of tribulations for the travelers that take on a universal valence, and in its inherent allusiveness to the Biblical narrative of exile, it serves as the archetype for the diasporic experience.[50]

As critic Gershon Shaked notes, "[Brenner's] stories usually described the wanderings of characters who believe that by changing places they might change their fortunes, only to discover that that is not the case."[51] Brenner's "Nerves" offers just such a migration narrative. The disaffected protagonist travels a circuitous path from his home in the Ukraine to New York, London, Antwerp, Berlin, Trieste, Alexandria, Cairo, and Port Said, before landing in Jaffa and disembarking in Haifa (despite his plan to continue on to Beirut.) The traveler concedes, "I didn't travel directly. There were a number of detours on the way."[52] This text functions like other narratives of Jewish migration—anti-epics—that emend the Zionist epic of return mapped and interpreted by Sidra Ezrahi in *Booking Passage*. Ezrahi writes, "the *anti-epic* follows the epic like a rudderless sailboat in the wake of a steamship, describing in its ellipses a skeptical parody of the redemptive itinerary."[53] In "Nerves," the disillusioned storyteller finds little comfort in Palestine, and indeed, having contracted malaria there, may be on the way to being counted among the pilgrims who came to the Holy Land only to meet their deaths.

Maintaining a parallel to the Biblical narrative of Exodus, "Nerves" describes how in Egypt the travelers encounter trying circumstances they must collectively overcome in order to make their way to Zion. Upon their arrival in Alexandria, they are swindled by a lame Egyptian Jew. From the port, they struggle to make their way to the train station, where they catch a train to Cairo, changing for Port Said. Laden with heavy burdens, the travelers must find their way from the train station to the harbor, and then negotiate fare for lighters to the ship. A local hotel employee with a cart takes pity on them and assists them free of charge. It is through these contrasting encounters in Egypt that the skeptical protagonist experiences the universal—a notion of good and evil that upon arrival in the Holy Land becomes a heartfelt (if temporary) revelation. The protagonist explains to his companion the import of his encounters in Egypt, "What I mean is ... good and evil, and all that they imply, in themselves ... Good and evil as two different worlds, two essences ... with an infinite abyss between them."[54]

However, although Egypt is where the protagonist first gains access to universal knowledge, the text nevertheless treats Egypt and its inhabitants with disdain. Brenner's use of a common Biblical reference recalling the taste of the "fleshpots of Egypt" as a metaphor for the experience of the Jews in exile, serves to underscore the distance the protagonist places between himself and the Egypt through which he travels.[55] Portrayal of Egypt's Jews, indistinguishable to the protagonist from other Eastern Jews, is also suspect. For example, he asks his interlocutor:

> Have you ever paid attention to the faces of some of our predatory Jews who haunt the cities of the Orient ... I mean those cocky, energetic, wolfish ones with their oily black hair and their sharp little mustaches that curl up at the edges? Have you noticed how they prowl when they walk, as if stalking prey?[56]

Such ugly stereotypes recur in the description of two other Levantine Jews the protagonist encounters. In the end of the journey, the joy of the travelers' successful arrival is tempered by a final swindle perpetrated by a Jewish hotel-owner and his brother, a fellow traveler whom the narrative describes as having "those slanting, typically Oriental eyes that glisten like the skin of some wet, dark reptile."[57]

Ammiel Alcalay has argued that Brenner, like other Ashkenazi immigrants of the period, "saw through" the landscapes of the East and the local inhabitants, "superimpos[ing] images from another world," the world of Eastern Europe they left behind.[58] Expanding on Alcalay's reading, Hanan Hever demonstrates that Brenner's ideology of literary universalism explicitly "reject[s] the representation of the local in literary writing" and "leaves no room for ethnicity."[59] Hever continues: "Brenner's universalism is the key to proper national writing—in this case, to Zionist writing, which must subject the particular case to the universalistic, all-human representation."[60] Brenner's stature as a writer and critic in shaping a Hebrew nationalist literary modernity served to perpetuate this ideology for decades. It is only in the 1980s, more than 60 years after Brenner's death, that the Israeli literary establishment began to recognize and embrace articulations of ethnicity.[61]

Both Alcalay and Hever contrast Brenner's ideology and aesthetic with that of his contemporary Yitzhaq Shami (1888–1949), an Arabic-speaking native of Hebron / al-Khalil, whose Hebrew fiction depicts local Arab culture.[62] In his novella, "The Vengeance of the Fathers" ["*Nikmat ha-avot*"] (1928), the protagonist, Nimr Abu al-Shawarab, sparks a blood feud by killing a rival and then flees to Cairo. The metropolis that Nimr encounters is populated by "masses of refugees and exiles from different lands and of different races."[63] The population in which Nimr finds himself is described as a "reveling Babel," "variegated masses" comprised of "Syrians, Negroes, Copts, Armenians, and Greeks. A vast mixture of strange races and costumes."[64] On summer evenings, along the banks of the Nile "a number of orchestras, Arab and European, played a confusion of gay and boisterous tunes and heartbreaking melancholy Oriental melodies full of longing and emotion."[65] The text describes a cosmopolitan city, notable for the diversity of its poor refugees and wealthy Europeanized minorities alike. For Alcalay, Shami's works represent a world where Arabs and Jews not only could but also did share language, geography, and cultural experience. This world, on the verge of disappearing, was also characterized by fluid movement of peoples across what later became physically and psychologically impenetrable borders between Israel and the Arab world.

This movement of people—including Jews, Ashkenazim and Sephardim, traveling between Palestine and Egypt—characterizes the representations of Egypt in Hebrew literature until those lines are broken. In "Nerves," although Brenner rejects the idiom Shami's writing reflects, the trajectory of the characters' travel also attests to trade and communication between points along the Levantine itinerary.

Modern Egypt similarly figures in works by several Ashkenazi authors who passed through or lived in Egypt in the first three decades of the twentieth century. During the First World War, the Ottoman authorities expelled thousands of Jews from Palestine and sent them to Egypt. Novelist Dvorah Baron was among the deportees. Some of Baron's writings, such as the stories "For the Time Being" [*"Le-'et 'atah"* (1943)] and "Since Yesterday" [*"Me-emesh* (1955)] reflect positively on the author's experience in Alexandria during the war years.[66] Ester Raab, referred to by Israeli critics as the first "native" female Hebrew poet, left Palestine in 1921 for Cairo where she lived for five years. Her short story "Rose Jam" [*"Ribat-shoshanim"* (1933)][67] sensually represents the fragrances of daily life in Cairo. These texts—and the experiences of their authors—map the well-trodden route between Palestine and Egypt.

Set during the British Mandate of Palestine, Gid'on Telpaz's short story "Port Said Rose Water" [*"Me veradim mi-port sa'id"*] (1972) also depicts Egypt as a way-station in a narrative of Jewish mobility that ends in Palestine.[68] In addition, this story introduces another recurring trope in the representation of Egyptian Jewry, reflections on the ethics of servitude.[69] In this story, a young widow returns to Palestine with her two children after living for several years in Australia. Her boat docks in Port Said where she reconnects with a former suitor, Aviezer Antebi, a wealthy bachelor, who attempts to resume their courtship. She resists his overtures and insists on continuing to Jerusalem where she opens a boarding house. In contrast to the hard-scrabble existence she faces in Palestine, Port Sa'id represents a life of ostentatious luxury. However, wealth raises certain moral challenges. As an act of goodwill Aviezer sends one of his servants to assist her. Despite her reservations, the widow engages the man's services before concern over appearances compels her to send him back to Egypt. In its echoes of the liberation theme of Exodus as well as ideologies consistent with labor Zionism, "Port Said Rose Water" rejects the *bourgeois* lifestyle of Egypt's Jews, and implicitly endorses an ethos of Jewish labor. In the parallel rebuffs of two prospective suitors, the story also hints at Ashkenazi prejudices against Sephardim. Mapping these two narrative threads onto one another, one sees how the story could be interpreted to grant Ashkenazim who reject servitude moral superiority over their Sephardi neighbors who employ servants. As discussed at greater length in the chapters that follow, the moral and cultural significance of the presence of servants becomes a central concern in literary works by Egyptian Jews published in Israel.

The fluidity of movement evident in representations of early twentieth century Egypt in Hebrew literature came to an end in 1948. Yitzhaq Ben-Ner's novel *The Man from There [Ha-Ish mi-sham]* (1967)[70] depicts the end of the era of free movement and the cultures of contact it fostered. The novel's protagonist is a Jewish soldier from the *yishuv* who had served in the British forces during the Second World War.

Injured in the war, he remains in Egypt for medical treatment. In 1948, when he belatedly learns of the imminent British withdrawal from Palestine, he boards a train to return home. As a result of the outbreak of war, the train cannot cross the border, and he gets caught behind enemy lines. A young doctor he meets on the train treats him and provides him a place of refuge with his fiancée's family. The narrative tension in the text revolves around a presumption of enmity—the contact between the Jewish Zionist and his Egyptian Arab hosts is portrayed as exceptional. The title of the novel establishes the dichotomy of essentialist geography: here versus there; Jew versus Arab; Israeli versus Egyptian.[71]

In these Hebrew literary works, Egypt is represented as a place of temporary residence. As Ben Ner's novel demonstrates, although narratives of cross-border movement persist, the establishment of the State of Israel seals off the points of contact. Jews from Egypt are absent from or marginal to these texts. It took the arrival of Egyptian Jews onto the Israeli literary and cultural scene to give voice to the community's past. A handful of works appear in Israel during the 1950s and 1960s that begin to articulate a collective identity of Egyptian Jews. These voices gain greater visibility following the 1967 war in which Israel's conquest of Egyptian territory leads to a desire for more knowledge about Egypt. The majority of works appearing in the wake of Israel's 1967 military victory reflect the atmosphere of the day.[72] According to Beinin's analysis of these works, they underscore the popularly accepted assumptions about Israel's cultural superiority over its defeated foes. These works also serve to inscribe Egyptian Jews into the Zionist narrative, as I discuss below. Two events in the late 1970s—the victory of the Likud party in the 1977 parliamentary elections on the strength of its support by Jews from the Arab–Islamic world, and the peace negotiations between Egypt and Israel—validate the Egyptian Jewish experience. The late 1970s and early 1980s saw the publication of many more works by Egyptian Jews than had previously appeared. In the remainder of this section I briefly map the articulations of Egyptian Jewishness in Hebrew literature and Israeli culture.

Egyptian Jewish essayist Jacqueline Shohet Kahanoff (1917–79) transforms into social theory the fluidity of movement that characterized earlier representations of Egypt in Hebrew literature. Kahanoff first introduced her ideas to the Israeli public in her cycle of four essays "A Generation of Levantines" published in the Israeli literary and cultural journal *Keshet* in 1959.[73] Through nostalgic reminiscences about her life in Cairo, Kahanoff represents the multi-cultural interactions and admixture of Eastern and Western cultures in her Iraqi–Tunisian family in Egypt as the ideal incarnation of a pluralistic society. Her essays advocate for Israeli society to embrace its cultural diversity. Kahanoff's writing paid particular attention to the nature of Ashkenazi cultural hegemony, and the limited opportunities granted to recent Jewish immigrants from Arab countries. In opposition to predominant cultural trends in Israel, she valorized cultural "cross-fertilization" and its potential to undermine hegemonic social discourses. By labeling her social model "Levantinism" (*levantiniyut*), Kahanoff appropriates a term that in Hebrew had taken on negative connotations as a description of the poverty and "backwardness" of Jewish immigrants from Arab countries. Kahanoff's essays call for the internalization of the trajectories blocked by geopolitical realities of the Arab–Israeli conflict.

Israeli literature about Egypt, not unlike Egyptian literature about Alexandria of the same period, takes on a territorially nationalist orientation after the 1967 Arab–Israeli war. As Joel Beinin writes, "Conquest of a substantial piece of Egyptian territory ... stimulated a desire for knowledge about Egypt that explained military victory as a consequence of civilizational superiority."[74] Egyptian Jews played a significant role in filling the knowledge gap. He identifies Rahel Maccabi's memoir *My Egypt* [*Mitzrayim Sheli*] (1968) as exemplifying this idiom. Maccabi (1915–2003) was born in Alexandria. In 1935 she immigrated to Palestine and settled on a kibbutz, establishing her "pioneering Zionist credentials."[75] According to Beinin's reading, "*Mitzrayim Sheli* affirms the Zionist national narrative: Some Egyptian Jews became good Zionists even before 1948; they were unaffected by contact with anything Arab, and their Jewish identity was preserved by leaving Egypt as soon as possible."[76] Maccabi's text not only "affirms the Zionist national narrative," as Beinin argues, but also simultaneously expands it. *My Egypt* inserts an Egyptian Jewish narrative, however Europeanized and disdainful of Arabs and Arab–Jewish culture, into the Ashkenazi-dominated Zionist imaginary. This effort by Egyptian Jews to write themselves into the national narrative characterizes the works produced in the period between the 1967 war and 1977.

Moshe Mizrahi's film *The House on Chelouche Street* [*Ha-bayit bi-rehov Shelush*] (1973), now considered a classic masterpiece of Israeli cinema, has perhaps done more than any other creative work to inscribe Egyptian Jews into the Israeli national master narrative. Ella Shohat describes the film as representing a "Jewish entity, which is at the same time Arab."[77] As Shohat argues, the film represents a breakthrough in its sensitive, non-stereotypical representation of Arab–Jewish culture. In Shohat's view, the film ends at a moment of rupture, the outbreak of hostilities in 1948 portraying "the major first steps toward Sephardi identity crisis" in which, "the two poles of Oriental Jewish identity—Arab and Jewish—are pressured to pull apart."[78] However, I would like to suggest that the film, in which a Ladino-speaking Ashkenazi man marries a Sephardi Egyptian Jewish woman on the eve of the establishment of the state of Israel, represents a narrative of suture rather than rupture. In the film, Sephardi Jews are brought into the Zionist fold—albeit on their own terms, and retaining their own language and culture. *The House on Chelouche Street* domesticates Sephardi culture's foreign elements—the narrative takes place in Palestine where the family has settled, not Egypt from whence they came. Finally, the men of the neighborhood—Ashkenazi and Sephardi alike—all take up arms when war breaks out.[79] Like Maccabi's memoir, *The House on Chelouche Street* aims to pluralize the national imaginary without unseating its major ideological underpinnings.

The 1977 Israeli parliamentary election, which brought the right-wing Likud party of Menahem Begin to power, generated a radical shift in Israeli national discourse, within and against which Egyptian Jewish and other Mizrahi writers were inscribing themselves. Political parties of the Socialist–Zionist movement had governed Israel for nearly 30 years, putting into place their own interpretation of

Jewish history and maintaining their dominant vision through various state appa-ratuses. The dissolution of a single hegemonic interpretation of Zionist ideology symbolized social changes already under way in Israel and hastened their impact on the society. The election was also noteworthy in that the Likud victory was largely attributable to its success in mobilizing the previously underrepresented Mizrahi population.[80]

This new government was characterized by its mandate from those who had been marginalized in Israeli society. Joel Beinin notes that the Labor party and MAPAM (the United Workers Party) responded to Likud efforts to write Mizrahim into national identity by "document[ing] the history of their activists in Middle Eastern countries."[81] The new regime's re-writing of Israeli history, according to Beinin, was neither more coherent nor necessarily any less Eurocentric than that of its predecessor.[82] Stereotypes of Oriental Jews persisted across the political spec-trum.[83] The ascendancy of Likud, even taking into account its perpetuation of these stereotypes, broke Socialist–Zionism's hold on the shaping of officially sanctioned cultural institutions, and granted some legitimacy to claims of marginalization articulated by Sephardi and Mizrahi intellectuals. This shift had the effect of plu-ralizing and validating the voices of Mizrahim in Israel, and was reflected in the emergence of a new wave of Mizrahi literature.[84]

The visibility of Egyptian Jews rose further the following year when Egyptian President Anwar Sadat flew to Israel to address the Knesset, launching peace negotiations between the former adversaries. Joel Beinin has demonstrated that the Egyptian Jewish community in Israel, "situated in th[e] cross-border zone," in Israel played a significant role in mediating the new circumstances brought on by the Egypt–Israel peace negotiations and treaty.[85] The recognition of Egypt as a negotiating partner, and the ensuing peace treaty validated Egyptian Jewish iden-tity. As Beinin documents, the late 1970s and early 1980s produced a significant number of works by Egyptian Jews—both in and out of Israel.[86] He notes:

> The Egyptian–Israeli peace agreement altered the insistently negative images associated with Egypt sufficiently to allow Egyptian Jews to begin the process of recalling and reconstructing their past and representing it to themselves, their children and the public.[87]

In Israel several Egyptian Jewish authors published works in this period. Reflect-ing a plurality of voices, the works produced by Egyptian Jews after the late 1970s represent a variety of subject positions. In 1978, Yitzhaq Gormezano Goren published his first novel, *Alexandrian Summer* [*Qayitz aleksandroni*]. Follow-ing a return visit to Egypt in 1980, poet Anda Harel-Dagan (née Andrée Wahba) published a collection of poetry entitled, *Cairo Poem* [*Po'ema qahirit*].[88] Poet Ada Aharoni, already active in the Israeli peace movement, published poetry, articles, and the novel, *Second Exodus*, that dealt directly with her own Egyptian origins.[89]

One writer inspired by the peace negotiations to publish his creative work repre-sented a significant divergence from the trend. Maurice Shammas wrote in Arabic about the Arab–Jews of *harat al-yahud*—a group not represented in any significant way in Egyptian Jewish writing in Hebrew. As already noted, by the 1950s, there were few prominent Jewish literati in Egypt writing in Arabic, although Jews remained involved in Egyptian music and cinema. Some Egyptian Jewish musicians have been prominent in the perpetuation of Arabic musical traditions in Israel, and others have been involved in the development of a hybrid Mediterranean-inflected musical genre popular among Mizrahim in Israel. Yet, unlike the experience of writers such as Shimon Ballas and Sami Michael documented by Nancy Berg, there were no notable Egyptian Jewish figures who had written literature in Arabic who, upon arrival in Israel, were confronted with the difficult choice between continuing to publish in Arabic and beginning to find their voice in Hebrew.[90] Ballas and Michael both continued writing in Arabic for the first years after their arriving in Israel, but by the mid-1960s had begun writing in Hebrew. Jacqueline Kahanoff who was the first Egyptian Jewish literary figure to appear on the Israeli scene, wrote in English and occasionally French. Others who immigrated at a younger age, or began writing after living in Israel for longer wrote in Hebrew. Maurice Shammas, who had written for the Arabic press in Egypt prior to his immigration to Israel, found employment with the Israeli Broadcasting Agency in its Arabic language section. He composed Arabic dramas for radio, and in 1979 published his first book, a collection of short stories in Arabic that depict the cultural life of the residents of Cairo's *harat al-yahud*. He later published a collection of poetry and a memoir, also in Arabic.[91] The major work published in Hebrew literature attesting to the integration of Jews into Egyptian Arabic culture, an historical novel about Ya'qub Sannu', was written not by an Egyptian, but by an Iraqi, Shimon Ballas.[92]

The following two chapters examine narratives of Jews' departure from Egypt produced for the Israeli–Hebrew reading public. My analyses build on scholarship that asserts that the Arab–Israeli conflict and the poor treatment of Mizrahi Jews in Israel are interrelated articulations of colonial power relations. The texts discussed in these chapters by Yitzhaq Gormezano Goren and Ronit Matalon, I argue, disrupt the binaries—Arab and Jew, Mizrahi and Ashkezani—in their exploration of cosmopolitan discourses.

In the next chapter I analyze at length Yitzhaq Gormezano Goren's novel *Alexandrian Summer* [*Qayitz aleksandroni* (1978)]. The novel represents Alexandria's culture of coexistence as a means of dispelling Israeli preconceptions about Egyptian Jews and the conditions under which they left Egypt. Through the trope of conversion the novel also questions the boundaries between Jews and Muslims, Israelis and Arabs, self and other.

7 A Mediterranean vigor that never wanes

Yitzhaq Gormezano Goren

Troubling the lines

Yitzhaq Gormezano Goren's *Alexandrian Summer* [*Qayitz aleksandroni*] (1978) portrays a middle-class Westernized Sephardi milieu in Egypt. Although the majority of the novel takes place in Egypt during the summer of 1951, the narrative situates itself within the context of the Israeli society in which it is published. Near the beginning of the novel the narrator articulates that he is motivated to tell this story to counter the Ashkenazi-cultural hegemony in Israel. He explains:

> I want to tell the story of the Hamdi-'Ali family. What is it really, this Hamdi-'Ali family? They are the joy of life, a Mediterranean vigor that never wanes. Yes indeed, Mediterranean. Perhaps because of this Mediterranean-ness I sit here and spin out this story. Here in the land of Israel bordering on the shores of the Baltic Sea. Sometimes you wonder if Vilna is the Jerusalem of Lithuania or if Jerusalem is the Vilna of the land of Israel. Thus, I wanted so much to tell the story of the Hamdi-'Alis, and the story of the city of Alexandria.[1]

This playful passage draws attention to the disconnect between Israeli cultural influences and its territorial locale as it claims a space within Israeli culture for Mediterranean narrative.

The novel's representation of Zionism is ambivalent. As Joel Benin expresses, in the novel "characters acknowledge that [...] there is no future for Jews in Egypt, but Gormezano Goren is ambivalent about the Zionist resolution of their problem."[2] The novel contrasts the idealistic vision of Israel shared by one family in Alexandria prior to immigration, with the grim reality faced by another family a few years later in Beersheba.

I argue in this chapter that the novel's "Mediterraneanness" reflects an anti-parochial, cosmopolitan urge. The novel represents Alexandria's culture of coexistence to dispel Israeli preconceptions about Egyptian Jews, and also to dispel preconceptions about the Arab "other." *Alexandrian Summer* hesitantly attempts to move beyond the "masking" tendencies of stereotyping rhetoric.[3] The novel sets up a binary conflict between essentialized Jews and Muslims only to break them down. Initially the novel follows closely the drama of the highly anticipated 1951 horse-racing season featuring competition between a Jewish jockey and a Bedouin jockey. The novel then shifts its attention to the internal conflict of the Jewish jockey's father, who converted from Islam to Judaism. Through this exploration of conversion, the novel, I argue below, "troubles the lines" between self and other, disturbing stereotyped binaries.[4]

Yitzhaq Gormezano Goren was born in 1941 in Alexandria. At the age of ten he immigrated to Israel with his family. In the process of integrating into Israeli society, the author's family shed the name—Gormezano—connecting them to the place from which their ancestors had issued generations earlier. Like many other immigrants to Israel in those years, they adopted a name—Goren—that signified acceptance of their new Israeli–Hebrew identity.[5] As an artist, the author has chosen to embrace both names, rejecting the radical rupture with the past signaled by discarding Gormezano, without rejecting the Israeli–Hebrew identity that the name Goren signifies.

Gormezano Goren's work as a novelist and dramatist, too, creates continuity, fusing the language-space of the past with that of the present. The multilingual texture of Sephardi speech in Turkey, Egypt, and Israel, finds expression in Gormezano Goren's Israeli–Hebrew literature. To reproduce verbal code switching in a monolingual text, the writer peppers the Hebrew narrative with words in Ladino, French, and English. Gormezano Goren has also been a force in Israel promoting creative works by other Sephardim and Mizrahim. In 1982, Gormezano Goren cofounded a theater company, *Bimat Kedem*, dedicated to expression of Mizrahi perspectives on stage. In an effort to expand the objectives of *Bimat Kedem*'s mission, in 1998 the company began publishing literary works under its own imprint.

Perhaps in emulation of, or response to, Lawrence Durrell's famed *Alexandria Quartet*, Yitzhaq Gormezano Goren, like Youssef Chahine, Ibrahim Abdel Meguid, and Edwar al-Kharrat produced a multi-volume, semi-autobiographical work representing life in Alexandria in the middle of the twentieth century.[6] Gormezano Goren published a trilogy of novels comprising *Alexandrian Summer, Blanche* [*Blansh*] (1986), and *On the Way to the Stadium* [*Ba-derekh la-itztadyon*] (2003).[7] The three novels share a common pool of Alexandrian Jewish characters. All three volumes of the trilogy modulate between the locus of the narrator, situated in present-day Israel, and that of the narrated events, in Alexandria from the 1930s to the 1950s. The relative balance between these loci shifts across the novels. Together, the novels describe the Alexandrian Jewish community's last years in Egypt and the transition to life in Israel.

In *Alexandrian Summer*, Israel of the late 1970s provides a critical frame through which events in Alexandria during the summer of 1951 are narrated. Three generations of the Gormezano family reside in a large apartment in Alexandria: Albert and Eugénie; their two youngest children, Anabella, a teenager, and Robby, aged ten; and Albert's mother. During the summer, the Gormezanos rent out rooms in their apartment to families visiting from Cairo. One set of guests, a Coptic family named Murad, play a minor role in the plot. The novel focuses on the adventures of the Gormezanos' other guests, the Hamdi-'Ali family: Joseph and Amélie, and their sons David and Victor. Joseph, born a Turkish Muslim, followed his beloved Amélie, a Sephardi Jew, to Alexandria, where he converted to Judaism in order to marry her. In his day, Joseph had a successful career as a jockey. David, his elegant and affected son, followed in his father's footsteps. *Alexandrian Summer* narrates the events surrounding David's involvement in the dramatic, politically charged racing season of 1951.

Gormezano Goren's second novel, *Blanche* engages with the effects of Zionism on the Egyptian Jewish community. The novel follows the romantic life of the title character, Blanche, who makes a brief but significant appearance in *Alexandrian Summer*, as discussed below. Blanche seeks economic and social advancement through sexual exploits. After her wealthy lover dies, she agrees to marry her earnest, idealistic suitor, Raphael. Fearing that Raphael's naïve attempts to establish a Zionist cell landed him on a police blacklist in Egypt, the couple immigrate to Israel. They settle in Beersheba where Blanche is cut off from the society that fed her desire. She experiences a nervous breakdown, and subsequently the marriage dissolves. The novel highlights the contrast between the flow of wealth in Alexandria and the bleak poverty of 1950s Beersheba.

The third novel, *On the Way to the Stadium*, straddles the periods covered by the previous two texts. Reproduced within the novel are fragments of a text purported to be an unfinished novel by Albert Gormezano, Robby's father, based on his life in Alexandria in the 1930s and 1940s. Interwoven with the textual fragments from this "found manuscript" is a multi-textured representation of the narrator / Robby's youth in Israel following his family's departure from Alexandria in 1951. The novel reflects on the nature of authorial voice and on the act of representation through the narrated events.

In what follows, I will focus exclusively on the first installment of the trilogy, *Alexandrian Summer*, the first novel in Hebrew to represent Egypt's cosmopolitan society. The publication of a novel that asserts both ethnicity and local specificity reflects the cultural re-alignments in Israel in the late 1970s. *Alexandrian Summer*, more than the two other novels of the trilogy, engages with the interrelationship between the cosmopolitan and empire. The novel unseats Israeli stereotypes of Muslims and Jews, and by extension, of Mizrahim and Ashkenazim. This dissolution of binaries is affected in the novel by the presence of a third term, the colonial power, which functions not as a mediator, but rather as a destabilizing force. As a point of departure, I begin my analysis of *Alexandrian Summer* establishing the ways in which the text delimits the distinctions between Jews and Muslims, foreigners and natives—the same opposition the novel ultimately attempts to unravel. Characters in the novel rely upon essentialized identities to make sense of social order. These stereotyped assumptions are articulated in the domestic sphere, among gossiping women, and in the public sphere of the race track. I then explore two moments in the novel that disrupt these binary constructions, hesitantly positing converted Levantine identities with the power to subvert the essentialized categories of Arab and Jew, colonizer and colonized.

The Jewish characters in the novel, including the narrator, who identifies himself as Robby's adult self, fundamentally see themselves as "European," and display a deep internalization of Orientalist attitudes toward native Egyptians. Drawing upon colonialist stereotypes of uncontrolled sexual urges of native peoples, Gormezano Goren's novel sensationalistically portrays the sexuality of the local population— particularly the Sudanese servants. Unlike Telpaz's "Port Said Rose Water," discussed in the previous chapter, which passes moral judgment on the practice of employing servants, Gormezano Goren's lively, and largely uncritical depiction of the Jewish *bourgeoisie's* employment of domestic help is intended to yank the chain of the Israeli Labor establishment.[8]

In the opening pages of the novel the reader is introduced to a group of elite Jewish women who play cards on a regular basis, and gossip in a mix of European languages. This group functions as a chorus of sorts throughout the narrative, establishing social norms, revealing background information on various characters, and discussing the implications of the events that transpire around them. Early in the novel, the card-playing women exchange stories about the sexual appetites of their black, Sudanese servants. One such story goes as follows:

> Once I had a maid of Bedouin origin—green eyes, *so* big. Then we hired a Sudanese servant, black like asphalt. One time, they cleaned the bathroom together. Don't ask. Suddenly I heard screams like labor pains. I ran. The door was locked. I called my husband Isadore and he got the doorman. We broke down the door. What did we find? Don't ask! The two of them … I am embarrassed to even hint what state they were in. She, the poor girl, her clothes completely torn, lay in the tub almost fainting, and he, naked and black, was hitting her with death-blows. Apparently she did not please him."[9]

This anecdote combines the teller's fascination with the overly active libido of Sudanese men and her fears of their presumed propensity for violence, particularly against women. The narrator, in effect, endorses the card-players' perspective by suggesting that the aristocratic society was so repressed that these women could hardly have dreamed such things up on their own, as indicated by the storyteller's "embarrass[ment] to even hint" at nakedness. The narrator sums up: "It is difficult for me to imagine that any one of them fantasizes to the point of weaving dreams around the proud masculinity of the impertinent black, but it is possible, it is possible."[10] Although admitting the prospect that the stories perhaps issued from the women's repressed fantasies—as the tale of one servant who propositions the lady of the house could, in fact, signify—the narrator inscribes his acceptance of the women's accounts by adopting their moralizing voice in describing the "impertinent" servant.[11]

The anecdote above, like the others related in the same context, denies the individuality of the servants, rendering them interchangeable and indistinguishable. In this particular tale, the servant remains unnamed. Elsewhere in the exchange of "horrifying" anecdotes, another woman further erases the individuality of the male servants by exclaiming, "they're all called Ahmad."[12] This indistinguishability of the "Other" is characteristic of the flattening tendency of the stereotype. As Critic Sander Gilman has described, "stereotypes arise when self-integration is threatened. They are therefore part of our way of dealing with the instabilities of our perception of the world."[13] Gilman continues that the subject establishes an imaginary, perceived impermeable boundary between the "self" and "Other" as part of the stereotyping process, perpetuating:

> [...] a needed sense of difference between the 'self' and the 'object,' which becomes the 'Other.' Because there is no real line between self and the Other, an imaginary line must be drawn; and so that the illusion of an absolute difference between self and Other is never troubled, this line is dynamic in its ability to alter itself as is the self.[14]

Throughout the novel the words "Arab" and "Muslim" are indiscriminately employed as interchangeable, and the "nativeness" of both categories remains as uninterrogated in the text as Jewish "foreignness." "Turkish," "Sudanese," and "Bedouin" characters are often also referred to as "Muslim," and are thus, transitively granted privileged access to this somewhat distorted notion of "nativeness" constructed, as it is, in contrast to Jewish foreignness. Copts don't come into play in this discourse at all. A Coptic family boards with Robby's family, along with the Hamdi-'Ali's during the summer. They are also an elite, Westernized family. However, the text never raises the question of their allegiance or "nativeness."

From the perspective of the Muslim Arab characters in the novel involved in the struggle for Egyptian independence, the Jews, are thus, aligned with the foreign powers the nationalists hope to overthrow. Although the racist implications of Orientalist attitudes internalized by Jewish characters become most apparent in the domestic sphere in the relations between wealthy Jews and their servants, anti-foreign attitudes, as portrayed in the novel, particularly in their anti-Jewish idiom, are manifested primarily in the public forum of the race track.

Alexandrian Summer depicts the rivalry between two jockeys—a Jew, David Hamdi-'Ali. and a Muslim, Ahmad al-Tal'uni. Set in 1951, a greater cultural struggle between Jews and "native" Egyptians underlies this competition on the race track. The characterizations of the two competitors clearly establish the elements of the conflict. The valences of these characterizations bear an indelible Orientalist stamp. David identifies with and internalizes the foreign view of Egypt, while Ahmad is cast as the object of the Orientalist gaze. As the competition between the jockeys heats up over the course of the season, Egyptian fans increasingly view the races as symbolic of the national struggle to throw off foreign rule.

David is introduced as cutting the figure of a "Hollywood star" in his white suit, clean, and still neatly pressed after a long journey through the hot, dusty desert.[15] David, "tall as a toreador, blond like a Frankish cavalier, and elegant like Rudolph Valentino," affects an attitude of "Olympian superiority."[16] David's privilege is derived from his likeness to "European" images of heroism and masculinity. Rudolph Valentino, the silent film star, one of whose most famous roles was as a Bedouin named Ahmad in *The Sheik* (1921), already points to a sort of self-referential playfulness that characterizes the novel's attempts to undermine the binaries it erects. In a description of David's experience in a nightclub, the narrative directly evokes the Orientalist literary tradition. Aroused by the seductive moves of a belly-dancer in the club, David recalls the words of French writer Gustave Flaubert who, in his description of his travels in Egypt, noted that the dancers also worked as prostitutes.[17] Proven correct in his assumptions, David succeeds in procuring the woman's services on the eve of a race.

The depiction of Ahmad is drawn from a familiar racially based, Orientalist vision of the Arab. Ahmad is described as a "desert savage,"[18] is described as "an unfortunate genetic mutation," "black, skinny and desiccated like a piece of carob that was dried out for several days in the sun."[19] The narrative sets Ahmad up as the fulfillment of the Orientalist imaginary, the ideal of Bedouin masculinity. He is discovered riding skillfully in the fantasia at a party thrown for the British consul, staging Bedouin culture for his consumption. The narrator describes the scene:

> Legend has it that one day the head of the tribe threw a party honoring the British consul who occasionally loved to dress up in the cloak of Lawrence of Arabia, come to the dark tents, sit oriental-style, and eat with his fingers. The sheik would organize a fantasia including all the '*shabab*,' the beautiful and strong youngsters of the tribe. Once, all of a sudden, in the middle of the performance, he appeared from the depths of the wild, black, mysterious desert, amazing everyone with his fiery riding, unlike anything anyone had witnessed from Mecca to Baghdad. The Muslims responded that he had been born in the heart of the desert.[20]

The consul's Orientalist vision represents a paternalistic romanticism, which Ahmad is happy to oblige.

The rivalry between Ahmad, the "native," and David, the "foreigner" plays out over the course of the racing season. The races become imbued with political significance in the context of Egypt's struggle for independence.[21] For the Egyptian fans, Ahmad achieves the symbolic status of national hero in his battle against David who comes to signify foreign domination.

David wins the first race and Ahmad the second. Following the second race the nationalistic tenor of the celebrations takes on distinctly anti-Jewish overtones:

> The crowd—the crowd went wild with an excess of enthusiasm, especially the Arabs. A few began to shout '*mat al-yahud.*' We were a little afraid, but thank God, there were only a few voices, a few young hot-heads, perhaps students from the Muslim brotherhood or the like.[22]

The Arabic expression "*mat al-yahud*" is translated within the text as "*mavet la-yehudim*" or "death to the Jews." Although the expression in Arabic could bear a passive significance, meaning that David's loss in the race signified a "downfall," that the Jews are "dead" or "done for," it is clear from the fear expressed by the Jewish characters in the novel that they interpret the expression as an active threat.

When confronted by the police the antagonistic voices "shut up immediately, like good children."[23]

When David wins the third race, "a hair-raising cry of despair broke loose from the black throat of the blood-thirsty Bedouin."[24] The narrative continues:

> Although there were signs in it of bad theater, it managed to shock the crowd for a moment. There were those who were disgusted by this common manner, and saw in it an inability to lose with grace, but the majority heard in this cry reverberations of something else entirely. After a time, in the courthouse, someone said that in that outcry was heard the cries of Egypt trampled under the feet of foreigners.[25]

In response to this perceived nationalist outburst, the anti-foreign sentiment of the crowd manifests itself as directed against the Jews. Once again shouting "*mat al-yahud,*" the crowd takes to the streets searching for Jews in cafés, and boarding trams "like Indians boarded the mail-train in the wild west."[26]

The representation of anti-Semitic rioting in the novel is in accordance with the widespread perception—particularly in Israel—that life for Jews in Arab countries was rife with persecution as had been the experience of Jews in Europe. Fueled by contemporaneous Arab opposition to Zionism and Israel, and a Zionist teleological view of Jewish history, this perspective, referred to by historian Joel Beinin as a "neo-lachrymose" historiography, perpetuates "a gloomy representation of Jewish life in the lands of Islam that emphasizes the continuity of oppression and persecution from the time of Muhammad and until the demise of most Arab Jewish communities in the aftermath of the 1948 Arab–Israeli war."[27] In this way *Alexandrian Summer* effectively perpetuates Orientalist discourses that also serve to fan fears of Jewish persecution; however, the novel also opens up the possibility for a more complex representation of the interaction among the various groups represented.

The narrator notes that several years later it was revealed that the riots were started by political agitators unified not only by their hatred "of the foreigners with rights and privileges" but also "first and foremost the British administration."[28] The introduction of a third term, the British, serves to disrupt the apparently clear identification and opposition already established. Whereas Jews perceive them-selves as essentially "European," adopting Orientalist contempt for the "natives," and Egyptians perceive the Jewish community as essentially "foreign," and, thus, aligned with sources of foreign rule, British characters see things differently, viewing both Jews and Arabs with equal disdain.

Indeed, on the day of the riots, in his attempt to deflect attention from the anti-Jewish sentiment expressed by the demonstrators, the narrator posits that the "real" source of anti-Semitic sentiment lies, rather, with the British.[29] The text describes that on that very day, while attending a picnic for employees of the Ford Motor Company, Robby's father, Albert, was denigrated by his supervisor, "a British man with clear anti-Semitic tendencies."[30] It is implied that the supervisor's prejudices propel Albert's eventual dismissal from his job, the event that convinces the fam-ily to leave Egypt. Rather than defusing the representation of the embattlement of the Jewish community, by introducing the issue of British anti-Semitism, in effect, the narrative ultimately endorses the fears expressed by the neo-lachrymose view—that both the locals and the foreign administration in Egypt were, at their core, anti-Semitic. However, the example of the British supervisor clearly serves to destabilize the as yet unchallenged identification of the Jewish community with the centers of foreign power.

Furthermore, although Ahmad becomes a symbol of nationalist aspiration for his fans, in fact, as the narrative makes clear, he remains quite visibly indebted to the British. On the visit of the British consul to the Bedouin tent, Ahmad impresses the consul's wife with his riding to the extent that she insists on bringing him to Alexandria to compete in the races. Ahmad quickly becomes the darling of British society. Well-trained in chivalry and sportsmanship, upon his first victory he lives up to his sponsor's expectations: "He rode over to the 'loge' of the English consul, to give 'homage' to his wife, like some kind of Ivanhoe in a tournament of knights."[31] Thus, Ahmad, too, demonstrates his internalization of British romantic notions in his expression of indebtedness to the figurehead of foreign rule.

But perhaps in an even more striking expression of the blurring of boundaries between groups is the portrayal of the character Joseph, David's father. In the third race, Ahmad accuses Joseph of having poisoned his horse in order to insure that his son would win. At the moment the Joseph hears the charges, he envisions Ahmad, his accuser, as a son who is acting out against parental authority, and not as an adversary.[32] As in this example, Joseph, through the second half of the novel, increasingly comes to represent the possibility of an internalized other. Joseph Hamdi-'Ali—known in Arabic as Yusuf—had been a jockey in his youth. It is repeatedly noted in the novel that he gave up his family, homeland (Turkey) and religion (Islam) for his Jewish wife. Through the novel, Yusuf/Joseph struggles with his conflicted identity. The act of conversion introduces an element of ambiguity.

Conversion undermines the ethno-politically charged stereotyping rhetoric of Muslim and Jew by opening up the possibility of crossing over between the categories. Critic Gauri Viswanathan has expressed that the act of religious conversion contains within it the potential to disrupt notions of identity, community, and nation:

> By undoing the concept of fixed, unalterable identities, conversion unsettles the boundaries by which selfhood, citizenship, nationhood, and community are defined, exposing these as permeable borders. Shifts in religious consciousness traverse the contained order of culture and subtly dislodge its measured alignments, belying the false assurance that only change from the outside has the power to disrupt. The indeterminacy of conversion poses a radical threat to the trajectory of nationhood.[33]

Conversion, as viewed by Viswanathan, is a mimetic act with subversive potential, much like Homi Bhabha's articulation of "mimetic desire."[34] According to Bhabha the colonial subject's mimicry of the colonizer injects ambivalence and indeterminacy into the relationship between them, providing the colonized with the subversive potential to undermine colonial power and authority. Conversion, like Bhabha's mimicry creates a "subject of difference that is almost the same, but not quite."[35] In *Alexandrian Summer*, in living as a Jew Yusuf/Joseph affects the outer trappings of the Westernized cosmopolitan culture identified with colonialism. As the flattening of the anti-Semitism onto anti-colonial rhetoric experienced at the racetrack, it is clear that the crowd sees Joseph as a traitor to both country and religion. His indeterminacy cannot shake up the power relations of the colonial system. However, his converted identity serves to undermine the essentialized binaries underpinning the relations between Egyptians and their others—colonizer and colonized; native and foreign; Muslim and Jew.

The indeterminacy that Yusuf/Joseph represents reaches its fullest articulation at the end of the novel. Through the novel, Yusuf/Joseph appears to be in a state of mental and emotional decline. He is described as increasingly withdrawn and disengaged from those around him as he attempts to quiet the conflict, and assimilate both faiths into his being. He experiences a powerful vision. Fearing the end of his life is near, Yusuf/Joseph is uncertain whose God, the God of which religion would be awaiting with his judgment:

> Many years ago he had turned his back on the religion of his ancestors, and followed his heart, after his own mistakes. Was it Allah sitting in the heavens on the supreme exalted throne who navigated him through the channels of the waters of paradise, or was it the God of the Jews? He was convinced that the father in heaven was one, as Abraham was the father of Ishmael and Isaac— one father for all, one God, but everyone sees him with his own eyes, one through the eyes of a Jew, another through the eyes of a Christian, and another through the eyes of a Muslim.[36]

Through the hallucination from which this passage is taken, Yusuf/Joseph begins to identify himself with Abraham, the progenitor of Judaism, Christianity, and Islam. Yusuf/Joseph attempts to maintain an ambiguity between the faiths.

At the climax of the novel, when Yusuf/Joseph stands facing the heavens, the narrative comes to resemble the language of the Biblical rendering of Abraham's tribulations in the face of God's demands to sacrifice his son. The representation of the *Aqedah*, or binding of Isaac is prevalent in modern Hebrew literature. The imagery has been employed for various effects in both poetry and prose, and has been much commented upon in the literary criticism.[37] In this context, the story evokes not only the Jewish narrative, but also the parallel narrative in the Islamic tradition, in which Ishmael/Isma'il is the one Abraham/Ibrahim brings as his sacrifice.

Like Abraham, Yusuf/Joseph is summoned by a disembodied voice. He ascends almost miraculously to the roof, and stands under the glint of the crescent-shape of a sickle, signifying both the sacrifice he—as Abraham—is called upon to make, as well as a reminder of the centrality of both Ibrahim and Yusuf in the

Islamic tradition. Yusuf/Joseph wonders: "[Is] this the beginning of the return?" His reflections continue:

> It had happened many years ago. Thirty years ago. A man got up and severed himself from the thread of his past, left his country and his kindred [*holekh lo me-artzo u-mi-moladeto*], and followed after a woman and after her religion to a strange land. There he took her for his wife, and after ten barren years, the will of punishment, Allah the gracious and forgiving remembered her [*poqed*], and she gave birth to a boy-child, and they called his name David in [the tradition of] Israel.[38]

The language of Gormezano Goren's text mirrors the Biblical narrative of Abram's command to leave his home: "*Lekh lekha me-artzekha u-mi-moladetkha*" "Go from your country and your kindred" (Genesis 12:1).[39] Also, Gormezano Goren's language reflects the use of the verb "*p.q.d*" in Genesis 21:1 to describe God's intervention in Sarah's barrenness. This choice of the biblical patriarch, the progenitor of both Judaism and Islam permits Yusuf/Joseph to be loyal simultaneously to both religious traditions.

As Yusuf/Joseph's fantasy continues, Layla, his beloved horse, springs forth out of a crashing brightness emanating from the horizon and flies to him on outstretched wings. As she approaches, he realizes she bears the face of Blanche, the title character of Gormezano Goren's second novel in the trilogy. The internalization of opposing forces is represented further by the depiction of the horse/woman, Layla/Blanche. Unlike the earlier representation of the competition between David and Ahmad in black and white, the horse/woman represents a composite image, a fusion of opposites: Layla, representing the blackness of night in both Arabic and Hebrew, and Blanche, representing whiteness, in French.

At its conclusion the fantasy transforms into a distorted mirroring of Muhammad's night ride, adding to the ambivalence of Yusuf/Joseph's converted identity:[40]

> Blanche–Layla invited him to ride on her naked back. He hesitated a moment and suddenly the angel Gabriel came to him, supported him under his arms and helped him mount.
> 'I am no longer young,' Yusuf said to the angel with an apologetic smile.
> 'Muhammad ascended to heaven riding on the back of Buraq,' whispered the angel in his ear, 'and Buraq also had the face of a man. '*al-mi'raj*' the miracle was called. And I was appointed to accompany him through all the spheres to the throne of honor.'
> Yusuf was afraid. Muhammad. But he … Here, here he almost fell off the back of the horse, he quickly grabbed her with all his might.[41]

Yusuf/Joseph envisions himself riding off to the heavens on the back of his beloved horse. The next morning his body is discovered on the street, and the coroner's report concludes that he died from the impact of the fall, although "miraculously," his body showed no outward signs of trauma, and his face bore an expression of bliss. It is unclear from the narrative if his fantasy leads him astray, in effect causing the plunge to his death, or if we are to understand that it instead led him toward salvation.

Either way one reads it, the internal conflict between the religious identities essentialistically defined, clearly represents a "dead end," never resolvable, but leading inevitably to the character's demise. His death signifies the untenability of the composite identity. In effect, his death signals the hegemony of the binary. Set as it is within the context of the Jewish community of Alexandria in 1951, Yusuf/Joseph's internal struggle between the Muslim and Jewish identities that had coexisted peacefully within him for many years, symbolizes the political and discursive shifts under way in Egypt in the early 1950s. Yusuf/Joseph's death—the failure to reconcile the conflicting forces—signifies the beginning of the end.

In the context of the narrative, too, Yusuf/Joseph's death marks an end of another sort. His death scene is followed only by a brief coda describing the departure of Robby's family for Israel just three months later. The loss of the mobile, converted potential represented by Yusuf/Joseph's internalized otherness, thus, also signals the demise of the Jewish community in Egypt.

Desire at play

The text also obliquely refers to another conversion narrative drawn from Pharonic times. In honor of David's victory in the first race, ten-year-old Robby plans a party for which he choreographs and performs a piece he calls "Nefertiti's dance."[42] Queen Nefertiti, along with her husband, the pharaoh Akhenaton, publicly espoused a vague monotheism that rejected the famous pantheon of ancient Egyptian gods. In a sense, the historically contentious conversion of Nefertiti and Akhenaton, which was met with great opposition and was overturned by the priests upon Akhenaton's death, parallels Yusuf/Joseph's internalized struggle. The reference to this historical proto-monotheism also provides a glimpse at a moment that predates the two monotheistic traditions between which Yusuf/Joseph's allegiances are split. Furthermore, as some historically baseless but prevalent theories suggest a link between Akhenaton and Moses, the gesture toward this ancient monotheism in the context of this novel could signify an attempt to locate a site for Jewish Egyptian nativeness issuing from ancient times.

The inclusion of "Nefertiti's dance" in the celebrations for David's victory also signals a "troubling" of the gender line.[43] From the time he was born, Robby's sister, who had desperately wanted the baby to be a girl, insisted on referring to him as "*ma petite fille.*"[44] When Robby dons the Nefertiti costume he had designed, the card-playing women exclaim that he looks like a girl.[45]

Robby's femininity is contrasted to the hypermasculinized, predatory practices of Victor Hamdi-'Ali, Yusuf/Joseph's youngest son. At the start of the novel Robby shielded by the repressed society remains sexually latent. Victor, however, is an 11-year-old boy with an overly active libido. Victor pursues Robby, and initiates sexual contact between them. Although Robby comes to enjoy the sexual play, he can never surmount his sense of guilt. As the two boys engage more frequently in sexual behavior, they become more careless, and are eventually caught in the act by Robby's mother. Fearing the threat of his father's intervention, Robby sublimates his desire.

Victor's hybrid origins are highlighted humorously in the narrative by the gossiping card-players. Victor is not only the product of a marriage between a converted Muslim and a Jew, but also, as the boy's "long head and face" resemble that of a horse, there is some speculation that his father was perhaps thinking about his beloved horse, Layla, at the moment of conception, or that the boy was, rather, the product of the union between man and beast.[46]

In *Alexandrian Summer* the hybridization of cultures is portrayed as an "unnatural," corrupting force, producing "animalistic" desires outside of the norms proscribed by the society. Within the context of a society that "strangled itself within webs of conventions, so that even the smallest of small hints of an act of carnality lets loose emotions and demons hidden in the depth of depths beneath the façon,"[47] homosexuality is identified as "dirty," "unnatural," "Arab behavior."[48] Shocked by her son's conduct, when she catches the boys in the act, Robby's mother rebukes them in a moralizing tone: "It is not acceptable in polite society, *N'est-ce-pas?* Perhaps among the Arabs, who knows."[49] In other words, the hypersexuality of the Muslim men—here we once again see the discursive slippage beween Arab and Muslim—described by the gossiping women, Robby's mother among them, is portrayed as an immutable and transferable trait, passed on from father to son.

If Yusuf/Joseph's death represents one end limit to the possibility of hybrid identities, Victor represents another. While the novel explores the possibility of internalization of otherness, hybridization leads either to a dead end, or its disruptive potential is repressed. Although this text confronts the disruptive possibilities of mobile, converted identities, it does not ultimately seek to overturn social norms.

8   Unmasking Levantine blindness
Ronit Matalon

This chapter represents a dialogue of sorts between the writings of novelist Ronit Matalon, the daughter of Egyptian Jewish immigrants to Israel, and those of essayist Jacqueline Shohet Kahanoff, whose works give voice to the experiences and desires of the immigrant generation. Jacqueline Shohet Kahanoff, mentioned in Chapter 6, was born in Egypt in 1917. She lived in the United States for ten years, during which time she completed a degree in journalism at Columbia University, and published her first novel, *Jacob's Ladder*, a semi-autobiographical bildungsroman depicting a Jewish girl growing up in interwar Egypt.[1] Kahanoff moved to Israel in 1954, where she began to work as freelance journalist for the English language press, as well as writing sociological reports for the Jewish Agency. In 1959, as noted in the previous chapter, she published a cycle of four essays, "A Generation of Levantines," that appeared in Hebrew translation in the Israeli literary and cultural journal *Keshet*.

In the "Generation of Levantines" essays, Kahanoff evokes colonialism in describing intra-Jewish cultural conflict in Israel. Long before Ella Shohat and other scholars in the late twentieth century succeeded in raising the issue, Kahanoff argued that the experience of Oriental Jews in Israel replicated a colonial relationship. In place of the colonizer / colonized binary she proposes a more multi-faceted model derived from her experiences in cosmopolitan Egypt. Yet, her attempt to establish a broad universal ultimately fails to transcend the colonial relationship. Kahanoff's model excludes the Arab–Islamic culture in which Egyptian cosmopolitanism flourished. As I argue in the following section of the chapter, Kahanoff's Levantinism functionally replaces one colonial discourse—Ashkenazi hegemony in Israel—with another—Levantine cultural superiority over Arabs.

In the last year of Kahanoff's life, the editor of *Keshet*, Aharon Amir, who had also translated into Hebrew her most important works, published a collection of her essays under the title *From East the Sun* [*Mi-mizrah shemesh*].[2] By the time of Anwar Sadat's visit to Egypt, Kahanoff was already stricken with the disease that would ultimately claim her life. She managed to write a couple of short pieces expressing hope for the future—a future that she imagined could allow for the Levantine integration she advocated in her writings.[3] After her death, her work began a slow decline into obscurity.

In 1986 a young writer, Ronit Matalon, published a long article about Kahanoff and her writings in the weekend supplement to the newspaper *Ha'aretz*, launching a campaign to revitalize Kahanoff's memory.[4] Matalon was born in Israel in 1959, the year that Kahanoff published the "Generation of Levantines" essays. Matalon's parents had immigrated to Israel from Egypt. She found in Kahanoff's work both an artifact of a shared family history, and the voice of a compelling social critic. Matalon's 1994 novel *The One Facing Us* [*Zeh 'im ha-panim elenu*] offers a tribute to Kahanoff.[5] The novel features a character named "Jacqueline Kahanoff," and includes, embedded in the narrative, two of Kahanoff's essays from the "Generation of Levantines" cycle.[6] What characterizes the representation of Kahanoff and her work in Matalon's writings is not sycophancy, but rather a respectful critical analysis. Matalon, I argue in this chapter, is attracted to Kahanoff's social theory of "Levantinism" as much for its failings as for its strengths.

Ronit Matalon, by contrast, explores Levantinism in all its ambiguity and contradictions, embracing its inability to transcend dominant paradigms. *The One Facing Us*, I argue in the second section below, extends Levantinism to its various logical conclusions, in particular exploring its indebtedness to and complicity with colonial discourses. Matalon's novel mediates between the binary of the colonizer / colonized relationship on the one hand, and a multiplicitous plurality, on the other hand, both contained, as I argue, within Kahanoff's notion of Levantinism.

The colonial-cosmopolitan Levantine

Jacqueline Kahanoff's "Generation of Levantines" valorizes cultural "cross-fertilization" as a means of undermining parochial social discourses. Kahanoff draws upon Egyptian cosmopolitan society as a social model for achieving cultural integration in Israel. Kahanoff's conception of the cosmopolitan is also filtered through her experience as a colonial subject—her work perpetually negotiates between the binaries invoked by colonial relationships, and the multiplicitous possibilities afforded by cosmopolitanism. Kahanoff situates herself against colonial power and against hegemonic discourses of unitary or narrowly defined national identities. Nevertheless, her vision of Levantine cosmopolitanism, much like the social model from which it is drawn, is indelibly marked and limited by colonial discourses.

The essays that comprise the "Generation of Levantines" cycle are: "Childhood in Egypt," "Europe from Afar," "Rebel, My Brother," and "Israel: Ambivalent Levantine." In the opening essay of the cycle "Childhood in Egypt," Kahanoff distinguishes between the traditional Levantines and her "Levantine Generation." The Levantines, by her definition, are Syrians, Greeks, and Jews, "those whom the Moslems called with superstitious respect and suspicion, the People of the Book."[7] By contrast, the "Levantine Generation," defined as "crossbreeds of many cultures" living under British rule in Egypt included Muslim Egyptians and Turks.[8] The "task and privilege" of this group "was to translate European thought and action and apply it to [their] own world."[9] Kahanoff continues by distinguishing her generation from those who came before: "We were the first generation of Levantines in the contemporary world who sought a truth that was neither in the old religions nor in complete surrender to the West."[10] In her view, Levantine hybridity does not merely combine influences but creates something new.

As the title suggests, the first essay, "Childhood in Egypt," describes Kahanoff's growing consciousness of her place within society as a child. The second essay, "Europe from Afar," continues to explore the self as a social being by representing her experiences during late adolescence in the 1930s. Kahanoff had educational ambitions that exceeded the social norm for women of her class. Restless and under-stimulated, Kahanoff and her peers sought out acceptable means of expression—opening an ill-fated clinic in *harat al-yahud* and taking classes. Her restlessness is mirrored in this essay by her representation of the society at large, a society ready-ing itself for change. In "Europe from Afar," Kahanoff also begins to express her voice as a social critic. From her "Levantine" position Kahanoff denounces social Darwinism and European brutality, but likewise criticizes Arab–Islamic culture for, in her view, rejecting everything European.[11]

The final essay of the cycle, "Israel: Ambivalent Levantine" picks up the trajec-tory of Kahanoff's personal narrative in Israel. Upon her arrival, Kahanoff finds a society built on a model of "absorption" rather than one of cultural integration. Jewish immigrants were asked to shed the trappings of their dispossessed, neu-rotic Diaspora past, in order to normalize themselves as healthy citizen-subjects of the Jewish state. As discussed in the previous chapter, in practice, this process of normalization meant acculturating Jewish immigrants from the Arab–Islamic world to an Ashkenazi-centric society. Further, Zionist leaders feared the impact these immigrants might have on Israeli culture. What Kahanoff valued—cultural crossbreeding—was commonly viewed with fear and loathing. In "Israel: Ambivalent Levantine," Kahanoff advocates for Israel to embrace rather than repel the "transformative" and "reconstructive" power of the Levantine hybrid:

> Israel could be Levantine in a more constructive sense by assembling its tre-mendous richness of backgrounds and cultures to create an art, a style of thought and living, a personality more truly its own. For this, an active, con-scious intellectual and moral reappraisal of what makes Israel would open new paths. There is nothing to fear from this type of Levantinization, to which we are destined by our very origins and composition, than this inhibiting fear itself. In effecting this new cultural synthesis, there is no model but what we make of ourselves by living together and attempting to find workable solutions to the problems confronting us.[12]

In a move far ahead of her time, Kahanoff equates the patronizing Israeli hege-monic discourse with a colonial civilizing mission. By articulating the parallels between the Levantines' position in Egypt under British stewardship, and in Israel under Ashkenazi power, she attempts to assert a transformative power with which the Levantines are imbued.

For Kahanoff the Levantines also hold promise not just in domestic social for-mation, but also in negotiating Israel's place within the Middle East. She posits region-wide Levantinization as the only hope for peace between Israel and the Arab states. She writes: "Israel 'wins' if it becomes the model of a well-integrated Levantine country, which refuses neither side its inheritance in creating its own values."[13] However, much like the critiques Kahanoff levies against Israeli absorption policy, what she intends as peace between equals, is cast in terms of a patronizing, civilizing mission.[14]

Kahanoff's colonizing impulse toward Arab culture is perhaps best illustrated in the third essay of the cycle, entitled "Rebel, My Brother." As described above, the first two essays in the "Generation of Levantines" cycle are drawn from Kahanoff's personal experiences during her childhood and adolescence in Egypt, whereas the final piece, somewhat more didactically, explores the possibilities for intercultural relations in her adopted country, Israel. "Rebel, My Brother" relates a narrative taking place during the intervening years of the early 1950s in Egypt, rather than continuing the anticipated trajectory of Kahanoff's life—by exploring for example, her own experiences in the United States and France, her decision to emigrate, or her early years in Israel.

The essay begins by describing the family's continued close ties with their ancestral Tunisian village, also home to Habib Bourgiba, at the time of narrated events a leader in the Tunisian independence movement, and by the time of the essay's publication, already the first president of independent Tunisia. After Kahanoff and her sister left Egypt, a Tunisian cousin, at Bourgiba's behest, approached her parents asking them to host some North African intellectuals passing through Cairo. The essay then proceeds to describe the close relationship that developed between Kahanoff's parents and their last guest, an Algerian revolutionary known to them by an assumed name. Eventually, in the process of narrating their story, the parents let slip the real name of their guest, Ahmad Ben Bella, the then imprisoned FLN mastermind who later became the first president of Algeria.

In this essay, Kahanoff foregrounds the gaps her narrative attempts to bridge. At one point, Kahanoff's husband disrupts the flow of the narrative. He patronizingly scolds his in-laws for having put themselves at risk to provide refuge to an Arab terrorist. The disruptive inclusion of the husband represents the voice of the cultural target audience. His presence serves to demarcate the extent of the expanse between perceived Israeli realities of the Arab–Israeli conflict, and the Levantine culture in which it was possible for Arab nationalists and Jews with ties to Israel to live amicably under the same roof. Although Kahanoff's husband also lived in Egypt, his family had emigrated there from Russia, and he did not share his in-laws' close relationship with Arab culture.

As the events unfold, the narrator envisions the image of her parent's boarder coming into focus as reflected in her bedroom mirror. However, the borders between self and other disintegrate as she comes to claim his reflection as her own. Kahanoff writes:

> An intense jealousy gripped me when mother told me, after her arrival in Israel, about the North African patriots who had lived in our house in such close relationships with her and my father. In her letters she had mentioned

'a nice group of youngsters—students from friendly countries—who fill the silent emptiness that the children left behind after they abandoned us.' The rebuke annoyed me, as did the thought of some stranger making himself at home in my room. Strange, I had a feeling of some essence looking at the mirror on my vanity, a face embellished by the shining glints of the polished frame of the mirror. Friend? Foe? I didn't know for sure. Yet, I felt that some cloudy connection existed between us.[15]

As the essay progresses, the figure reflected in the mirror becomes more distinct, identified first by his narrative, then his name, and finally the full representation of his image. By the end of the essay Kahanoff's narrator comes to recognize herself reflected in the image of this "other" she constructs, appropriating his image as a universal symbol of her Levantine generation. She comes to see the image as whole, providing some unity to her own fragmentary identity. However, through this process the narrator achieves her own individuation as she denies Ben Bella his.

As her mother describes, Ben Bella was on a flight from Egypt to Tunisia with other FLN leaders when their plane was diverted to France and they were all taken into custody. Kahanoff's narration also represents an appropriation, diversion, and entrapment—indeed a hijacking of sorts.

In the essay, the mother offers to share his photograph:

She picked up a bag that contained pictures of her nearest and dearest. From among the faces which had surrounded the days of my youth, surfaced a sheet of paper from which peered a brownish, pleasant face with fine features, a refined mouth, sad, deep eyes, and an expression of quiet, cultivated splendor, surrounded by bold green and red Arabic letters. The face in the mirror surrounded by fire, is the face of my generation.[16]

The words framing Ben Bella's image remain unformed, unrecognized, untranslated, circumscribing the muteness of the photograph. The letters on the flyer, not even acknowledged as words, are evacuated of their function as linguistic signs, instead serving only as culturally specific markers of the struggle for independence: the green and red of Algerian nationalism, the choice of Arabic over French. In the end, Ben Bella's image in the narrative is just as entrapped in multiple discursive framings as his physical confinement. In order to universalize the image, Kahanoff's narrator evacuates any specific content from the flyer, and by extension the struggle to which Ben Bella was dedicated.

Kahanoff effectively denies Ben Bella his subjectivity as she hijacks his story, and in doing so she reveals her own colonial complicity. According to Israeli literary critic Dolly Benhabib, although Kahanoff's body of work is largely devoted to exposing legacies of colonialism in its various forms—from the effects of European Imperial rule to Israeli "colonization" of its disenfranchised Jewish minorities—Kahanoff never recognizes her own colonizing tendencies in her treatment of Arab culture.[17] Indeed, Kahanoff projects a social cohesion of Jews through a model derived from "Levantine civilizations" but devoid of the majority culture of the same Levant. Although Arab culture served as a host, it is described as somewhat superfluous to the (explicitly non Arab-Islamic) Levantine "bridge" culture which flourished within it.

The final passage of "Rebel, My Brother" tightens the circle of appropriation by enlisting the mother as complicit in the entrapment of her "adopted" son, "Mother asked: 'Would you like the picture?' I said yes. That was the face of my generation, which fought such a desperate battle to be free, to be whole. ... We smiled at each other over the swarthy face between us."[18] The Algerian freedom fighter is multiply entrapped in the narrative: captured and imprisoned by his "colonizing mother," discursively framed in the Arabic of the flyer, and finally caught between the mother's narrative and her daughter's re-telling. By the end of the essay, in order to advance the case of Levantinism's potential as articulated throughout the "Generation of Levantines" essays, Kahanoff's narrator takes full possession of Ben Bella's image and his story.

Levantinism revisited

Ronit Matalon, whose Egyptian Jewish parents belonged to Kahanoff's "Generation of Levantines,"[19] could be said to belong to a "post-Levantine" generation. In contrast to the mainstream Israeli society of her youth that rejected her parents' cultural heritage, Matalon embraces and explores Levantinism's cultural potential. Matalon affords herself a critical distance from both the Zionist discourses that pervaded her education and the Levantine legacy. *The One Facing Us* explores the sources of Levantinism's weaknesses, particularly the ambivalence of its complicity with colonialism or colonizing discourse. Such a confrontation with the premises of Levantinism does not serve to undermine the notion, but rather to come to terms with its sites of ambivalence. Likewise, *The One Facing Us* also adopts a deterritorializing vision of national belonging that decenters Zionism's rooted relationship to place.[20]

Ronit Matalon's novel, *The One Facing Us*, tells the story of an Egyptian Jewish family at a remove of several decades from their departure. The novel is framed by the visit in 1979 of 16-year-old Esther to her uncle Jacquo Cicurel in Cameroon. Just as thousands of Israelis, many from Egypt, were flocking to visit Egypt in the wake of the peace treaty between the two countries,[21] Esther engages in her family history tour in Douala. The narrative interweaves the girl's discomfort with the inequities of life in postcolonial Cameroon with discoveries about her family who had dispersed over five continents after leaving Cairo in the 1940s and 1950s. The novel unfolds as a narration accompanying the photographs—some recorded as missing—leading off each chapter. Unlike for Kahanoff, photographs in Matalon's work are shared and traded, not possessed. Fractured reminiscences and stories told by various members of the family about one another are filtered through Esther's narration. Esther, a generation removed from family life in Cairo, is nevertheless imprinted by the stories of those times and by the people who populate them.

Esther's grandparents' generation of Levantine elites is described in the novel as "frozen in a sort of strange, ceremonial death of inner contradictions that negate one another."[22] The members of the last generation to live in Egypt, including Robert, Esther's father and each of the five Cicurel siblings—Marcelle, Inès (Esther's mother), Edouard, Moïse, and Jacquo—each represent a different logical extension of these contradictory impulses in their varied choices and conflicting ideological positions. In the text, there is no privileged inheritor of postdispersion Levantinism. Each character displays certain exaggerated character traits, caricatured embodiments of their internalization of a Levantine legacy. This critical distancing and portrayal of multiple Levantinisms has the effect of de-essentializing the term, of moving consideration of the notion outside of the exclusive, binary, othering realm of Israeli political discourse. In what follows, I begin my analysis of the novel by identifying and interpreting the "post-Levantine" options each character represents. The final section explores the novel's representation of the outer limits of the Levantine option.

Robert, Esther's father, "already out of place," always already an anachronism, carries on as if a "man of leisure." His lifestyle in Cairo permitted the cultivation of loose affiliations, the possibility of wandering and creating a new persona in each locale:

> From the age of 12 he wandered, diligent, perceptive, adaptable, and savvy about people and life, he found himself other homes. He was constantly changing occupations or working several at a time: he worked in sales and marketing, he was a journalist, a translator, and a consummate, perpetual student who picked things up here and there, dexterously making the most of his often meager knowledge and granting it the capacity to distinguish his personality. Different groups from the fringes of society always attracted his attention, although he coveted a life of wealth, pampering, and ease: Marxists and Trotskyites, the Copts, the Arab nationalists, Cairo's drug dealers and pimps, theater and movie actors—he ran with them all, drinking, carousing, influencing and being influenced, spurning his Jewishness in favor of Arab national identity and pan-Arabism that always excited him—until his final years, Gamal Abdel Nasser was his great hero.[23]

Driven by dissatisfaction, Robert gives in to his wanderlust, in Cairo roaming the streets, searching outwardly for a sense of fulfillment.

Preferring the transnational pan-Arabism to any derivation of Jewish nationalism, he found that once in Israel, his opportunities for remaking himself were curtailed:

> Here there was a particular place and image. Not in Cairo: there were a thousand possible places, nevertheless he never missed it, he created anew the shifting illusion of a thousand places, a thousand shifting possible places.[24]

Jacquo Cicurel had long recognized that Robert's loose affiliations translated into unreliability and instability in personal relations, and therefore he opposed his friend's marriage to Inès. Throughout the novel Robert frequently abandons family responsibilities. After promising to care for his ailing mother, he leaves her at the train station in Cairo with his sister who was about to depart for America. He is also an absentee husband and father, preferring on occasion to sleep on a park bench rather than come home to his family.

Likewise, Robert's political activism is intermittent and short-lived. Frustrated with life in the *ma'abara*, he leads demonstrations demanding "bread and work" for Mizrahim.[25] To pacify him, the Israeli government offers him a cushy post with little responsibility and lots of perks. Ultimately, he finds he is not interested in maintaining a sedentary life in Israel, and takes flight again. Several years later upon his return, when he loses a bid for city council, rather than continuing to pursue other political opportunities, he disappears once more. Robert embodies the multiply identified and perpetually dissatisfied Levantine, with his short attention span and inability to make and maintain connections.

Marcelle, Esther's maternal aunt, lives in Paris. She is a kleptomaniac and compulsive liar who steals photographs from her family members. Her character blurs the boundaries of memory by taking a broad narrative license. She hunts for lost treasures, gathering leftover bits and pieces—like the used appliances she seeks in every district of Paris. Together with her husband Henri, a Holocaust survivor from Poland, Marcelle travels the world, visiting relatives in every port.[26] The manic pace of Marcelle's travels, matched only by the frenzy with which she narrates the tall tales of her adventures, add a comic touch to the parodic rendition of the wandering Jew. Encircling the globe several times a year, Marcelle and Henri visit and gather relatives to create a vague anchoring in their rootlessness. Marcelle's Levantinism, thus, is subsumed into a broader discourse of post-Holocaust Jewish life, picking up the pieces in the aftermath of the great destruction and displacements experienced by Jews in the twentieth century.

Inès, Esther's mother, takes on the role of "homemaker," creating a welcoming environment even in the tent she occupied with Robert in the *ma'abara* in 1950s Israel.[27] Yet, just as in the transit camp, "home" for Inès is not a fixed place, but mobile, uprootable, constantly in flux even when she inhabits a fixed structure in Beersheba. Disturbed by a photograph of her brother Jacquo's cramped and cluttered office in Cameroon "her vigilant pragmatic instinct" kicked in "to march immediately with a hammer, screwdriver, and broom and enter right into the very center of the photograph."[28] Her impulse is not merely to clean, but to "expand," "dismantle," "tear up," or in her words "to turn his world upside-down," to transform the space / place into something other.[29]

Inès re-landscapes her small garden behind her house in Beersheba, uprooting trees, digging holes, planting anew,[30] to the extent that she defamiliarizes the space of home. Once, when Marcelle, as was her wont, arrived unannounced in the middle of the night, she could no longer identify the house because Inès had cut down the great cypress tree in the front yard.[31] Another time when Inès decides to remove an unwanted bush by burning it, the fire threatens to burn down the house.[32] This destructive gardening threatens the structure of the house, as it metaphorically threatens the placeness of "home." Inès perpetually re-enacts her displacement, her Levantine denial of fixity of place and the binding ties of home.

Edouard, Inès's youngest brother, was only 13 when the family emigrated from Egypt. His character displays a mix of Levantine charm and an Israeli cockiness rooted in a deep self-doubt,[33] Edouard becomes consumed by his desire for power. At one point, Edouard goes to work for his brother Jacquo who at the time was running a factory in Gabon. Edouard fails to learn the subtleties of mixed fear and respect toward black workers driving his brother's management strategy.[34] Upon his return to Israel, he finds an outlet for his heavy-handedness, his "core of personal and political extremism."[35] He takes a job with the police force, working his way up to the post of chief of the interrogation unit in the occupied Gaza strip. He chooses to live in Gaza, where he embraces aspects of his own Arab identity: "He speaks Arabic almost exclusively with a strange, demonstrative aggression, denouncing at every opportunity both the 'Ashkenazi assimilation" of Uncle Moïse and mother, and the naïveté of their compromising position regarding 'the Arabs here.'"[36] Ammiel Alcalay describes this scenario as a complex internalization and displacement of derision for Arab culture:

> One can hum the tunes of Farid al-Atrash, Umm Kulthum, or Muhammad 'Abd al-Wahab one minute, and serve as an interrogator in which the Palestinian subject becomes an object of misplaced rage the next. Such is the nature of Israeli working-class dislocation and each turn of the screw in both the hegemonic cultural structure and the continuing occupation, always amply abetted by the industry of official imagery, only serves to further mutilate memory itself as an entirely new history and set of relations is constantly being produced.[37]

The character of Edouard in broad strokes represents the stereotypical "reactionary" and "despotic" Mizrahi.[38] In the novel, Moïse, the eldest sibling, and Inès shake their heads at the transformations their brother has undergone, described by the narrator as taking place "slowly, away from the family."[39] Yet, Inès concedes that the seeds for such attitudes could have been present in their shared universe: "Perhaps they were there and we didn't know," she muses to Moïse, "maybe we didn't see."[40]

Moïse, a Zionist ideologue already in Cairo, identifies *bourgeois*, Egyptian Levantine society as a dead-end street: "There's no way out […], not individually and not collectively. […] The choices before us are very clear, you'd have to be blind not to see them: you can be a Zionist or a Communist. Those are the only two options."[41] Yet, Moïse fails to recognize his own unwavering, and sometimes inhumane commitment to his beliefs. His own "natural instinct for authority"[42] overrides all other impulses. Unwavering in his principles, he insists on killing the family's German shepherd in Cairo because it had stolen a piece of meat and could therefore no longer be trusted.[43] By concluding the passage describing his principled cruelty with a mention of his departure six months later to a kibbutz,[44] the narrator highlights the interconnection between his penchant for heavy-handed, unfeeling authority and his Zionist ideology. In his embracing of the ideals of Socialist–Zionism, Moïse abandons the "humanity" that characterized the Levantine lifestyle of his father and brother Jacquo.

For Moïse, the logic of ideology unquestioningly supersedes the irrationality of emotion. In contrast, his father, in his tendency toward a vague, sympathetic humanism, distrusted Zionism, "placing it with a clear conscience above all other enemies. He could not spurn a human face; a human face, in his eyes, always deserved compassion, unlike an idea, abstraction or an ideology."[45] More than literally, Jacquo the younger, named after his father, carries on the family name— even though Moïse was the eldest, their mother, Fortuna, was known in Cairo as Umm Jacquo,[46] and throughout the novel the second son is identified by the family name, Cicurel. Father and son also share a resistance to nationalism, preferring rather a vague "humanism" that transcends national borders:

> [Grandfather Jacquo] did not hide his preference for Uncle Cicurel and 'that Africa of his,' which he felt suited the *esprit de la famille* better, anyhow, than the Zionist dream, which he conceived of as a foreign element, a betrayal of the family spirit.[47]

Although Jacquo gains approval from the family patriarch for his brand of Levantinism, it is not privileged in the text as a preferable model, rather one, like the others, rife with inherited inconsistencies and blind spots, as explored in greater detail in the following section.

Levantine blindness and colonial complicity

The novel privileges the scopic realm in its exploration of Levantinism, evoking sight and blindness, the look and the gaze. Blindness, both literal and figurative, appears somewhat endemic to the various incarnations of Levantinism and generations of Levantines represented in the novel. Esther's great-grandfather, a man of letters in Egypt who had translated Shakespeare into Arabic, lost his sight. Fortuna, Esther's grandmother, also blind, reminisces about life in Cairo, when she could still see, by paying Esther, to describe family pictures. The insistent metaphorical Levantine blindness is passed along from generation to generation, as if a hereditary trait. Zuza, Robert's niece raised in America, comes to Israel to interview relatives; in a dialogue with Inès, rife with misunderstandings, Zuza articulates her own insistent refusal to see the imprint of the past: "To really see a picture very well, you need to turn your eyes from it, or simply close them, simply."[48]

In postcolonial Cameroon, Levantine blindness bears within it the social weight of colonial complicity. The closing scene of the novel provides a key to understanding and reading the role of the visual—in both seeing and refusing to see—in the constitution of Levantine identities in the novel. Jacquo and Marie-Ange Cicurel host a Christmas party, an event also marking the niece's imminent departure, as well as the arrival of five-year old Cedric, the Cicurels' grandson, from France. One guest, a Jewish veterinarian, attempts to relate how he once assisted in cataract surgeries on blind Malawian children: "In Malawi, the doctor continues, heaping pieces of cold salmon in lemon sauce onto his plate, there was an odd story, one of those things that could perhaps only happen in Africa."[49] His story is deferred several times in the narrative by champagne toasts in honor of the various festivities and, as in the passage above, by descriptions of the sumptuous feast. In broken fragments he relates that when the children regained their eyesight, they sought ways to re-induce the blindness. He remarks uncomprehendingly of the willful acts of blindness, "the children did not want to see."[50] Yet we are aware how he, like the others gathered at the feast, cannot see beyond their plates piled high with delicacies flown in from France[51] to draw into focus the black hands serving them.[52]

In the midst of this tension between the self-destructive impulses of the children and the willed blindness of the white (post-) colonialists gorging themselves, Uncle Cicurel—who had completely ignored the veterinarian's narrative—turns to his friend Sendrice, a Greek Cypriote who had lived many years in Alexandria, and proprietarily asserts their identity: *"Nous les Orientaux."*[53] With these concluding words of the novel, Cicurel, thus, closes the circle of complicity, articulating the connection between his own brand of Oriental / Levantine identity, enacted through this gathering—his French-born grandson on his knee, a multi-national guest list, feasting on vast quantities of expensive imported delicacies—and the willful acts of blindness implicated within it.

Although this blindness is enacted through colonial discourses, it is nevertheless a metaphor reserved for the "Levantines." In contrast, the refusal of Marie-Ange, Jacquo's wife, to acknowledge her dehumanizing of blacks is rather characterized by deafness. Marie-Ange, cast as entirely foreign to Levantinism, represents "the colonial woman"—daughter of subsistence farmers in Bretagne, she followed her first husband to the promise of wealth in Africa.[54] She met Jacquo after the death of her first husband when she was stranded in Gabon with a small child. Unlike the visual constitution of the Levantine existence, the world of Marie-Ange, the perennial gossip, comes into being through oral / aural transmission. For example, although she sees Esther frequently talking to the servants, it is only after she hears rumors about it that she scolds her niece for creating a scandal.[55] Esther describes Marie-Ange's personality as follows:

> She is not what you think, the Madame. [...] No loose malice circulates within her, rather deafness, an exaggerated deafness towards language and its phrases, a deafness free of blemishes, sewed-up well on all sides, a deafness that has become a kind of personality, this deafness sort of came into being out of itself, with cities, bridges, neighborhoods, villages, a legal code, traffic signs, alley cats, everything, all the errors, the mis-steps, the clumsiness, the deeds and words that miss the mark, and all the possible *faux pas*.[56]

Marie-Ange, in her deafness, thus, effectively embodies the "governmentality" of "racist stereotypical discourse, in its colonial moment."[57]

Esther, the visitor, positions herself as an outside critic of race relations in Cameroon. The black servants make her feel uncomfortable, and she frequently vocalizes criticisms of whites' treatment of blacks. In defiance of the wishes of her aunt, Marie-Ange, initially the girl spends a great deal of time socializing with the servants, particularly the cook, Julien. Yet, in her naiveté Esther does not recognize the intrusiveness of her enactment of "liberalism," aggressively asserting / inserting her authority / privilege in others' private space.

One day in the kitchen, the cook Julien tries to explain to Esther his nephew's political involvements and insistence on resisting the lingering effects of colonialism. Esther dismisses his claims out of hand, and signals her careless disregard for the details of Julien's narrative and family relations by misidentifying the boy as a cousin. In the context of this discussion Esther also transgresses the bounds of their interactions by implying an intimacy they do not share. In an act mirroring a cruel trick Cicurel played many years earlier on his hired playmate, a dark-skinned Egyptian girl whom he informed could lighten her skin if she scrubbed hard enough, Julien reacts to Esther's flippancy by squeezing her hand around the piece of steel wool she was using to wash up, drawing droplets of blood.[58]

When Esther finds out Julien's first child has been born, she buys as a gift "the largest panda bear she could find."[59] She invades his private space, delivering the inappropriate gift to his home in an impoverished district of Douala. Julien, tripping over the bear in the dark, is startled by the beast lurking in the shadows of the hall. The not-so-cuddly animal also reflects the animality of Esther's attraction to Julien.[60] In the tense interaction in the hut, Esther for the first time looks at Julien, and momentarily comes to recognize his subjectivity through the contempt and rage she sees in his eyes:

> I looked at his face, something I had never dared to do. His eyes were white-white without pupils, burning with a boundless hatred, contempt and hatred. I knew that I would never forget those eyes, the empty white look of hatred: no one had ever looked at me like that. I couldn't understand what I had done to deserve it.[61]

As Homi Bhabha writes of the articulation of subjectivity through the visual in Franz Fanon's exploration of race and the colonial condition: "In the objectification of the scopic drive there is always the threatened return of the look [. ...] To put it succinctly, the recognition and disavowal of 'difference' is always disturbed by the question of its representation or construction."[62] Afraid of the consequences, from that moment on, Esther fulfills the prediction of her acculturation to the white (post-)colonial lifestyle[63] in her deliberate, complicitous refusal to look, her adoption of an empty gaze that sees right through the black servant "like through air,"[64] and denies his articulation of subjectivity through the visual.

The novel explores the ambivalent place of Levantine characters in colonial discourses, inferring parallels between Levantines as colonial subjects on both sides of the divide. In Africa, as in Egypt, the Levantines, as described above, are cast as complicitous with the colonizing power, although distinguishable from it. However, in the Israeli context, the relationship is reversed—the Levantine is cast as the ethnic / racial other. In the novel Cicurel's patronizing insistence that he provides the African workers in his factory with "bread and wages"[65] echoes hollowly with the cries for "bread and work" of Robert's Mizrahi demonstrators before the Labor party headquarters in Israel.

Such racialized discourse commonly cropped up in 1950s political discourse in Israel, focusing on metaphors of the colonial economy, rather than the complicity of the postcolonial moment. David Ben-Gurion was recorded on numerous occasions likening Jews from Arab countries to the black slaves brought over to America.[66] In the early 1970s with the establishment of the Israeli Black Panthers, some Mizrahim inverted the valence of this racialized discourse, modeling their struggle after the American black power movement.[67] *The One Facing Us* also gestures toward a comparison between the African Americans and Mizrahim in Israel by Inès' likening of Zuza's desire to record the family history to Alex Haley's *Roots*. Yet, some of the nuances of the comparison are lost on Zuza, intent as she is on molding the story into a teleological narrative like Haley's; Zuza sees her own story, beginning with the oppression of Oriental women, conclude with Western feminist liberation.

In sum, *The One Facing Us* recognizes the limitations of Levantinism as envisioned by Jacqueline Kahanoff and draws out the discontinuities implicit in a notion adopted uncritically from one culturally specific context to another. In a sense, Matalon restores to Levantinism its multiple possibilities—both within and outside of Israel—through its representation of the varied and distinct logical extensions of the Levantine, decades after dispersion of the Jews from Egypt. Matalon's vision of the Egyptian Jewish diaspora mirrors its point of origin both in its diversity and in its incongruities, affected by Israel and Zionism but not circumscribed by either.

9   Conclusion

The limits of Egyptian cosmopolitanism

In August 2007 a feature-length Egyptian documentary, *House Salad* [*Salata baladi*], long in the making, debuted at the Locarno Film Festival. The film, directed by Nadia Kamel, like the works discussed in the previous pages, offers a view of Cosmopolitan Egypt. One of its many distinct features is its portrayal of the persistent vestiges of Egypt's cosmopolitan past buried in plain sight in Egypt's present. Kamel's cosmopolitanism is at once local and personal, as the film offers explorations of her rich family heritage, and the diversity of political opinions and religious affiliations it contains.

Kamel's mother, Nai'la (née Mary Rosenthal) is the Egyptian-born daughter of an Italian Catholic woman and an Egyptian Jewish man. Upon her marriage to Sa'ad, the director's father, she converted to Islam and adopted a new name. Mary/Na'ila and Sa'ad who, among other things, both worked as journalists, were communist activists, an affiliation for which both have been arrested and jailed. Mary/Na'ila and Sa'ad's marriage, reaching across ethno-national and religious lines, represents a link in a long chain of such unions stretching back into the family's past and forward to the younger generation. Kamel's sister, Dina, married a Palestinian named 'Ali Sha'ath, the son of Nabil Sha'ath, a leading figure in Fatah who, among other roles, served as the first Foreign Minster of the Palestinian Authority. Constructed around the family stories Mary/Na'ila tells Dina's son Nabil, named after his paternal grandfather, the film is as much anchored in the relationships between the living generations as it is in family history. In her blog, the director writes about her motivation to make the film: "In a world where my family's identities are being squeezed into irreconcilable positions, I needed to document my history before I became apologetic about it and the myth of its extinction was realized."[1]

In resisting the "myth of extinction" the film argues that not only does Egyptian cosmopolitanism live on through narrative and memory, but also in its very populace, embodied by Egyptians like Nadia Kamel whose family's ethno-national and religious origins are complex and varied. In resisting the "native/foreign," "us/them," "self/other" binaries the film transforms the vision of "nativeness that embraces difference" offered by the Lichtenstern & Harrari postcard discussed in

Chapter 1 into an investigation of the multiplicitous self. The nation, Kamel asserts through this film, is defined, not threatened, by these perceived differences.[2]

Kamel's pluralistic vision of the nation is implied in the title of the film. The term *"salata baladi"* refers to the humble chopped salad that is a mainstay of the Egyptian diet. However, in this context, Kamel draws out a tension between the terms. *"Salata,"* salad, implies a mixture, while *"baladi"* means "native" or "indigenous," referring in every day usage to a form of traditional authenticity. The title, thus, imbues the mixture of nationalities and identities that characterized Cosmopolitan Egypt with a nativeness it has often been denied.

House Salad is framed by Kamel's reaction to Nabil's first attendance at morning prayers during *'id al-adha*. On that day, the sheikh's *khutba*, sermon, expressed a xenophobic view of non-Muslims that made Kamel bristle. The film, she notes in her opening voiceover, is an attempt to counter that prevalent discourse in an effort to educate Nabil and his generation of a time in Egypt's recent history when relations between religious communities was less contentious. Kamel, thus, makes explicit the relationship between her desire to produce a film on Egypt's cosmopolitan past and the rising discourse of intolerance in Islam as it is presently practiced in Egypt. As I have argued in the preceding pages, the rise of such discourses in Egypt's mosques has in part fueled the countervailing rise of cosmopolitan nostalgia among the Leftist writers and intellectuals whose work I discussed.

In the course of filming, Mary/Na'ila expresses a desire to see the members of her family who left Egypt decades earlier. Some members of the Italian branch of the family settled in Italy, while members of the Egyptian Jewish branch settled in Israel. In keeping with her staunch support for the Palestinian cause, Na'ila had cut ties with members of her Jewish family who had immigrated to Israel. After much soul-searching and family discussion, Mary/Na'ila decides that a visit to her Jewish relatives would not compromise her political commitments. Although the closure imposed on Gaza prevents them from visiting members of their son-in-law's family, they take the opportunity to visit other friends in Ramallah. The filmmaker accompanies her parents, recording the family reunions, which constitute more than half of the film.

House Salad has received a great deal of attention in Egypt, not for its cinematic achievements, but in response to the filmmaker's decision to shoot in Israel. Although many prominent Egyptian personalities have come to Kamel's defense,[3] the Egyptian press and public have found her guilty of engaging in "normalization," in other words, engaging in an act that tacitly or explicitly endorses the normalization of relations with Israel. Many Egyptians opposed, and continue to oppose, the Egyptian–Israeli peace accords signed in 1979, in large part because they did not redress the plight of the Palestinians. Although the treaty established diplomatic relations between the two countries, with economic ties and agricultural initiatives ensuing, many Egyptian professional syndicates opted to express their opposition by refusing to accept "normalized" relations with Israel.[4] Following the outbreak of the al-Aqsa Intifada in October 2000 in the era of satellite television, the daily violence of the Palestinian territories—particularly acts carried out by

Israelis against Palestinians—became increasingly more visible to the Egyptian public, further fueling the anti-normalization fervor.

Public outrage over perceived acts of normalization is expressed in the pages of newspapers as well as in the meetings of professional syndicates that ban their members from contact with Israel or Israelis. In an article covering a press conference held in November 2007 by the organizers of the Cairo International Film Festival to announce the films selected for competition, one reporter noted that, "as usual, 'normalization with Israel' was the most prominent guest."[5] At issue was the application submitted by the producers of the Israeli feature film, *The Band's Visit [Bikor ha-Tizmoret]* (2007),[6] about an Egyptian Police band hired to play at an Arab cultural event in Israel, which was predictably denied entry into the festival. *House Salad* was also rejected on grounds that the festival screens only feature films, not documentaries.[7] Kamel and her cameraman, who did not accompany her to Israel, faced charges, later dismissed, by the filmmaker's union for breaking their policy opposing acts of normalization.[8]

As two other scandals from Autumn 2007 demonstrate, the accusations of "normalization" extend beyond visiting Israel or having direct contact with its officials. The first scandal broke in October 2007 when news leaked that an Egyptian actor, 'Amr Waked, was appearing in a BBC–HBO mini-series, "House of Saddam," alongside Yigal Naor, an Israeli Jew of Iraqi origin, who played the role of Saddam Hussein. Egyptians were incensed by Waked's willingness to participate in this venture. Then, on October 30, 2007, the Egyptian opera singer Jabir al-Baltaji performed at a secular celebration held at the *Sha'ar ha-shamayim* synagogue in central Cairo marking the building's centennial and the completion of renovations. Al-Baltaji was accused of engaging in an act of normalization by performing in the presence of the Israeli and American ambassadors to Egypt. Also galling to his detractors was that his performance in effect desecrated the work of a much beloved nationalist poet of the Egyptian vernacular, Salah Jahin, whose poetry, set to music, al-Baltaji sang in multiple languages, including Hebrew. Like Kamel, Waked and al-Baltaji both faced inquests into the accusations of normalization by their respective professional syndicates.[9]

As this adversarial posture demonstrates, the persistence of the Israeli–Palestinian conflict continues to shape the prevailing political atmosphere in Egypt. The same could be said for Egyptian memories of European colonialism and experiences of neo-colonialism. The revival of interest in Egypt's cosmopolitan past among the literati and filmmakers discussed in these pages emerges out of and into this cultural environment. Recognizing that acts of memory are not politically neutral, these writers and filmmakers, each in their own way, have attempted to shift the discourse, to distinguish between foreign minorities resident in Egypt and the colonial powers ruling it, and between Jews native to Egypt and the Zionist leadership. In the process, these texts also interrogate both colonial rule and the Arab–Israeli conflict as forces shaping modern Egypt. Nevertheless, these works remain in the minority in Egypt, overshadowed by the prevailing adversarial discourse.

In Israel, the literary works discussed in the preceding chapters have been met with a range of responses from indifference to critical acclaim. The political climate in Israel since the late 1970s has been receptive to literary and filmic works that represent life in the Jewish diaspora prior to immigration nostalgically, including those that reflect on cosmopolitan Egypt. However, such memories of coexistence are frequently relegated to the past, divorced from the thorny politics of Jewish–Arab relations in Israel or between Israelis and the Palestinians living under Israeli occupation.

In *House Salad*, there is a conversation that takes place in the home of Mary's cousin Peppo, which reveals a great deal about how cosmopolitanism, particularly Egyptian cosmopolitanism, is viewed in present-day Israel. Peppo's commitment to Zionism had drawn his family to Palestine from Egypt in 1946. Seated in his living room, the kippah-wearing Peppo reminisces in French: "From Greece, from Turkey, from Syria, from Morocco, from Romania. Jews from all over the world came to Egypt."

MARY (OFF SCREEN, IN FRENCH): "I read a book that said that the Jews preferred to be in Egypt, even if …"
PEPPO (INTERRUPTING, IN ARABIC): "It was the mother of the world (*umm al-dunya*)!"
(CUT TO BENNY, PEPPO'S YOUNGER ISRAELI RELATIVE)
BENNY (IN ENGLISH): "Egypt, it is not new[s], was cosmopolitan."
NADIA (OFF SCREEN, IN ENGLISH): "You're not cosmopolitan any more?"
BENNY: "No. Here, no. We are local … local patriots."

Just as the film brings to the fore Egypt's actually existing cosmopolitanism, Kamel succeeds in revealing Israel's own source of cosmopolitanism, undercutting Benny's words as he utters them. As a polyglot nation, with a Jewish populace comprised of immigrants from around the world (to say nothing of its Muslim and Christian citizens), Israel's diversity is undeniable. Here, as in all the boisterous reunion scenes in the film, the various members of Mary's extended family code-switch between Arabic, French, English, and Italian.

Indeed, in Peppo's opening remark, one could easily replace the prepositional phrase "to Egypt" with "to Israel": "Jews from all over the world came *to Israel*." How is it, then, that Jewish immigration to Egypt results in a cosmopolitan society—Peppo's use of "*umm al-dunya*" is here offered as an expression of a place that harbors many nations, much like Plutarch's narrative of the founding of Alexandria—whereas Jewish immigration to Palestine and then Israel results in a society of "local patriots?" As Benny's comment suggests, the inward-looking nature of the decades-long struggle to construct a coherent national identity indeed had the effect of suppressing sources of Jewish diversity, cultural difference, and cosmopolitan transnationalism. Even as literature of Jewish diversity flowers in Israel, cosmopolitanism's "myth of extinction," to use Kamel's terms, have effectively been realized.

The persistence of these oppositional discourses should come as no surprise. In this book I have intentionally brought together in a comparative framework texts from cultures in conflict to underscore the cosmopolitan possibilities that those texts contain. This book has proposed an alternative counter-narrative to the hostility, confrontation, and animosity that characterizes much discussion of the Middle East. The works discussed in this book all represent minority voices, both in the sense that they represent forgotten minorities, and also in the sense that their cosmopolitan outlook runs counter to the majority views in their respective cultures. These works critically engage with Egypt's cosmopolitan past, mining it for contemporary political relevance. This cosmopolitanism—even as it differs from author to author and text to text—avoids sliding into a gimlet-eyed embrace of naïve "why can't we all get along" coexistence.

Whither (not wither) Egyptian cosmopolitanism?

In the introduction to this book, I described cosmopolitanism in Egypt as a short-lived phenomenon fostered by Imperial rule. This model led us along an historical arc that begins in the mid-nineteenth century and ends in the mid-twentieth century. This periodization of Egypt's cosmopolitan era has, for better or worse, been adopted by many historians, following the lead of Robert Ilbert. To define cosmopolitanism as I have done draws attention to the European and Europeanized minorities that inhabited Egypt. I have chosen this approach to explore the valences attached to the memory of these communities as represented in postdispersion literature and film. Further, this model enables me to interrogate the nature of the relationship between the presence of these communities, the memory of their presence, and the colonial encounter. It is these issues that I have foregrounded in my analysis of texts that represent Egypt's diversity during the era in question.

Nevertheless, some may find fault with my approach for placing European power at the center of my analyses, even as I focused on works by non-Europeans. Cosmopolitanism, as I demonstrated in the book's opening pages, is a contested concept, both among critical theorists and in popular usage. Through its recent history, cosmopolitanism has been criticized from the Left as a concept with questionable political relevance, as it has been attacked from the Right for fostering subversive discourses. Defining the notion of the "cosmopolitan" differently than I have done in these pages, one could find many other sources and expressions of cosmopolitanism in Egypt throughout its history.

Egypt, given its geographic position straddling two continents, has, since its earliest history, served as an entrepôt between peoples and cultures. Some of Egypt's sources of diversity in the period represented by the texts I have been discussing indeed predate the substantial waves of European migration that began in the second half of the nineteenth century. In postrevolutionary Egypt, even as the colonial-cosmopolitan era was coming to a close, other transnational discourses and affiliations were emerging. The Egyptian administration's embrace of Arab Socialism and pan-Arabism offered models of ideological and ethno-linguistic regional realignment that transcended national borders. Egypt's involvement with the Non-Aligned Movement also signaled a commitment to transnational agendas that extended beyond the Arab Middle East.

In the present day, Egypt's cities continue to host diverse populations, although the resident minority and foreign populations are no longer predominantly European or

Europeanized as they were in the colonial-cosmopolitan era. Nevertheless, it would be inaccurate to claim that after the dispersal of the foreign-minority communities in the mid-twentieth century that Egypt became a monolithic (or even mono-lingual) ethno-national entity. Egypt's institutions of higher education attract students from around the world. In addition to the more well-known, longstanding academic institutions, in 1990 an international francophone university, the Université Senghor, which as its name suggests attracts students from across Africa, opened its doors in Alexandria. Populations of North Africans and *shawam* whose ancestors settled in Egypt have long been fully integrated into Egyptian society. Egypt hosts a significant population of Palestinians, and many Sudanese have found refuge in Egypt from fighting in their native country. The residency status of these populations, however, like that of the resident foreigners of an earlier era, remains precarious. A significant number of Egyptians also seek employment abroad, further expanding the circle of transnational contact and identification. Such experiences, both for foreigners resident in Egypt and Egyptians residing abroad, are mostly temporary and contingent, highlighting the unequal power relations between citizens and non-citizens, and underscoring the continued hegemony of the state system. Yet, they reflect examples of actually existing forms of cosmopolitanism evident in Egypt after the end of the colonial-cosmopolitan era—itself rife with inequality—discussed in the pages of this book.

Diane Singerman and Paul Amar, the editors of the book *Cairo Cosmopolitan*, find the term "cosmopolitan" appealing for its ability to focus on the transnational character of urban environments like Egypt's capital. The social science scholarship of contemporary Cairo represented in that book "present[s] evidence of vernacular, bottom-up cosmopolitanisms of enhanced agency and claims-making practices" such as people and groups "publicly and visibly demanding justice, accountability, representation, citizenship, and political and social rights."[10] Sa'ad Kamel, Nadia's father who features prominently in *House Salad*, embodies this form of local activism informed by transnational ideologies and commitments, independent of his multi-national household. Mona Abaza, a sociologist whose work appears in the *Cairo Cosmopolitan* volume, wrote in a 2005 journalistic profile that Sa'ad Kamel represents "the promise of a cosmopolitan and progressive yet grassroots Egypt that, perhaps understandably, has not been fulfilled. He embodies an increasingly extinct oppositional attitude—free thinking, engaged but undogmatic, and ultimately sincere."[11] Whereas this sort of political and social engagement also underpins the thinking and writing of Edwar al-Kharrat, as articulated in Chapters 3 and 4, a study of cosmopolitan Egypt that privileges Abaza, Singerman, and Amar's definition of the "cosmopolitan" would look very different from the present volume.

Cosmopolitanism, as I have defined it in the pages of this book, is historically and discursively inseparable from empire. In Egypt, the period often referred to by historians as the "cosmopolitan era" is equally inseparable from the European colonial encounter. As I have hoped to demonstrate, the recollection and representation of this era is perpetually being negotiated—within Egypt and outside its boundaries among its former inhabitants. The literary and filmic works discussed in this book that interrogate this relationship serve to undermine the romantic myths of coexistence with their avoidance of all things Egyptian, as well as the familiar *bourgeois* narratives of privilege and loss. In approaching the material in this way I have aimed to demonstrate that cosmopolitanism is dynamic and protean, and that it resists clear identification with either side of the colonial or postcolonial binary. As such, it continues to remain a relevant, if problematic and contested, discourse in our neo-colonial, globalized world.

Notes

1 Introduction

1 For more on postcards of Arab women produced for the European male gaze see: Malek Alloula, *The Colonial Harem*, trans. Myrna Godzich and Wlad Godzich (Minneapolis: University of Minnesota Press, 1986).

2 [sing. *gallabiya*] As this book is aimed at a broad academic readership, I have adopted a simplified version of the IJMES system for transliterating Arabic and Hebrew into English. This method minimizes the use of diacritical marks that might confuse the non-specialist reader, but provides enough detail for those familiar with the language to identify sources. I favor commonly accepted transliterations for proper names when they exist, including names of authors published in English translation. The first time a literary text or film is mentioned, I refer to it by its transliterated title as well as its title in translation. Subsequent references to a text are made in English. Generally, when available I cite from published translations of texts, also providing the page numbers in the original. All other translations are my own.

3 Timothy Mitchell, *Colonising Egypt* (Berkeley: University of California Press, 1988).

4 Residents of *bilad al-sham*, the Arab lands of the Eastern Mediterranean: Syrians, Palestinians, Lebanese and Jordanians (pl. *shawam*).

5 Rudolf Agstner, "Ein Wiener Ansichtkartenverleger in Ägypten" *Biblos* (Vienna) 50:1 (2001), 7–8.

6 Samir Raafat, "R.I.P. Annie Gismann 1911–96" *Egyptian Mail*, March 23, 1996, http://www.egy.com/people/96-03-23.shtml.

7 Agstner, "Ein Wiener Ansichtkartenverleger in Ägypten," 7–8.

8 Janet Abu-Lughod, *Cairo: 1001 Years of the City Victorious* (Princeton: Princeton University Press, 1971), 209.

9 David Hollinger, *Postethnic America: Beyond Multiculturalism*, (New York: Basic Books, 1995), 3.

10 Edward Said, *Orientalism* (New York: Random House, 1978), and *Culture and Imperialism* (New York: Alfred A. Knopf, 1993).

11 Amanda Anderson, "Cosmopolitanism, Universalism, and the Divided Legacies of Modernity," In *Cosmopolitics: Thinking and Feeling Beyond the Nation*, Pheng Cheah and Bruce Robbins, eds, (Minneapolis: University of Minnesota Press, 1998), 266.

12 Anderson, "Cosmopolitanism," 267.

13 I am using the word "empire" with a lower case "e" to distinguish it from Michael Hardt and Antonio Negri's use of "Empire" with a capital "E" in *Empire* (Cambridge: Harvard University Press, 2000). Hardt and Negri distinguish between old forms of colonialism and imperialism and the new globalized order that, in their view, demands a redefinition of sovereignty. Imperialism, they note, "was really an extension of the sovereignty of the European nation-states beyond their own boundaries," whereas

"Empire" is "decentered and deterritorializing," establishing "no territorial center of power." (xii). Although their postnational view of the world political–economic order is thoroughly cosmopolitan and offers possibilities for conceiving of global capitalism in the early twenty-first century, I do not rely upon their understanding of "Empire" because it downplays the ways in which the nation remains a significant discursive term, one that continues to command popular imagination. As we see in the texts discussed in this book, the nation defined against past colonial domination and present neo-colonial interests represents a key term of analysis.

14 Anderson, "Cosmopolitanism," 268.
15 Scott Malcomson, "The Varieties of Cosmopolitan Experience," In *Cosmopolitics*, 233.
16 Malcomson, "Varieties," 233.
17 Anderson, "Cosmopolitanism," 268.
18 David Harvey, "Cosmopolitanism and the Banality of Geographical Evils" *Public Culture*, 12:2 (2000), 533.
19 Walter Mignolo, "The Many Faces of Cosmo-polis: Border Thinking and Critical Cosmopolitanism," *Public Culture* 12:3 (2000), 722.
20 Ibid.
21 Seyla Ben Habib, *The Rights of Others: Aliens, Residents and Citizens* (Cambridge: Cambridge University Press, 2004); Julia Kristeva, *Nations without Nationalism*, Leon Roudiez, trans. (New York: Columbia University Press, 1993).
22 Martha Nussbaum, "Patriotism and Cosmopolitanism" *Boston Review* (Oct-Nov 1994); Bruce Robbins, *Feeling Global: Internationalism in Distress* (New York: New York University Press, 1999).
23 Timothy Brennan, *At Home in the World: Cosmopolitanism Now* (Cambridge: Harvard University Press, 1997), 23.
24 Brennan, *At Home in the World*, 15
25 See for example: Roel Meijer, Introduction, in: *Cosmopolitanism, Identity and Authenticity in the Middle East* (Surrey: Curzon Press, 1999), 1–2; and Robin Ostle, "Alexandria: A Mediterranean Cosmopolitan Center of Cultural Production," Fawaz and Bayly, eds., *Modernity and Culture From the Mediterranean to the Indian Ocean*. (New York: Columbia, 2002), 314.
26 The topic has been of interest to historians of earlier periods as well. See, for example, Maya Jasanoff, "Cosmopolitan: A Tale of Identity from Ottoman Alexandria," *Common Knowledge* 11:3 (2005), 393–409.
27 Henk Driessen, "Mediterranean Port Cities: Cosmopolitanism Reconsidered," *History and Anthropology* 16:1 (March 2005), 138.
28 Robert Ilbert, "Cités cosmopolites: la fin d'un modèle?" *Qantara: le magazine de l'Institute de monde arabe*, (April 1994), 37.
29 Ilbert, "Cités cosmopolites," 38.
30 Robert Ilbert, "Alexandrie, cosmopolite?" In *Villes ottomanes à la fin de l'empire*, Paul Dumont and François Georgeon, eds. (Paris: Editions l'Harmattan, 1992), 185.
31 Robert Ilbert, "A Certain Sense of Citizenship," In *Alexandria 1860–1960*, Robert Ilbert and Ilios Yanakakis, eds., Colin Clement, trans. (Alexandria: Harpocrates Publishing, 1997), 30.
32 Robert Ilbert, "International Waters," In *Alexandria 1860–1960*, 14.
33 The term he uses in French to describe Alexandrian society is *communauté citadine*.
34 Hollinger, *Postethnic America*, 3–4.
35 *C.f.* Khaled Fahmy, "For Cavafy with Love and Squalor: Some Critical Notes on the History and Historiography of Modern Alexandria," In *Alexandria Real and Imagined*, Anthony Hirst and Michael Silk, eds. (London: Ashgate, 2004), 271–72.
36 Benedict Anderson, *Imagined Communities* (London: Verso, 1983).
37 By referring to the minority communities as "an extraterritorial phenomenon," I am not here contradicting Ammiel Alcalay's primary assertion that the Levant constitutes a "native" Jewish space [*After Jews and Arabs: The Remaking of Levantine Culture*

(Minneapolis: University of Minnesota Press, 1993), 27]. However, as discussed below, Jews were among the constituencies benefiting from European protection and citizenship while residing in Egypt during the colonial-cosmopolitan era. Although the majority of Egypt's Jews could be counted among those native to the Levant so eloquently described by Alcalay, they were not considered native to Egypt, as defined by the ideologies of mid-twentieth century nationalism. There are, of course, exceptions among the minority of Egyptian Jews whose families had resided in Egypt for innumerable generations, and the members of prominent families whose roots dated back to at least the eighteenth century who refused foreign protection. However, as Alcalay notes, such nativeness did not protect them from the historical transformations under way throughout the region.

38　The term *"millet,"* which can also mean "nation," was also undergoing a shift in usage. Following the dissolution of the Ottoman Empire, in modern Turkish the term has come exclusively to mean "nation" in the modern, political sense of the term. Andrew Hess, *"Millet,"* in John Esposito (ed.), *The Oxford Encyclopedia of the Modern Islamic World*, vol 3 (New York: Oxford University Press, 1995), 107–8.

39　For a more extended discussion of the simultaneous processes of separation under way throughout the region between majority Arab Muslim populations and Jewish minorities, see Ammiel Alcalay, *After Jews and Arabs*, 195–219.

40　André Raymond, "The Role of the Communities (*tawa'if*) in the Administration of Cairo in the Ottoman Period," in *The State and its Servants: Administration in Egypt from Ottoman Times to the Present*, Nelly Hanna, ed. (Cairo: American University in Cairo Press, 1995), 32–43; Abu Lughod, *Cairo*; and Thomas Philipp, *The Syrians in Egypt 1725–1975* (Stuttgart: Franz Steiner Verlag, 1985).

41　Bruce Masters, *Christians and Jews in the Ottoman Arab World: The Roots of Sectarianism* (New York: Cambridge University Press, 2001), 61–65.

42　For more on the clustering of communities in certain trades, see Charles Issawi, "The Transformation of the *Millets* in the Nineteenth Century," Benjamin Braude and Bernard Lewis, eds., *Christians and Jews in the Ottoman Empire: The Functioning of a Plural Society*, Vol. 1 (New York: Holmes and Meier, 1982), 261–86; and Robert Tignor "The Economic Activities of Foreigners in Egypt, 1920–50: From *Millet* to Haute Bourgeoisie." *Comparative Studies in Society and History* 22:3 (Jul 1980), 416–49.

43　Raymond, "The Role of the Communities," 36.

44　My thinking here is influenced by Seyla Ben Habib, *The Rights of Others* (Cambridge: Cambridge University Press, 2004)

45　Ernest Renan, "What is a Nation?" (1882) in *Nation and Narration*, Homi Bhabha, ed., Martin Thom, trans. (London; New York: Routledge, 1990), 11.

46　*Orientalism* (New York: Pantheon Books, 1978), 130–48; and "Islam, Philology, and French Culture: Renan and Massignon" in *The World, The Text and The Critic* (Cambridge: Harvard University Press, 1983), 268–89.

47　Islamist groups in Egypt have not "forgotten" this "difference," however.

48　Eve Troutt Powell, *A Different Shade of Colonialism: Egypt, Great Britain, and the Mastery of the Sudan* (Berkeley: University of California Press, 2003).

49　Timothy Mitchell, *Rule of Experts* (Berkeley: University of California Press, 2002), 183.

50　Ibid., 37.

51　Ibid., 82.

52　Gabriel Baer, *Studies in the Social History of Modern Egypt* (Chicago: University of Chicago Press, 1969), 226–28.

53　Ehud Toledano, *State and Society in Mid-Nineteenth Century Egypt* (Cambridge: Cambridge UP, 1990), 16–17.

54　P. J. Vatikiotis, *The History of Modern Egypt*. Fourth edition. (Baltimore: Johns Hopkins University Press, 1991), 63.

55　Fahmy, *All the Pashas' Men*, 314

56 Kemal Karpat, "*Millets* and Nationality: The Roots of the Incongruity of Nation and State in the Post-Ottoman Era," Benjamin Braude and Bernard Lewis, eds., *Christians and Jews in the Ottoman Empire: The Functioning of a Plural Society*, Vol. 1 (New York: Holmes and Meier, 1982), 163.

57 Karpat, "*Millets* and Nationality," 141–69.

58 For more on immigration and population statistics see: Muhammad Rif'at al-Imam, *al-Arman Fi Misr (1896–1961)* (Cairo: Jam'iyat al-Qahira al-Khayriyya al-Armaniyya al-'Amma, 2003); Alexander Kitroeff, *The Greeks in Egypt 1919–1937: Ethnicity and Class* (Oxford: Ithaca Press, 1989), 11–31; Gudrun Krämer, *The Jews in Modern Egypt, 1914–1952* (Seattle: University of Washington Press, 1989), 8–13; Philipp, *The Syrians in Egypt 1725–1975*, 166–76; and Mercedes Volait, "La Communauté Italienne et ses Édiles," *Revue de l'Occident Musulman et de la Méditerranée* 46:4 (1987), 137–55.

59 Shimon Shamir, "The Evolution of the Egyptian Nationality Laws and their Application to the Jews in the Monarchy Period" in *The Jews of Egypt: A Mediterranean Society in Modern Times* (Boulder: Westview Press, 1987), 37.

60 Vatikiotis, *The History of Modern Egypt*, 38.

61 On 11 June 1882 a Maltese Alexandrian stabbed an Arab Alexandrian following an argument. The melee that broke out between Greek and Arab onlookers devolved into large-scale riots throughout the city. By the time the fighting was quelled, approximately 50 Europeans and an estimated 250 Egyptians lay dead. The rioting is not reducible to interethnic tensions, but must rather be seen in the context of larger social and political struggles under way in Egypt. Quelling interethnic strife served as a pretext for the British invasion. However, the British were much more concerned about unseating Ahmad 'Urabi, a nationalist military officer, who had risen to the position of Minister of War in February 1882. For more on 'Urabi and the threat he posed to the European powers see: Juan Cole, *Colonialism and Revolution in the Middle East: The Social and Cultural Origins of Egypt's 'Urabi Movement* (Princeton: Princeton University Press, 1993). For more on the increase of British involvement in Egypt throughout the nineteenth century see: Michael Reimer, *Colonial Bridgehead: Government and Society in Alexandria 1807–1882* (Boulder: Westview Press, 1997).

62 James Harry Scott, *The Law Affecting Foreigners in Egypt*. Revised edition. (Edinburgh: William Green and Sons, 1908), 91–98.

63 David Landes, *Bankers and Pashas: International Finance and Economic Imperialism in Egypt* (Cambridge: Harvard UP, 1958), 91.

64 Talal Asad, *Formations of the Secular: Christianity, Islam, Modernity* (Stanford: Stanford UP, 2003), 211.

65 Robert Mabro, "Alexandria 1860–1960: The Cosmopolitan Identity," in *Alexandria Real and Imagined*, 247–62.

66 Shamir, "Evolution of the Egyptian Nationality Laws," 33–67.

67 For greater detail on this process, see Ibid.

68 Israel Gershoni and James Jankowski, *Redefining the Egyptian Nation, 1930–1945* (Cambridge: Cambridge University Press, 1995), 3.

69 Joel Beinin, *The Dispersion of Egyptian Jewry: Culture, Politics, and the Formation of a Modern Diaspora* (Berkeley: University of California Press, 1998), 37.

70 Ibid. For a more extensive discussion of this transformation in Egyptian nationalist tendencies see: Gershoni and Jankowski, *Redefining the Egyptian Nation*.

71 Tignor, "The Economic Activities of Foreigners in Egypt," 416–49.

72 Vitalis has demonstrated that from the economic liberalization policies instituted by the British beginning in 1882 through the rise of capitalist venture groups simultaneous with the Egyptianization of state bureaucracy after 1922, local capitalists, regardless of their nationality, were motivated by the same economic interests and involved in foreign trade and other ventures both supporting and compromising Egyptian attempts to localize business. Vitalis adds that Egyptian capitalists, many of whom provided

the financial power behind the Egyptianization of the economy in the mid-twentieth century, were also largely involved simultaneously in ventures at odds with a "nationalist" economics. Robert Vitalis, *When Capitalists Collide: Business Conflict and the End of Empire in Egypt* (Berkeley: University of California Press, 1995).

73 Khaled Fahmy, "Towards a Social History of Modern Alexandria," In *Alexandria, Real and Imagined*, 281–306.
74 Krämer, *The Jews of Modern Egypt*, 206. See also: Shamir, "Evolution" 59.
75 Shamir, "Evolution" 57–62; and Beinin, *Dispersion* 36–39. As both Shamir and Beinin note, this situation left approximately 40,000 Jews "stateless."
76 Mabro, "Alexandria 1860–1960," 250–52.
77 Beinin argues that the new regime initially sought to protect the religious minorities, by extending them what he refers to as a "neo-*dhimmi*" status. Beinin, *Dispersion*, 36–39.
78 Fahmy, "Towards a Social History," 281–306.
79 Brennan, *At Home*, 39.
80 Brennan, *At Home*, 42.
81 (New York: Columbia University Press, 2006).
82 (Routledge: London, 2008).
83 Jenine Abbushi Dalal's controversial article "The Perils of Occidentalism: How Arab Novelists are Driven to Write for Western Readers" *Times Literary Supplement* (24 April 1998) prompted discussion over to what extent Arab authors write with the translation market in mind. Although the size of the book market in Egypt is substantial, the interest in contemporary literature is quite limited. Distribution within Egypt and in other Arab countries can be spotty. Translation offers authors the opportunity for broader readership, and the possibility of royalties and international travel.
84 Ammiel Alcalay's *After Jews and Arabs* convincingly argues for a reading of Jabès' work in a Levantine context, 59–75. Two later studies privilege Jabès' Egyptianness by exploring his life and writing during his years in Cairo. See Daniel Lançon *Jabès L'Égyptien* (Paris: Jean Michel Place, 1998); and Stephen Jaron, *Edmond Jabès: The Hazard of Exile* (Oxford: Legenda, European Humanities Research Centre, University of Oxford, 2003).
85 Alcalay, *After Jews and Arabs*, 23.
86 Alcalay, *After Jews and Arabs*, 201.
87 (Beirut: Dar al-Mustaqbal al-'Arabi, 1985).
88 (Beirut: Dar al-Adab, 1990).
89 (Cairo: Dar al-Hilal, 1996).
90 (Cairo: Dar al-Hilal, 2000).
91 Beinin, *The Dispersion of Egyptian Jewry*, 207–40.
92 (Tel Aviv: 'Am 'Oved, 1978).
93 (Tel Aviv: 'Am 'Oved, 1995).

2 Literary Alexandria

1 "*Al-Malik yuzih al-sitar 'An timthal jadihi Isma'il*," *al-Ahram*, 5 Dec 1938, 1–2. "Italian Gift to Alexandria," *Times* (London), 5 Dec 1938, 14e. Fu'ad's state visit was reciprocated by King Victor Emmanuel III and Queen Helena of Italy six years later in 1933. For more on the reciprocal state visits between Egypt and Italy see: Yunan Labib Rizk, "Close to Italy," *al-Ahram Weekly* 670 (25–31 December 2003), http://weekly.ahram.org.eg/2003/670/chrncls.htm.
2 He later relocated to Istanbul where he died in 1895.
3 For more on the incident and on the Imperialist subtext of Aida see: Edward Said, *Culture and Imperialism* (New York: Vintage Books, 1994), 111–32.
4 Hala Halim, "Dance to the Music of Time," *Al-Ahram Weekly* (2–8 July 1998), http://weekly.ahram.org.eg/1998/384/cu1.htm.

5 The statue of Mehmed Ali caused an uproar at the time because of its exorbitant expense, and because the representation of human form was seen as an affront to Islam. The liberal, nationalist, Muslim cleric, Muhammad 'Abdu issued a *fatwa* granting permission for the display of statues of state figures, permitting the first statue of a leader to be erected in the modern Arab world. Mohamed Awad, "The Metamorphoses of Mansheyah," *Mediterraneans*, 8/9 (1996): 48.

6 Anouchka Lazarev, "Italians, Italianity and Fascism," trans. Colin Clement *Alexandria 1860–1960: The Brief Life of a Cosmopolitan Community*, ed. Robert Ilbert and Ilios Yanakakis (Alexandria: Harpocrates Press, 1997), 80.

7 "Italian Gift," *Times* (London), 14e.

8 In an ironic twist to the reciprocal visits, when Victor Emmanuel III was deposed in 1946 he went into exile in Alexandria where he died a year later. When Farouk was deposed in 1952, he went into exile in Italy where he died in 1965.

9 According to the 1937 census, of the 47,706 Italians subjects living in Egypt, 6034—approximately 8%—were Jews. Mercedes Volait, "La Communauté Italienne et ses Édiles," *Revue de l'Occident Musulman et de la Méditerranée* 46, no. 4 (1987): 140.

10 Lazarev, "Italians, Italianity and Fascism," 81–83. This division in the Italian community in Alexandria is also portrayed in Fausta Cialente's novel *Ballata Levantina* (Milan: Feltrineli, 1961) published in English as *The Levantines*, trans. Isabel Quigly (Cambridge: The Riverside Press, 1962).

11 Lazarev, "Italians, Italianity and Fascism," 81–83.

12 Awad, "Metamorphoses," 56–57.

13 For more on the dedication ceremony see: Halim, "Dance to the Music of Time."

14 Benedict Anderson, *Imagined Communities* (London: Verso, 1983), 9.

15 Halim, "Dance to the Music of Time." As Halim also notes, a statue of Nubar Pasha who briefly served as Prime Minister under Isma'il, also stored for many years at the museum, was similarly restored in 1998. Nubar was a statesman of Armenian origin who represented Egypt in the negotiations over the establishment of the Mixed Courts in 1875. He later served two additional terms as Prime Minister in 1884–88 and 1894–95.

16 I discuss the turn of the millennium renovations at greater length in "Recuperating Cosmopolitan Alexandria: Circulation of Narratives and Narratives of Circulation," *Cities* 22, no. 3 (2005): 217–28. See also Alexander Stille, *The Future of the Past* (New York: Farrar Straus and Giroux, 2002), 246–73.

17 Reports on the size of Egypt's Greek population since the late 1960s range from several hundred to a few thousand. According to the Greek Ministry of Foreign Affairs, 3800 Greeks resided in Egypt in 2005. Although not noted, this statistic may also include diplomatic staff in temporary residence as well as the permanently resident Greek population of Egypt. Greek Ministry of Foreign Affairs, *Bilateral Relations-Egypt*, http://www2.mfa.gr/www.mfa.gr/en-US/Policy/Geographic+Regions/Mediterranean+-+Middle+East/Bilateral+Relations/Egypt (accessed 7/23/06).

18 Shwikar 'Ali, "*Wa-azma hawl timthal al-iskandar bil-iskandariyya*," *al-Ahram*, 12 May 2000.

19 Amal al-Jayar, "*Abu al-haul raqdan taht qadmay al-iskandar*," *al-Ahram*, 24 Aug 2001.

20 Robert Mabro, "Nostalgic Literature on Alexandria," in *Historians in Cairo*, ed. J. Edwards, (Cairo: American University Press, 2002), 237–63.

21 Plutarch, *The Life of Alexander the Great*, trans. J. Dryden, ed. A. Clough (New York: Modern Library, 2004), 26–27.

22 Plutarch, *Life*, 9.

23 Jean-Yves Empereur, *Alexandria Rediscovered*, trans. Margaret Maehler (London: British Museum Press 1997), 36.

24 Plutarch, *Life*, 26.

25 Ibid.

26 Plutarch, *Life*, 27.

27 Cited in: Plutarch, *Life*, 27.
28 John Rodenbeck, "Literary Alexandria," *The Massachusetts Review*, 42, no. 4 (Winter 2001–2), 571.
29 Michael Haag, *Alexandria: City of Memory* (New Haven: Yale University Press, 2004), 11.
30 For references to other twentieth century Alexandrian writers see: *Mediterraneans* 8/9 (1996); Eglal Errera "The Dream of Alexander and the Literary Myth," in *Alexandria 1860–1960*, 128–43; Mabro "Nostalgic Literature," 237–63; John Rodenbeck, "Literary Alexandria," 524–72.
31 Durrell, *Justine*, 188.
32 Durrell, *Justine*, 9.
33 Hesiod, *Theogony*, trans. Dorothea Wender (London: Penguin, 1987), 33.
34 *The Oxford English Dictionary*.
35 Durrell, *Justine*, 14.
36 Eglal Errera, "The Dream of Alexander," 135.
37 Haag, *Alexandria: City of Memory*; David Roessel, "A Passage through Alexandria: The City in the Writing of Durrell and Forster," in *Alexandria, Real and Imagined*, ed. Anthony Hirst and Michael Silk (Aldershot, Hampshire: Ashgate Publishing, 2004), 323–36.
38 Khaled Fahmy, "For Cavafy, with Love and Squalor: Some Critical Notes on the History and Historiography of Modern Alexandria," in *Alexandria, Real and Imagined*, 263–80.
39 "International Waters," in *Alexandria 1860–1960*, 15.
40 Robin Ostle, "Alexandrian Iconography: Muhammad Nagi," *Mediterraneans*, 8/9 (Autumn 1996), 170.
41 Marilyn Booth, *Bayram al-Tunisi's Egypt: Social Criticism and Narrative Strategies* (Exeter: Ithaca Press, 1990), 31–132.
42 Richard Jacquemond, *Entre Scribes et Écrivains: Le Champ Littéraire dans L'Égypte Contemporaine* (Paris: Acts Suds, 2003), 30.
43 Najib Mahfuz, *Al-Summan wa al-kharif* 2nd ed. (Cairo: Maktabat Misr, 1964); Naguib Mahfouz, *Autumn Quail*, trans. Roger Allen and John Rodenbeck (New York: Anchor Books, 1990).
44 Mahfuz, *Al-Summan*, 83; Mahfouz, *Autumn Quail*, 78.
45 Mahfuz, *Al-Summan*, 83; Mahfouz, *Autumn Quail*, 78.
46 Mahfuz, *Al-Summan*, 106; Mahfouz, *Autumn Quail*, 96.
47 Najib Mahfuz, *Miramar* (Cairo: Maktabat Misr, 1967): Naguib Mahfouz, *Miramar*, trans. Fatma Moussa-Mahmoud (Washington: Three Continents Press, 1991).
48 See for example the postface by Trevor Le Gassick in the second edition of the English translation of *Miramar*, 150–54.
49 Azza Kararah provides a more extensive reading of the vestiges of cosmopolitan Alexandria in *Miramar* in "Egyptian Literary Images of Alexandria," in *Alexandria, Real and Imagined*, 313–20.
50 *Qisas sakandariyya fial-ma'raka* [Alexandrian Stories on the Battlefield] (Alexandria: al-hay'a al-mahalliyya li-ri'ayat al-funun wa-al-adab wa-al-'ulum al-ijtima'iyya, 1967), 13.
51 *Qisas sakandariyya*, 10.
52 Jacquemond, *Entre Scribes et Écrivains*, 214–16.
53 'Abd al-'Alim al-Qabani, "*Kafafis ... sha'ir al-iskandariyya al-'alami fi al-'asr al-hadith*," *Amwaj* (June 1978): 35–48.
54 (Cairo: Dar al-hilal, 1984).
55 (Cairo: Dar al-hilal, 1997).
56 It is worth noting that this trend is not driven by writers just appearing on the scene, nor is it limited to a single "generation" of writers. The writers mentioned below began their literary production between the 1960s and the 1980s.

57 (Cairo: Maktabat misr, 1996).
58 Husni Sayid Labib, *Riwa'i min bahri* [Novelist from Bahri], Kitabat naqdiyya 113 (Cairo: al-hai'a al-'amma li-qusur al-thaqafa, 2001), 29.
59 Interview with author 16 March 2003. Ukasha's 1989 serial, *"al-Raya al-bayda"* ["The White Flag"] set in contemporary Alexandria is discussed at length in Walter Armbrust's *Mass Culture and Modernism in Egypt* (Cambridge: Cambridge University Press, 1996), 11–36. The phenomenon of corruption in urban development the series depicts, however, is understood, according to Armbrust's examples, as an articulation of a national, not local, problem.
60 Interview with author 15 July 2002. *Amkina* (Alexandria: Sa'ud Jarub, 1999). See also 'Ala Khalid *"Iskandariyya nihayat 'asr, bidayat 'asr,"* *Akhbar al-adab*, al-Bustan, 388, 17 December 2000, 1–8; and *"Sirat maqha"* *Akhbar al-adab*, al-Bustan,. 439, 9 December 2001, 1–8.
61 (Cairo: al-hay'a al-misriyya al-'amma lil-kitab, maktabat al-usra, 2002).
62 Trans. Fakhri Labib (Cairo, Kuwait: Dar su'ad al-sabah, 1992). According to the editor's notes on the back cover of *Mountolive*, only *Justine* and *Balthazar* had previously been translated into Arabic. Labib's translation made the entire quartet available to Arab readers for the first time.
63 Trans. Hassan Bayumi (Cairo: al-hai'a al-'amma li-qusur al-thaqafa, 1999).
64 *Hayati fi misr* [My Life in Egypt], trans. Muhammad Abu Rahma, (Alexandria: Green Leaf, 1998). *Kleopatra, Kranzler und Kolibris* (Allschwill: E. Zimmerli Hardman, 1999).
65 (Dec. 1996).
66 (Feb. 1995).
67 For a scholarly discussion of the preservation efforts in Cairo undertaken since the 1992 earthquake see: Galila El Kadi and Dalila El Kerdany, "Belle-époque Cairo: The Politics of Refurbishing the Downtown Business District," in *Cairo Cosmopolitan*, ed. Diane Singerman and Paul Amar (Cairo: American University in Cairo Press, 2006), 345–71.
68 (Cairo: Palm Press, 1995).
69 *Cairo, the Glory Years: Who Built What, When, Why and For Whom*, (Alexandria: Harpocrates Press, 2003).
70 (Cairo: American University in Cairo Press, 1999).
71 (New York: Farrar, Straus and Giroux, 1999).
72 (Syracuse: Syracuse University Press, 2000).
73 (New York: Alfred A. Knopf, 1999).
74 (New York: Harper Collins, 2007).
75 (Cairo: Mirit lil-nashr wa-al-ma'lumat, 2002); *The Yacoubian Building*, trans. Humphrey Davies (Cairo: American University in Cairo Press, 2004).
76 In light of the novel's popularity, an upstart production company, Good News Productions optioned *Yacoubian Building* for its debut film. The film version of *Yacoubian Building*, released in 2006, features an ensemble cast of Egypt's biggest stars—Yusra, 'Adil Imam, and Nur al-Sharif—themselves a testament to an earlier era of Egyptian cinema. The film reportedly cost more to produce than any prior Egyptian film. The gamble paid off. Fueled by the popularity of the novel, a successful marketing campaign, and a swirl of controversy, the film was a box-office hit in an era of waning cinema attendance.
77 al-Aswani, *Ya'qubiyan*, 21; Al Aswani, *Yacoubian*, 11.
78 al-Aswani, *Ya'qubiyan*, 22; Al Aswani, *Yacoubian*, 12.
79 Mr. Talal, the Syrian owner of a clothing store, represents a transnational relic of a different sort. He arrived in Egypt following the unification of Egypt and Syria under the UAR, and not during the cosmopolitan era. al-Aswani, *Ya'qubiyan*, 64; Al Aswani, *Yacoubian*, 43.

80 The "Big Man's" residence is described as "an impregnable citadel," "reminiscent of the royal palaces ['Azzam] had seen as a child", implying that this shadowy character who requires pay-offs for large import contracts is the leader of the land. al-Aswani, *Ya'qubiyan*, 321; Al Aswani, *Yacoubian*, 226. The "Big Man's" inaccessibility and detachment from the concerns of his populace is underscored by his appearance, Oz-like, as a booming, disembodied voice, seeing but unseen, "echoing loudly throughout the hall" in which 'Azzam waited. al-Aswani, *Ya'qubiyan*, 324; Al Aswani, *Yacoubian*, 229.

81 al-Aswani, *Ya'qubiyan*, 242; Al Aswani, *Yacoubian*, 170–71.

82 al-Aswani, *Ya'qubiyan*, 108; Al Aswani, *Yacoubian*, 76.

83 al-Aswani, *Ya'qubiyan*, 55–56; Al Aswani, *Yacoubian*, 37.

84 al-Aswani, *Ya'qubiyan*, 115; Al Aswani, *Yacoubian*, 80–81.

85 al-Aswani, *Ya'qubiyan*, 131–32; Al Aswani, *Yacoubian*, 93.

86 al-Aswani, *Ya'qubiyan*, 266; Al Aswani, *Yacoubian*, 188.

87 al-Aswani, *Ya'qubiyan*, 345–46; Al Aswani, *Yacoubian*, 243.

88 al-Aswani, *Ya'qubiyan*, 348; Al Aswani, *Yacoubian*, 245.

89 French phrases in this exchange are transliterated into Arabic script in the text. al-Aswani, *Ya'qubiyan*, 92–93; Al Aswani, *Yacoubian*, 64–66.

90 al-Aswani, *Ya'qubiyan*, 48; Al Aswani, *Yacoubian*, 32.

91 al-Aswani, *Ya'qubiyan*,220; Al Aswani, *Yacoubian*, 156.

92 al-Aswani, *Ya'qubiyan*, 134; Al Aswani, *Yacoubian*, 95.

93 For example, in 1995 Professor Nasr Abu Zayd was convicted of apostasy and ordered to divorce his wife, prompting the couple to flee Egypt.

94 Sectarian violence escalated in 1992, claiming an estimated 1100 lives in the period up to 1997. In 1994 an Islamist radical attacked on Nobel laureate Naguib Mahfouz.

95 Bruce Robbins, *Feeling Global: Internationalism in Distress* (New York: NYU Press, 1999), 7.

96 Amanda Anderson, "Cosmopolitanism, Universalism, and the Divided Legacies of Modernity," in *Cosmopolitics: Thinking and Feeling Beyond the Nation*, ed. Bruce Robbins and Pheng Cheah (Minneapolis: U. Minnesota Press, 1998), 266.

97 Edwar al-Kharrat, *Turabuha za'faran* (Beirut: Dar al-Mustaqbal al-'Arabi, 1985); Edwar al-Kharrat, *City of Saffron*, trans. Frances Liardet (London: Quartet, 1989).

98 Edwar al-Kharrat, *Ya banat iskandariyya* (Beirut: Dar al-Adab, 1990); Edwar al-Kharrat, *Girls of Alexandria*, trans. Frances Liardet (London: Quartet, 1993).

99 Ibrahim 'Abd al-Majid, *La ahad yanam fi al-iskandariyya* (Cairo: Dar al-Hilal, 1996); Ibrahim Abdel Meguid, *No One Sleeps in Alexandria*, trans. Farouk Abdel Wahab (Cairo: American University in Cairo Press, 1999).

100 Ibrahim 'Abd al-Majid, *Tuyur al-'anbar* (Cairo: Dar al-Hilal, 2000); Ibrahim Abdel Meguid, *Birds of Amber*, trans. Farouk Abdel Wahab (Cairo: AUC Press, 2005).

3 Poetics of memory: Edwar al-Kharrat

1 "Cultural Authenticity and National Identity," *Diogenes*, 52 (May 2005): 21–24. Another piece by al-Kharrat is also included in this issue: "Alexandria, My Mediterranean," trans. Jean Burrell, *Diogenes* 52 (May 2005), 19–20.

2 "Cultural Authenticity," 22.

3 Ibid.

4 "Cultural Authenticity," 24.

5 Ibid.

6 Edwar al-Kharrat, *Turabuha za'faran* (Beirut: Dar al-mustaqbal al-'arabi, 1985); Edwar al-Kharrat, *City of Saffron*, trans. Frances Liardet (London: Quartet, 1989).

7 Edwar al-Kharrat *Ya banat iskandariyya*. (Beirut: Dar al-adab, 1990); Edwar al-Kharrat, *Girls of Alexandria*, trans. Frances Liardet (London: Quartet, 1993).

8 "Iskandariyyati ... madinat za'faran" *Iskandariyyati: madinati al-qudsiyya wa-al-hushiyya* (Cairo and Alexandria: Dar wa-matabi' al-mustaqbal, 1994), 5–14.

9 Al-Kharrat, "*Iskandariyyati*," 6.

10 Ibid.

11 *Justine*, 185.

12 *Clea*, 97.

13 For example, al-Kharrat objects to how characters in the *Quartet* "fluctuate at times between violence, on the one hand, and submissiveness and obsequiousness, on the other," following the familiar Orientalist formula. "*Iskandariyyati*," 7.

14 *Balthazar*, 151.

15 (Cairo: Matba'at atlas, 1959). As Marina Stagh notes, the first edition of this volume was subject to censorship. For more on this issue see: Stagh *The Limits of Freedom of Expression* (Stockholm: Almqvist & Wiksell International, 1993), 171–83.

16 *Gallery 68* was irregularly published between May 1968 and February 1971. In a 1994 essay Samia Mehrez describes the importance of the influence of *Gallery 68* on Egyptian poetry of the 1970s, as well as al-Kharrat's own intervention on behalf of the new idiom the young artists represented: "Experimentation and the Institution: The Case of *Ida'a 77* and *Aswat*," in *The View from Within: Writers and Critics on Contemporary 'Arabic Literature*, ed. Ferial Ghazoul and Barbara Harlow (Cairo: American University of Cairo Press: 1994) 177–96. See also, Elisabeth Kendall, *Literature, Journalism and The Avant-Garde: Intersection in Egypt* (London; New York: Routledge, 2006). Al-Kharrat's continued efforts in promoting emergent writers of the 1980s and 1990s are evidenced, for example, in numerous articles as well as in his critical monographs: *al-Hassasiyya al-jadida: maqalat fi al-zahira al-qisasiyya* [*New Sensitivity: Essays on The Narrative Phenomenon*] (Beirut: Dar al-Adab, 1993) and *al-Kitaba 'abra al-naw'iyya* [*Writing Beyond Genre*] (Cairo: Dar Sharqiyat, 1994).

17 (Beirut: al-Mu'assasa al-'Arabiyya lil-Dirasat wa-al-Nashr, 1980); Translated as *Rama and the Dragon*, trans. Ferial Ghazoul and John Verlenden (Cairo: American University in Cairo Press, 2002).

18 Ahmad Khurays, *Thuna'iyyat Idwar al-Kharrat al-Nassiyya* [Idwar al-Kharrat's Textual Duets]. (Amman: Azmina, 1998).

19 Al-Kharrat's writings, both critical and literary, have sparked much debate over genre. The subtitle of *City of Saffron* is "Alexandrian Texts" ("*nusus iskandraniyya*"). Al-Kharrat resists categorizing the work as either a collection of stories or a novel. Although my reading takes into consideration the effect of narrative texture on meaning, debates over genre *per se* do not have any direct bearing on the issues here under consideration. For more on questions of genre see: Khurays, *Thuna'iyyat;* Magda al-Nowaihi "Memory and Imagination in Edwar al-Kharrat's *Turabuha Za'afaran*" *Journal of Arabic Literature* 25 (1994): 34–57; Samia Mehrez "Experimentation and the Institution," 177–96.

20 al-Kharrat *Turabuha*, 127; *City*, 107.

21 al-Kharrat *Turabuha*, 180; *City*, 154. Minor modification made to Liardet's translation.

22 al-Kharrat *Turabuha*, 179; *City*, 153

23 Ibid.

24 al-Kharrat *Turabuha*, 105; *City*, 87.

25 al-Kharrat, *Turabuha*, 142; *City*, 120–21.

26 al-Kharrat, *Turabuha*, 10; *City*, 4.

27 al-Kharrat, *Turabuha*, 10; *City*, 4. Minor modification made to Liardet's translation.

28 al-Kharrat, *Turabuha*, 19; *City*, 11.

29 al-Kharrat, *Turabuha*, 22; *City*, 13.

30 Biblical scholars generally agree that Mary Magdalene was not the unnamed harlot identified in Luke 7: 35–50. However, overwhelmingly, popular representation has focused on her as the icon of repentance and forgiveness.

31 al-Kharrat, *Turabuha*, 65; *City*, 50. Minor modification made to Liardet's translation.
32 al-Kharrat, *Turabuha*, 73; *City*, 57.
33 al-Kharrat, *Turabuha*, 73; *City*, 57.
34 al-Kharrat *Turabuha*, 33; *City*, 23.
35 al-Kharrat, *Turabuha*, 33; *City*, 23.
36 al-Kharrat, *Turabuha*, 201; *City*, 173.
37 al-Kharrat *Turabuha*, 33; *City*, 23.
38 al-Kharrat *Turabuha*, 123; *City*, 103.
39 al-Kharrat, *Turabuha*, 32; *City*, 22–23.
40 Rob Wilson, "A New Cosmopolitanism Is in the Air: Some Dialectical Twists and Turns." *Cosmopolitics*, ed. Pheng Cheah and Bruce Robbins (Minneapolis: University of Minnesota Press, 1998), 353.
41 al-Kharrat, *Ya Banat*, 118–19; *Girls*, 10–11. Modifications made to Liardet's translation.
42 al-Kharrat, *Ya Banat*, 163; *Girls*, 151. Minor modification made to Liardet's translation.
43 al-Kharrat, *Turabuha*, 33; *City*, 23.
44 al-Kharrat, *Ya Banat*, 112; *Girls*, 102.
45 al-Kharrat, *Ya Banat*, 178; *Girls*, 164–65.
46 al-Kharrat, *Ya Banat*, 38; *Girls*, 30.
47 al-Kharrat, *Ya Banat*, 127; *Girls*, 115–16.
48 al-Kharrat, *Ya Banat*, 112; *Girls*, 102. Athenios is a Greek salon de thé across from Ramla Station in central Alexandria. Like other streets whose names evoked Egypt's former rulers or the colonial-cosmopolitan era, the name of Fu'ad 1st Street was changed; it is now called *shari'al-hurriyya*.

4 Polis and cosmos: Ibrahim Abdel Meguid

1 "Inter-faith Conference Opens in Cairo to Boost Islam's Image," *Agence France Presse*, Jul 24, 1996.
2 No Jewish leaders were invited to participate in the conference. The limited press coverage the conference received in the West noted this exclusion, undermining the message of tolerance and coexistence the conference espoused.
3 *La ahad yanam* fi al-iskandariyya (Cairo: Dar al-hilal, 1996).
4 'Abd al-'Aziz Muwafi, "*Asatir wa-Bahith 'An Zaman Da'i'*," *al-Hayat* (23 August 1996), 16.
5 Hala Halim, "Alexandria Re-Inscribed," Review of *No One Sleeps in Alexandria*, by Ibrahim 'Abd al-Majid. *Al-Ahram Weekly* 472 (9–15 March 2000), *http://weekly.ahram.org.eg/2000/472/bk1_472.htm*.
6 *Tuyur al-'Anbar*, (Cairo: Dar al-Hilal, 2000).
7 Interview with the author, March 17, 2003.
8 My use of the concept "spacetime" is based on the writings of David Harvey who calls for "the dynamic unification of 'dead' spatiality with 'live' narrative" in David Harvey, "Cosmopolitanism and the Banality of Geographical Evils," *Public Culture* 12, no. 2 (2000): 555.
9 See: Daniel Lançon, *Jabès L'Égyptien* (Paris: Jean Michel Place, 1998), which documents the frequency with which Éluard's work is evoked in the context of Cairene francophone literary meetings, as well as in Jabès' private papers.
10 Hala Halim, "Alexandria Re-Inscribed."
11 'Abd al-Majid, *La Ahad Yanam*, 58; Abdel Meguid, *No One Sleeps*, 52–53. Tellingly, one Egyptian critic of the novel dates Alexandria's cosmopolitanism to the start of the Second World War, and identifies it entirely with the arrival of foreigners as part of the war effort: "Alexandria became a cosmopolitan city filled with all the races of the world: the English, Australians, Blacks, ATS girls, the French, Cypriotes, New Zealanders, and Indians because the world events penetrated to create this giant mixture …" Amjad Rayyan, *Riwayat al-tahawwulat al-ijtima'yiyya: La ahad yanam fi al-iskandariyya*

l-ibrahim 'abd al-majid namudhajan [The Novel of Social Change: The Example of Ibrahim 'Abd al-Majid's No One Sleeps in Alexandria], Kitabat naqdiyya 99, (Cairo: al-hai'a al-'amma li-qusur al-thaqafa, 2000), 16.

12 'Abd al-Majid, *La ahad yanam*, 58; Abdel Meguid, *No One Sleeps*, 52–53.

13 'Abd al-Majid, *La ahad yanam*, 128; Abdel Meguid, *No One Sleeps*, 123.

14 Literarily, Rushdi's quest also evokes ancient Egyptian myth of Isis searching for the body of her lover Osiris, as well as the wanderings of Qais/Majnun Layla in the Arabic tradition. I would like to thank Professor Mohamed Berairi of the Department of Arabic Literature at Cairo University Bani Suwayf for sharing his insight on this intertextuality with me.

15 'Abd al-Majid, *La ahad yanam*, 124; Abdel Meguid, *No One Sleeps*, 118. Minor adjustment made to Abdel Wahab's translation.

16 'Abd al-Majid, *La ahad yanam*, 57–58; Abdel Meguid, *No One Sleeps*, 52.

17 'Abd al-Majid, *La ahad yanam*, 206. Abdel Meguid, *No One Sleeps*, 201.

18 'Abd al-Majid, *La ahad yanam* 83; Abdel Meguid, *No One Sleeps*, 77.

19 'Abd al-Majid, *La ahad yanam*, 28; Abdel Meguid, *No One Sleeps*, 23.

20 'Abd al-Majid, *La ahad yanam*, 296–97; Abdel Meguid, *No One Sleeps*, 293.

21 'Abd al-Majid, *La ahad yanam*, 14–15; Abdel Meguid, *No One Sleeps*, 8.

22 'Abd al-Majid, *La ahad yanam*, 124; Abdel Meguid, *No One Sleeps*, 118–19.

23 For a geneology of the slogan see: Reuven Snir, "'We Are Arabs Before We Are Jews': The Emergence and Demise of Arab-Jewish Culture in Modern Times," *EJOS* 8, no.9 (2005): 25, n106.

24 'Abd al-Majid, *La ahad yanam*, 131; Abdel Meguid, *No One Sleeps*, 126.

25 Reprinted from *Recuperating cosmopolitan Alexandria: Circulation of narratives and narratives of circulation*, Deborah A. Starr, 2005, with permission from Elsevier.

26 'Abd al-Majid, *Tuyur*, 7. I take issue with the translation of the word *'anbar* by Farouk Abdel Wahab in the published English translation of the novel, *Birds of Amber* (Cairo: AUC Press, 2005). In Arabic, *'anbar* can mean either "ambergris," its earliest meaning, or "amber." Both substances appear in the novel. However, Abdel Meguid avoids confusion in the Arabic by utilizing "*kahraman*" to signify amber and "*'anbar*" to signify ambergris; see respectively: 'Abd al-Majid, *Tuyur al-'anbar*, 156–57 and 239. The translation error is particularly apparent in the pivotal scene, discussed below, from which, I believe, the novel's title is derived. To confuse matters further, Abdel Wahab translates the adjective "*'asali*," "honey-colored," as "amber" as well; see: 'Abd al-Majid, *Tuyur al-'anbar*, 67; Abdel Meguid, *Birds*, 57. As a result of this and other translation issues, I have opted not to rely on the published translation in my analyses. All translations from *Tuyur al-'anbar* are my own.

27 'Abd al-Majid, *Tuyur*, 7.

28 'Abd al-Majid, *Tuyur*, 106–7.

29 Mohammed Awad, "The Metamorphoses of Mansheyah," *Mediterraneans* 8/9 (1996): 53.

30 'Abd al-Majid, *Tuyur*, 128.

31 'Abd al-Majid, *Tuyur*, 186–87.

32 'Abd al-Majid, *Tuyur*, 140–41.

33 Although the novel indicates that the statue of Isma'il was removed by the Revolutionary regime in the 1950s, as noted in the previous chapter, it was not actually removed until 1966.

34 'Abd al-Majid, *Tuyur*, 191.

35 'Abd al-Majid, *Tuyur*, 74.

36 'Abd al-Majid, *Tuyur*, 213–28.

37 'Abd al-Majid, *Tuyur*, 423–32.

38 'Abd al-Majid, *Tuyur*, 213–14.

39 'Abd al-Majid, *Tuyur*, 420–22.

40 'Abd al-Majid, *Tuyur*, 440–42.

41 Pepper's tale of his ancestor's adventures echoes several of the Sinbad stories from the *Thousand and One Nights* [*Alf layla wa-layla*]. The ambergris birds are somewhat reminiscent of the *rukh* (roc), a mythical bird who makes an appearance in voyages two and five. An island where Sinbad lands in voyage six is described as flowing with ambergris.
42 'Abd al-Majid, *Tuyur*, 449–50.
43 'Abd al-Majid, *Tuyur*, 451–54.
44 'Abd al-Majid, *Tuyur*, 454.
45 'Abd al-Majid, *Tuyur*, 140–41.
46 'Abd al-Majid, *Tuyur*, 464–65.
47 My usage of "centripetal" and "centrifugal" in describing modes of circulation differs somewhat from that of Edward Dimendberg. Drawing upon the work of Henri Lefebvre, Dimendberg identifies "'centripetal space'" with "the traditional metropolis with its fabric of neighborhoods, familiar landmarks, and negotiable pedestrian spaces" threatened by postwar development in the United States. "Centrifugal" space Dimendberg associates with the automobile and its corollaries: highways and suburbs. Dimendberg, "Kiss the City Goodbye" in *Sites and Stations: Provisional Utopias*, ed. Stan Allen and Kyong Park (New York: Lusitania Press, 1995), 56.

5 Why New York?: Youssef Chahine

1 Chahine deliberately uses the term "*al-naqd al-dhati*" rather than "*al-sira al-dhatiyya*." Walid Shamit, *Yusuf Shahin: Haya lil-sinima* (Beirut: Riyad al-rayyis lil-kutub wa-al-nashr, 2001), 197. For a discussion of the valences of the terms in the Arabic literary tradition see *Interpreting the Self: Autobiography in the Arabic Literary Tradition*, ed. Dwight Reynolds (Berkeley: University of California Press, 2001).
2 Al-Kharrat's family is Coptic, and Chahine's is Catholic, of Lebanese origin. There have been many previous works that document Chahine's life and career, the most comprehensive of which is Ibrahim Fawal's monograph on the director, upon which I rely heavily in my review of Chahine's biography and filmography. Ibrahim Fawal, *Youssef Chahine*, World Directors Series, (London: British Film Institute, 2001).
3 Begun as a satellite campus of Fuad I University in Cairo (later Cairo University) in 1938, it consisted of the faculties of Arts and Law. Engineering was added in 1941, a year before the campus was rededicated as its own institution, named Farouk I University—the name it bore in the years al-Kharrat and Chahine attended. Following the 1952 revolution, it was renamed University of Alexandria. *Alexandria University*, "Historical Background," *http://www.alex.edu.eg/history.jsp* (accessed 27 December 2005).
4 Fawal, *Youssef Chahine*, 199.
5 Ibrahim al-'Aris, *Rihla fi al-sinima al-'arabiyya wa-dirasat ukhra*, (Beirut: Dar al-farabi, 1979), 73.
6 Shamit, *Yusuf Shahin*, 203.
7 Chahine also articulates his love of Cairo on-screen. In his voiceover near the opening of *Cairo as Seen by Chahine* [*al-Qahira munawwara bi-ahliha* (1992)], he states, "J'aime le Caire si profondément que quand on pose la question comment, je ne pouvais pas chercher les mots." [I love Cairo so deeply that when one asks me how much, I cannot find the words.]
8 David Kehr, "Youssef Chahine," *Film Comment* 32, no. 6 (1996): 24–27.
9 Dir. Vincente Minnelli, Roy del Ruth, *et al.*
10 Dir. Vincente Minnelli.
11 Dir. Roy del Ruth. The clips that appear in *Alexandria ... Why?* from *An American in Paris*, and *Born to Dance* as well as the one from *Easy to Love* (1953) that appears in the opening montage were all featured in *That's Entertainment, Part II* (1976; Dir. Gene Kelley). This film comprised of musical numbers from the heyday of MGM

undoubtedly served as the source from which Chahine sampled, as evidenced by the narrator's voiceover introducing Eleanor Powell in the clip from *Born to Dance*.

12 Joel Gordon, *Revolutionary Melodrama: Popular Film and Civic Identity in Nasser's Egypt* (Chicago: Middle East Documentation Center, 2002), 17, n8.

13 Fawal, *Youssef Chahine*.

14 See, for example: Joseph Massad, "Art and Politics in the Cinema of Youssef Chahine," *Journal of Palestine Studies* 28, no.2 (1999), 91; and Shamit, *Yusuf Shahin*, 157–76.

15 According to Ibrahim Fawal, the family relations in the films, *An Egyptian Story* in particular, diverges from those of Chahine. See Fawal, *Youssef Chahine*, 136.

16 For example, in *An Egyptian Story* Yahia has two children, Akram and Jamila, while in *Alexandria ... New York*, he and his Egyptian wife were never able to conceive. Both facts play significant dramatic roles in the respective films. Hala Halim also notes that the protagonist's surname shifts from Yahia Shukry Murad in *An Egyptian Story* to Yahia al-Iskandarani in *Alexandria Again and Again*. "On Being Alexandrian," *Al-Ahram Weekly* 581 (11–17 April 2002) http://weekly.ahram.org.eg/2002/581/cul. htm (accessed 10/17/05). In *Alexandria ... New York* he is identified as Yahia Shukry.

17 Philippe Lejeune, *On Autobiography*, trans. Katherine Leary (Minneapolis: University of Minnesota Press, 1989).

18 John Paul Eakin, *Fictions in Autobiography* (Princeton: Princeton University Press, 1985), 3.

19 Eakin, *Fictions in Autobiography*, 5–6.

20 Rachel Gabara, "Mixing Impossible Genres: David Achkar and African Auto Biographical Documentary," *New Literary History* 34, no. 2 (2003), 333.

21 Gabara, "Mixing," 337.

22 Gabara, "Mixing," 337

23 Gordon discusses the period of nationalization and its demise in *Revolutionary Melodrama*, 207–41.

24 His production team from 1985 to 2004 comprised his niece and nephew, Marianne and Gabriel Khoury, and French producer Humbert Balsan. Balsan, who also produced the works of several other Arab filmmakers, committed suicide in February 2005. For more information on aspects of production, see: Thierry Jousse, "Visite de la maison Chahine: Propos de Gabriel Khoury," *Cahiers du cinéma*, special supplement, (Oct 1996), 22; and Cedric Anger and Thierry Jousse, "Produire Chahine: Propos de Humbert Balsan," *Cahiers du cinéma*, special supplement (Oct 1996), 36–37.

25 Gordon, *Revolutionary Melodrama*, 208.

26 Translation of: "*Y al mar, espejo de mi corazón, las veces que me ha visto llorar la perfidia de tu amor*." Although the opening sequence features an instrumental rendition of the song, it reappears with the Spanish lyrics as the crowning dance number of Yahia's *Ziegfeld Follies*-inspired variety show. Words and music by Alberto Domínguez, 1934. The English lyrics, composed by Milton Leeds, 1941, and featuring in a recording by Glen Miller and his Orchestra, are not a direct translation from the Spanish. *Popular Music, 1920–1979: A Revised Cumulation*, ed. Nat Schwartz and Bruce Pollock. (Detroit: Gale Research Co., 1985). I would also like to thank Ana Cordova for her assistance in translating the Spanish lyrics.

27 Dir. Charles Waters.

28 Later in the credits, images of waves gently lapping the Alexandrian shore are intercut with footage of rioting crowds in Europe from Frank Capra and Anatole Litvak's *The Nazis Strike* (1943), the second installment of the "Why We Fight" series. This montage establishes a contrast between the violent crowd mentality prevailing in Europe and the placid calm of Alexandria.

29 Song composed by John Kander with lyrics by Fred Ebb.

30 "*New York b-tiqtal kul hanin*" ["New York Kills All Nostalgia"] composed by, Faruq al-Sharluby, performed by 'Ali al-Hajjar.

31 Ibrahim Fawal, *Youssef Chahine*, 119.

32 Chahine also explores intercultural contact in the twelfth century Jerusalem and Andalusia in *Saladin* [*Nasir Salah al-Din*] (1963) and *Destiny* [*al-Masir*] (1997), respectively. Both films have been read as analogues to contemporary socio-political issues.

33 In an interview following the release of the film, Chahine comments that he read *Justine*, but not the rest of Durrell's *Alexandria Quartet*, and that he had the novel in mind while working on the screenplay. al-'Aris, *Rihla*, 200

34 One recent exception is a small-release Greek film, *Alexandria* (2001), Dir. Maria Ilióu.

35 See the discussion of this series in Chapter 2.

36 Dir. Henri Barakat.

37 Dir. Hussayn Kamal.

38 Dir. Khayri Bishara.

39 *Al-Summan wa-al-kharif* [*Autumn Quail*], dir. Hussam al-Din Mustafa (1967); *Miramar*, dir. Kamal al-Shaykh (1968). For a discussion of the novels on which these films are based, see Chapter 2.

40 "New Cinema, Commercial Cinema, and the Modernist Tradition in Egypt" *Alif* 15 (1995), 104.

41 Ibid.

42 See Ibid. 81–129, and Armbrust, *Mass Culture and Modernism in Egypt*, (Cambridge: Cambridge University Press, 1996).

43 "On Being Alexandrian."

44 Fawal, *Youssef Chahine*, 188.

45 Shamit, *Yusuf Shahin*, 172.

46 However, as Wendy Brown reminds us, "tolerance discourse reduces conflict to an inherent friction among identities and makes religious, ethnic, and cultural difference itself an inherent site of conflict, one that calls for and is attenuated by the practice of tolerance." *Regulating Aversion: Tolerance in the Age of Identity and Empire* (Princeton: Princeton University Press, 2006), 15.

47 Although the term "*jinsiyya*" can also mean "citizenship," it is clear in Chahine's comments as well as in his films that the issue of concern is primarily one of identity and identification rather than of legal status or documentation. For some members of Egypt's foreign-minority communities, nationality—in terms of national identification—and citizenship were not necessarily the same.

48 Shamit, *Yusuf Shahin*, 172.

49 As addressed in the following chapter, there has been some debate amongst historians about the extent of support for Zionism amongst the population of Egyptian Jews. See, for example: Joel Beinin, *The Dispersion of Egyptian Jewry*, (Berkeley: University of California Press, 1998); Gudrun Krämer, *The Jews in Modern Egypt, 1914–1952*. (Seattle: University of Washington Press, 1989); and Michael Laskier, *The Jews of Egypt, 1920–1970: In the Midst of Zionism, Anti-Semitism, and the Middle East Conflict* (New York: New York University Press, 1992).

50 The Egypt–Israel peace negotiations set in motion by Egyptian President Anwar Sadat's visit to Jerusalem in 1977 were met with deep ambivalence and suspicion. Egyptian President Anwar Sadat flew to Jerusalem on November 19, 1977. The Camp David Accords outlining the steps necessary to attain a peace treaty were signed by U.S. President Carter, Israeli Prime Minister Begin and Sadat on September 17, 1978, and the treaty itself was signed on March 26, 1979.

51 Samir Nasri, "The battles of Youssef Chahine," *al-Nahar* 29 Oct 1979, cited in *Cahiers du cinéma*, special supplement (Oct 1996), 46–47.

52 Fawal, *Youssef Chahine*, 48.

53 Al-'Aris, *Rihla*, 201–2; also cited in English translation in Fawal, *Youssef Chahine*, 129.

54 The *New York Times* report of the 1979 Berlin Festival also posits other political undercurrents to the film's success. *Alexandria ... Why?*, like the Golden Bear winner, Peter

Lilienthal's *David* (Germany) and several other entries offer introspective reflections of the past, particularly the Second World War and its aftermath. Cold War politics also played out at the festival—the East Bloc boycotted the competition in protest of the screening of the American Vietnam war film, *The Deer Hunter*. Yet, despite the reduced competition, the American entries were passed over for awards. Ellen Lentz, "Germans Sweep Film Festival," *New York Times*, 6 Mar 1979, C7.

55 Timothy Brennan. *At Home in the World: Cosmopolitanism Now* (Cambridge, MA: Harvard University Press, 1997), 21.
56 Brennan, *At Home in the World*, 4.
57 Shohat reads the presence of these figures as establishing a contrast between Egyptian Jews and Ashkenazim. *Israeli Cinema*, 279, n.7.
58 Shohat, *Israeli Cinema* 279, n. 7; and Maureen Kiernan, "Cultural Hegemony and National Film Language: Youssef Chahine," *Alif* 15 (1995): 145.
59 Shamit, *Yusuf Shahin*, 169.
60 According to Fawal, the representation of medical treatment in London is based on an article by Yusuf Idris. *Youssef Chahine*, 49.
61 The scene is intended to represent the political demonstrations of Feb–Mar 1946.
62 According to one reporter, prior to *Alexandria ... Why?*, Chahine held a reputation in the Arab world as "the spiritual father of committed (engagé) Arab cinema." Nasri, "The battles of Youssef Chahine," 46–47.
63 Fawal, *Youssef Chahine*, 131.
64 Armbrust, *Mass Culture and Modernism*, 24–26.
65 As already noted, the timeline of the film diverges from the release dates of Chahine's films in reality. In *An Egyptian Story* the nationalization of the Suez Canal and the ensuing military conflict takes place between the release of *Cairo Station* and *Jamila*—films both released in 1958.
66 The reference is perhaps even more apparent in Chahine's 1999 film *The Other* [*al-Akhar*] which features a montage of New York scenes—including similar aerial footage of apartment blocks at night—also accompanied by "Rhapsody in Blue."
67 It was only a few years after this fictionalized rejection by an American studio was said to take place that Omar Sharif, whom Chahine is credited with discovering and cast in the starring role of his film *The Blazing Sun*, made his break in the British film *Lawrence of Arabia* (1962) and went on to a successful international acting career.
68 Fawal, *Youssef Chahine*, 163.
69 Fawal, *Youssef Chahine*, 167–68.
70 *Le sixième jour* (Paris: Julliard, 1960)
71 There are references to *Cairo Station* in the movie, and in one scene it can be shown playing on Egyptian television. However, the difference lies in the fact that Yahia is not shown on the set of this film, nor in the process of writing, shooting, or editing any films that Chahine has actually made.
72 There has been much speculation about Chahine's sexual orientation. The expressions of homosexual desire evident in his Alexandria films are often interpreted as autobiographical. There is yet much critical work to be done on the implications of the fluidity of desire on his representation of Alexandria.
73 The romantic implications of the scene are further underscored by the soundtrack. 'Amr and Yahia dance to "Walking My Baby Back Home," words and music by Roy Turk and Fred Ahlert, 1930. It was also the title song of a 1953 musical featuring Donald O'Connor and Janet Leigh.
74 Halim identifies this return to Hellenistic Alexandria as iconoclastic in an Egyptian context. "On Being Alexandrian."
75 In *Alexandria ... Why?* he recites from Act III, scene iv; *An Egyptian Story* Act III, scene i; and *Alexandria Again and Forever*, Act II, scene ii. As evidence of what is perhaps an over-exuberance for *Hamlet* in Chahine's films since the 1970s, in *An 'Egyptian Story* Yahia and his interlocutor, a British driver, Andrew, misquote Shakespeare and

misidentify a verse from *Richard II* (Act V, scene v)—"I wasted time and now doth time waste me"—as a line from *Hamlet*.

76 In Chahine's lexicon, *Hamlet* does not always function as a model of solipsistic inaction. In *The Sparrow*, after getting wind of a local corruption scheme, the journalist Yusuf exclaims, "Something is rotten in the state of Denmark" (Act I, scene iv). In this case, the invocation of *Hamlet* is intended as explicit commentary on contemporary Egyptian politics, and serves as a call to action.

77 As the articles in a special issue of *Critical Survey* (Dec 2007) on Arab Shakespeares demonstrate, there is a burgeoning field of scholarship devoted to the study of Arab interpretations of Shakespeare's plays and adaptations thereof. Margaret Litvin's work in particular traces a history of modern Arab Hamlets, focusing on the ideological underpinnings of the plays. See, for example, "Vanishing Intertexts in the Arab *Hamlet* Tradition," *Critical Survey* 19, no. 3 (2007): 74–94. I thank Litvin for suggesting that Chahine's self-involved Hamlet as portrayed in this film might be more indebted to French interpretations of Shakespeare than to contemporaneous Arab interpretations.

78 Nadia's interpretation of the play and the underlying events mirrors that of Ahmad Shawqi's nationalist, anti-colonial play *Masra' Kilyubatra* [*The Death of Cleopatra*] (1927). For more on this play's representation of the contemporaneous Egyptian political situation see: Waddah Al-Khatib, "Rewriting History, Unwriting Literature: Shawqi's Mirror-Image Response to Shakespeare," *Journal of Arabic Literature*, 32, no. 3 (2001): 256–83.

79 Fawal, *Youssef Chahine*, 171.

80 Fawal, *Youssef Chahine*, 50.

81 Fawal, *Youssef Chahine*, 53.

82 Brown, *Regulating Aversion*, 7.

83 There is some confusion of Yahia's age in the film. In a scene near the end of the film, prior to Yahia's return to Egypt he identifies himself as 75 years old. However, all other details in the film would suggest that he is supposed to be 70 at that juncture. The present time of the film is approximately late 2000. Although not explicitly referenced in the Arabic edition of the film, the date of Yahia's arrival at the Pasadena playhouse is identified as 1948 in the French titles on the DVD. It is implied that he spent two years in Pasadena, making his graduation date, and thus the date of his return to Egypt 1950, or exactly 50 years prior to his triumphant return to New York, as is noted on multiple occasions through the film. In a faculty meeting at the Pasadena Playhouse a few months before graduation, the dean mentions that Yahia is 19 years old.

84 Many aspects of this film, including the dating of the filmmaker's recognition by the New York Film Forum, diverge from the details of Chahine's life. The retrospective of Chahine's works by the New York Film Forum occurred in 1998.

85 In addition to its direct political critique, *Alexandria ... New York* turns its back on the former colonizer and the present-day neo-colonial power in another way as well—language use. *Alexandria ... Why?* and *An Egyptian Story* aimed at natural language use, switching between Arabic dialogue among Arabic speakers and English in conversation with or among non-Arabic speakers. Although the majority of *Alexandria ... New York*, takes place in America, and represents much dialogue among non-Arabic speakers—such as between Ginger and Alexander, or among the faculty at the Pasadena Playhouse—the film renders all dialogue in Arabic. As such, Ginger's son is called "Iskandar" in dialogue, but is identified as "Alexander" on posters for the New York City Ballet. It is worth noting that the film to date has no American distributor, and has never been released on DVD in the UK or North America. For more on multilingualism in film, including mention of language use in *Alexandria ... Why?* see: Ella Shohat and Robert Stam, "The Cinema After Babel: Language, Difference, Power." *Screen* 26, no. 3–4 (1985): 35–58. This turn away from a multi-lingual texture

is consistent with the anti- or counter-modernist aesthetic in Egypt Walter Armbrust traces in *Mass Culture and Modernism in Egypt*.

86 Although it is unlikely that Chahine and his co-writer Khalid Yusuf would have been aware of it, Alexander Penn is also the name of a Marxist Hebrew poet of Russian origin (1906–72) who was the cofounder of the first Jewish film studio in Palestine in 1927. See Hagit Halperin, *Shalekhet kokhavim: Aleksander Pen, hayyav v-yetzirato 'ad 1940* (Tel Aviv: Papyrus, 1989), 140–41.

87 Daniel Williams. "Anti-Americanism a Hit With Egyptian Audiences." *Washington Post*, 20 Aug 2004, A1.

88 Ahmad Yahia, the actor who plays Alexander, danced the role of John in productions of *Zorba* by the Cairo Opera Ballet in 2004 and 2005. Amal Choucri Catta, "Greek Delight," *Al-Ahram Weekly* 578 (19–24 Feb 2004) *http://weekly.ahram.org. eg/2004/678/cu4.htm* (accessed 26 Sept 2005); and "Dancing the Sirtaki," *Al-Ahram Weekly* 710 (30 Sept – 6 Oct 2004) *http://weekly.ahram.org.eg/2004/710/cu2.htm* (accessed 30 Sept 2005). The scenes of *Zorba* performances in *Alexandria ... New York* were filmed at the Cairo Opera House. It is also worth noting that Alexander / Ahmad Yahia danced the role of John, the foreigner, who is scorned by the villagers because of his haughtiness; his affair with a local woman ends tragically in her death.

89 Michelle Hartman, "'Besotted with the Bright Lights of Imperialism?': Arab Subjectivity Constructed Against New York's Many Faces," *Journal of Arabic Literature*, 35, no. 3 (2004): 277.

90 Hartman, "Besotted," 293.

91 Emma Lazarus's 1883 sonnet "The New Colossus," passages of which are engraved on a plaque at the base of the statue, vaunts Liberty as a symbol of America's pluralism and commitment to immigration.

92 Adonis, in his poem "A Grave for New York" ["*Qabr min ajl New York*,"] also explores this tension in interpreting the figure of the Statue of Liberty. "New York, / A woman— the statue of a woman / in one hand she holds a scrap to which the documents we call / history give the name 'liberty,' and in the other she smothers / a child whose name is Earth." *A Time Between Ashes and Roses*, trans. Shawkat Toorawa (Syracuse: Syracuse University Press, 2004), 124–25. See also Toorawa's afterword in the same volume for a discussion of the poem.

93 Massad, "Art and Politics," 92.

94 Population estimates vary based on sources. According to Gudrun Krämer, the Jewish population in Egypt peaked in the 1940s with an estimated 75,000 to 80,000 people. *The Jews in Modern Egypt, 1914–1952*, 9.

95 Presumably Henri Curiel (1914–78), the well-known Egyptian Communist leader, who was exiled to France in 1950 where he died at the hand of unidentified assassins. Curiel, however, was not actually from Alexandria; he was born in Cairo and lived there throughout his years in Egypt. Hala Halim identifies another loose reference to Curiel in *Alexandria ... Why?*, in the choice of name, Sorel, of the wealthy Jewish family, whose offspring (Sarah) is a Jewish, anti-Zionist, leftist Egyptian activist. "On Being Alexandrian." For more on Curiel see: Beinin, *The Dispersion of Egyptian Jewry*, 142–78.

96 As Robert Vitalis asserts, Alexandria remains a cosmopolitan city, with an influx from North Africa, East Africa, and elsewhere in the Middle East, as well as from the Egyptian countryside—what it has lost is its European-identified population. "Alexandria Without Illusions," in *Cosmopolitan Alexandria*, ed. Deborah Starr (Forthcoming).

6 Gazing across Sinai

1 Castel-Bloom, *Sevivah 'oyenet* [*Hostile Surroundings*] (Tel Aviv: Zemora-Bitan, 1989), 93–109.

2 Castel-Bloom, *Sevivah 'oyenet*, 94.
3 Gudrun Krämer, *The Jews in Modern Egypt, 1914–1952* (Seattle: University of Washington Press, 1989), 9.
4 My characterization of Egyptian Jewish history in the mid-twentieth century is heavily influenced by the Joel Beinin's *The Dispersion of Egpytian Jewry: Culture, Politics, and the Formation of a Modern Diaspora* (Berkeley: University of California Press, 1998). Beinin contends that the 1956 Sinai-Suez War followed by widespread nationalization of businesses precipitated the dispersion of the Egyptian Jewish community. Previous historians placed greater emphasis on the events of the late 1940s and early 1950s: the conflict in Palestine, the rise of the Arab–Israeli conflict, and the Free Officer's Revolt.
5 Beinin, *Dispersion of Egyptian Jewry*, 88.
6 Maurice Shammas also writes about Israeli air raids on Cairo in *'Azza, hafidat nifirtiti* ['Azza, Nefertiti's Granddaughter] (Shafa'amru: Matba'at Dar al-Mashriq lil-Tarjama wa-al-Tiba'a wa-al-Nashr, 2003), 103–4.
7 Castel-Bloom, *Sevivah 'oyenet*, 102.
8 There have been several detailed scholarly studies documenting the history of Egyptian Jews. For a discussion of the transformations the community underwent in the nineteenth century see: Landau *Jews in Nineteenth-Century Egypt* (New York: New York University Press, 1969). For more on the apex of the community and its decline, see Krämer, *The Jews in Modern Egypt*. For a cultural history of Egyptian Jews after dispersion see: Beinin, *Dispersion of Egyptian Jewry*.
9 Beinin, *Dispersion of Egyptian Jewry*, 207–40.
10 Landau, *Jews in Nineteenth-Century Egypt*, 6–25.
11 Beinin, *Dispersion of Egyptian Jewry*, 2.
12 Krämer, *Jews in Modern Egypt*, 9.
13 Krämer, *Jews in Modern Egypt*, 8–29. Jean-Marc Oppenheim, "Egypt and the Sudan" *The Jews of the Middle East and North Africa in Modern Times*, ed. Reeva Simon, Michael Laskier and Sara Regeur (New York: Columbia University Press, 2003), 413.
14 Krämer, *Jews in Modern Egypt*, 222.
15 Krämer, *Jews in Modern Egypt*, 182–204; In *Dispersion of Egyptian Jewry*, Beinin also deals with the topic extensively. For a somewhat divergent opinion, see, Michael Laskier, *The Jews of Egypt, 1920–1970: In the Midst of Zionism, Anti-Semitism, and the Middle East Conflict*, (New York: New York University Press, 1992).
16 Beinin, *Dispersion of Egyptian Jewry*, 121.
17 Krämer, *Jews in Modern Egypt*, 36–49.
18 For a comprehensive list of Jewish periodicals, see: Thomas Mayer, "The Image of Egyptian Jewry in Recent Egyptian Studies," in *The Jews of Egypt: A Mediterranean Society in Modern Times*, ed. Shimon Shamir (Boulder: Westview Press, 1987), 208.
19 Juan Cole, *Colonialism and Revolution in the Middle East: Social and Cultural Origins of Egypt's 'Urabi Movement* (Princeton: Princeton University Press, 1993), 225–26.
20 Irene Gendzier, *The Practical Visions of Ya'qub Sanu'* (Cambridge: Harvard University Press, 1966), 140.
21 Cole, *Colonialism and Revolution*, 226. It is also worth noting that the Hebrew novelist of Iraqi origin, Shimon Ballas based his historical novel *Solo* on the life of Sannu'. See: Ballas, *Solo* (Tel Aviv: Sifriyat Po'alim, 1998). For more on the role Sannu' played in Egyptian anti-colonialism see: Ziad Fahmy, "Francophone Egyptian Nationalists, Anti-British Discourse, and European Public Opinion, 1885–1910. The Case of Mustafa Kamil and Ya'qub Sannu'," *Comparative Studies of South Asia, Africa and the Middle East*, 28, no. 1 (2008): 170–83.
22 Sasson Somekh, "Participation of Egyptian Jews in Modern Arabic Culture, and the Case of Murad Faraj," in *Jews of Egypt*, ed. Shamir, 138.

23 Beinin, *Dispersion of Egyptian Jewry*, 81–82. See also: Somekh, "Participation of Egyptian Jews in Modern Arabic Culture," 139 n8. Other Jewish musicians of stature in Egypt during the first half of twentieth century include Ibrahim Sahlun, Zaki Murad, and Zaki Surur.

24 Salah Tantawi, *Rihlat hubb ma'a Layla Murad* [A Journey of Love with Layla Murad]. (Cairo: Rose al-Yusuf, 1979), 87.

25 For more on Jabès's life and literary production in Egypt see: Daniel Lançon, *Jabès L'Égyptien*. (Paris: Jean Michel Place, 1998) and Stephen Jaron, *Edmond Jabès: The Hazard of Exile* (Oxford: Legenda, European Humanities Research Centre, University of Oxford, 2003).

26 Ammiel Alcalay, *After Jews and Arabs: The Remaking of Levantine Culture* (Minneapolis: University of Minnesota Press, 1993), 64.

27 Jacqueline Kahanoff, *"Tarbut Nefel," Masa*, 25 May 1973, 6.

28 Shimon Shamir, "The Evolution of the Egyptian Nationality Laws and their Application to the Jews in the Monarchy Period" in *Jews of Egypt*, ed. Shimon Shamir, 50.

29 Beinin, *Dispersion of Egyptian Jewry*, 208.

30 Beinin, *Dispersion of Egyptian Jewry*, 88.

31 Beinin, *Dispersion of Egyptian Jewry*, 207.

32 Ibid.

33 Ella Shohat, "Sephardim in Israel: Zionism from the Standpoint of Its Jewish Victims." *Social Text* 19/20 (1988): 1–35.

34 Ella Shohat, "Sephardim in Israel," 13.

35 Ella Shohat, "Sephardim in Israel," 3.

36 Shohat, "Sephardim in Israel," 1–35; Shohat, *Israeli Cinema*.

37 Alcalay, *After Jews and Arabs*.

38 Yehouda Shenhav, *The Arab Jews: A Postcolonial Reading of Nationalism, Religion, and Ethnicity* (Stanford: Stanford UP, 2006), xi.

39 André Aciman also describes the internal hierarchy among Jews in Egypt in *Out of Egypt* (New York: Riverhead Books, 1994), 132–33.

40 Shenhav, *Arab Jews*, 53–55.

41 Shenhav, *Arab Jews*, 55.

42 Ibid.

43 Ibid.

44 Shenhav, *Arab Jews*, 56.

45 Ella Shohat, "Sephardim in Israel," 2.

46 For further discussion on the establishment, orientation and impact of *Te'oryah u-viqoret* see Laurence Silberstein, *The Postzionism Debates: Knowledge and Power in Israeli Culture* (New York: Routledge, 1999), 165–206.

47 Sidra Ezrahi, *Booking Passage* (Berkeley: University of California Press, 2000), 3.

48 Aharoni, *The Second Exodus: A Historical Novel* (Bryn Mawr: Dorrance, 1983).

49 See Jacqueline Shohet, "Such is Rachel," *The Atlantic Monthly* 10 (1946): 113–16 and *Jacob's Ladder* (London: Harvill Press, 1951), 234–39, 419–26. See also Jacqueline Kahanoff, "Passover in Egypt," *Bulletin of the Israeli Academic Center in Cairo*, 23 June 1998: 26–29; published in Hebrew as "Pesah ba-mitzrayim" in *Mi-mizrah shemesh* (Tel Aviv: Hadar, 1978), 20–23. It is worth noting a reversal of the anticipated trajectory evident in *Jacob's Ladder* in which the grandfather sets off to Palestine where he hopes to live out his last days. But, confronted with the poverty and squalor in Jerusalem, he returns to Egypt where he celebrates the *seder* with his family.

50 "*'Atzabim*" in *Ketavim*, vol. 2 (Tel-Aviv: Hotza'at ha-Qibutz ha-Me'uhad, 1977), 1229–61; "Nerves," trans. Hillel Halkin, in *Eight Great Hebrew Short Novels*, ed. Allan Lelchuk and Gershon Shaked (New Milford, CT: The Toby Press, 2005), 33–66.

51 Gershon Shaked, *Modern Hebrew Fiction*, trans. Yael Lotan (Bloomington: Indiana UP, 2000), 51.

52 Brenner, "*'Atzabim*," 1235; "Nerves," 41.

53 Ezrahi, *Booking Passage*, 8.
54 Brenner, "'*Atzabim*," 1250; "Nerves," 56.
55 Brenner, "'*Atzabim*," 1231; "Nerves," 37.
56 Brenner, "'*Atzabim*," 1243; "Nerves," 49.
57 Brenner, "'*Atzabim*," 1243; "Nerves," 48.
58 Alcalay, *After Jews and Arabs*, 53.
59 Hanan Hever, "Yitzhak Shami: Ethnicity as an Unresolved Conflict." *Shofar* 24, no.2 (2006): 126.
60 Ibid.
61 Hever, "Yitzhak Shami," 127.
62 See: Alcalay, *After Jews and Arabs*, 52–59, 206–14; Hever, "Yitzhak Shami," 124–39.
63 Yitzhaq Shami, *Nikmat ha-avot* (Tel Aviv: Hotza'at Yahdav, 1975), 107; Yitzhak Shami, "The Vengeance of the Fathers" Richard Flanz trans. *Eight Great Short Hebrew Novels*, 143.
64 Shami, *Nikmat ha-avot*, 126; "Vengeance of the Fathers," 159.
65 Ibid.
66 Nurit Govrin, "The Encounter of Exiles from Palestine with the Jewish Community of Egypt During World War I, as Reflected in their Writings," in *Jews of Egypt*, ed. Shimon Shamir, 177–91.
67 "*Ribat-shoshanim*" *Moznayim* 44: 4 (1933), reprinted in Ester Raab, *Kol ha-prozah*, ed. Ehud Ben-Ezer (Hod Ha-Sharon: Astrolog, 2001), 308–11; "Rose Jam," trans. Y.L.H., *Sleepwalkers and Other Stories: The Arab in Hebrew Fiction*, ed. Ehud Ben-Ezer (Boulder: Lynne Rienner, 1998), 37–40.
68 *Me veradim mi-port sa'id* (Jerusalem: Agudat Shalem, 1972), 22–45.
69 Servants are also visibly present in the Egyptian writings of Ester Raab mentioned above.
70 (Tel Aviv: 'Am 'Oved, 1967); *The Man from There*, trans. Dorothea Shefer (New York: Sabra Books, 1970)
71 The 1986 film *Avanti Popolo* (Dir. Rafi Buka'i), set during the 1967 war, inverts the equation by depicting Egyptian soldiers caught behind Israeli lines. For more on this film see: Shohat, *Israeli Cinema*, 249.
72 Telpaz's "Port Said Rose Water," published in 1972, as discussed above does not reflect this majority perspective.
73 Kahanoff wrote in English. Her essays published in *Keshet* were translated into Hebrew by the journal's editor, Aharon Amir. The "Generation of Levantines" essays include: "*Yaldut ba-mitzrayim*" ["Childhood in Egypt"] 1:2 (Winter 1959), 72–79; "*Eropa mi-rahoq*" ["Europe from Afar"] 1:3 (Spring 1959), 50–59; "*Ahi ha-mored*" ["Rebel, My Brother"] 1:4 (Summer 1959), 52–62; "*Shahur 'al gabe lavan*" ["Black on White"] 2:1 (Fall 1959), 121–32. Of these essays, to date only one has been posthumously published in English, the language in which it was written: "Childhood in Egypt." *Jerusalem Quarterly* 36 (Summer 1985): 31–41. Kahanoff's work is discussed at greater length below in Chapter 8.
74 Beinin, *Dispersion of Egyptian Jewry*, 53.
75 Beinin, *Dispersion of Egyptian Jewry*, 52. Rahel Maccabi, *Mitzrayim sheli* (Merhavyah: Sifriyat Po'alim, 1968). The first two chapters of the memoir were initially published in *Keshet* 9, no. 4 (Summer 1967): 126–42; and *Keshet* 10, no.1 (Fall 1967): 125–43.
76 Beinin, *Dispersion of Egyptian Jewry*, 53.
77 Shohat, *Israeli Cinema*, 169.
78 Ibid.
79 One character in the film recruits members of the neighborhood to join the Irgun, and he drafts some of the teenage boys, including the protagonist, Sami, to help hang posters. The sympathetic representation of Irgun supporters is also notable in a work

produced in the early 1970s when Socialist–Zionism still maintained its hegemony over the Israeli national master narrative. In this matter, too, the film favors Jewish unity over infighting.

80 For an analysis of the demographic forces behind the election, Shlomo Swirski, "The Oriental Jews in Israel: Why Many Tilted toward Begin," *Dissent* 30 (1984): 77–91.
81 Beinin, *Dispersion of Egyptian Jewry*, 212.
82 Beinin, *Dispersion of Egyptian Jewry*, 212.
83 Ella Shohat, *Israeli Cinema: East/West and the Politics of Representation* (Austin: U. Texas Press, 1987), 115.
84 For more see: Nancy Berg, "Sephardi Writing: From the Margins to the Mainstream," in *The Boom in Contemporary Hebrew Literature*, ed. Alan Mintz (Hanover, N.H.: Brandeis University Press, 1997), 114–42.
85 Beinin, *Dispersion of Egyptian Jewry*, 1.
86 Beinin, *Dispersion of Egyptian Jewry*, 215.
87 Beinin, *Dispersion of Egyptian Jewry*, 220.
88 (Tel Aviv: 'Eked, 1981). For a discussion of this text see: Beinin, *Dispersion of Egyptian Jewry*, 227–31.
89 (Bryn Mawr: Dorrance, 1983). For a discussion of this text see Beinin, *Dispersion of Egyptian Jewry*, 220–27.
90 Nancy Berg, *Exile from Exile: Israeli Writers from Iraq* (Albany: SUNY Press, 1996). Both authors also address this topic on-screen in the documentary film *Forget Baghdad* (2002), Dir. Samir.
91 Maurice Shammas, *Al-Shaykh shabtay wa-hikayat min harat al-yahud* [Sheik Shabbtai and Stories from Harat al-Yahud] (Shafa'amru : Matba'at Dar al-Mashriq lil-Tarjama wa-al-Tiba'a wa-al-Nashr, 1979); *Sab'a sanabil hazila* [Seven Lean Sheaves] (1989); and *'Azza*. For more on Shammas's prose writing see: Deborah Starr, "Sensing the City: Representations of Cairo's *Harat al-Yahud*," *Prooftexts* 26, no. 1–2 (2006): 138–62.
92 Ballas, *Solo*.

7 Mediterranean vigor: Yitzhaq Gormezano Goren

1 Yitzhaq Gormezano Goren, *Qayitz alexandroni* (Tel Aviv: 'Am 'Oved, 1978).
2 Beinin, *Dispersion of Egyptian Jewry*, 57.
3 Homi Bhabha, *The Location of Culture* (London: Routledge, 1994), 82.
4 As will become more apparent below, I am thinking here of Judith Butler's usage of the term "troubling" in *Gender Trouble: Feminism and the Subversion of Identity* (New York and London: Routledge, 1990).
5 In his documentary film, *66 Was a Good Year for Tourism* (1992), the author's nephew, Amit Goren, credits his Ashkenazi mother with pressuring his father, Yitzhaq's older brother, to adopt an Israeli–Hebrew name to replace the Sephardi–Diaspora name.
6 Durrell's *Alexandria Quartet* has never been translated in its entirety into Hebrew. *Justine* was first translated in 1968 by Abraham Birman (Tel Aviv: Mizrahi). Widely circulating translations of *Justine* and *Balthazar* by Aharon Amir were both published in 1988 (Jerusalem: Keter).
7 Yitzhaq Gormezano Goren, *Qayitz*; *Blansh* (Tel Aviv: 'Am 'Oved, 1986); *Ba-Derekh la-Itztadyon* (Tel Aviv: Kedem, 2003).
8 These passages about servants pack less of a punch in the context of contemporary Israeli society in which the number of home health aids and house cleaners of Thai and Philippine origin proliferates. The text's engagement with Orientalist assumptions about the families' Nubian and Sudanese servants, however, remain relevant.
9 Gormezano Goren, *Qayitz*, 16.
10 Gormezano Goren, *Qayitz*, 17.
11 Ibid.

12 Gormezano Goren, *Qayitz*, 16.
13 Sander Gilman, *Difference and Pathology: Stereotypes of Sexuality, Race and Madness* (Ithaca: Cornell University Press, 1985), 18.
14 Gilman, *Difference and Pathology*, 18.
15 Gormezano Goren, *Qayitz*, 13.
16 Gormezano Goren, *Qayitz*, 12.
17 Gormezano Goren, *Qayitz*, 105.
18 Gormezano Goren, *Qayitz*, 148.
19 Gormezano Goren, *Qayitz*, 59.
20 Gormezano Goren, *Qayitz*, 60.
21 This novel also implicitly evokes *Ben Hur*, also a national and personal conversion narrative put to the test through a horse (chariot) race. In the 1959 film version starring Charlton Heston, there is also a latent homoerotic desire between the opponents Judah Ben Hur and Quintus Arrius. I would like to thank Shai Ginsburg for pointing out these parallels.
22 Gormezano Goren, *Qayitz*, 114.
23 Ibid.
24 Gormezano Goren, *Qayitz*, 147.
25 Ibid.
26 Gormezano Goren, *Qayitz*, 152.
27 Beinin, *Dispersion of Egyptian Jewry*, 14.
28 Gormezano Goren, *Qayitz*, 151.
29 Gormezano Goren, *Qayitz*, 152.
30 Ibid. In this context it is worth noting that Henry Ford, the founder of the corporation, had well-known anti-Semitic views.
31 The words "loge" and "homage" appear in transliteration in the text. Gormezano Goren, *Qayitz*, 114.
32 Gormezano Goren, *Qayitz*, 150.
33 Gauri Viswanathan, *Outside the Fold: Conversion, Modernity, and Belief* (Princeton: Princeton University Press, 1998), 16.
34 Bhabha, *The Location of Culture*, 86.
35 Ibid.
36 Gormezano Goren, *Qayitz*, 136.
37 See: Ruth Kartun-Blum, *Profane Scriptures: Reflections on Dialogue with the Bible in Modern Hebrew Poetry* (Cincinnati: Hebrew Union College Press, 1999), 17–65; and Edna Amir Coffin, "The Binding of Isaac in Modern Israeli Literature," *Michigan Quarterly Review* 22, no. 3 (1983): 429–44.
38 Gormezano Goren, *Qayitz*, 194. David's regal nature could also derive from his Biblical namesake. The Biblical David, too, is descended from a convert, Ruth.
39 Based on the translation of *The Oxford Bible*.
40 The Qur'an refers to Mohammed's night journey in Sura 17:1. Hadith literature expands on this narrative, introducing further elements, including the horse *Buraq*.
41 Gormezano Goren, *Qayitz*, 196.
42 Gormezano Goren, *Qayitz*, 39.
43 Butler, *Gender Trouble*.
44 French in the original. Gormezano Goren, *Qayitz*, 111.
45 Gormezano Goren, *Qayitz*, 42.
46 Gormezano Goren, *Qayitz*, 23–24.
47 The French word "façon" appears transliterated into Hebrew in the original. Gormezano Goren, *Qayitz*, 17.
48 Gormezano Goren, *Qayitz*, 134. Joel Beinin also makes this point, *Dispersion of Egyptian Jewry*, 56.
49 "*N'est-ce-pas*" appears in French in the original. Gormezano Goren, *Qayitz*, 134.

8 Unmasking Levantine blindness: Ronit Matalon

1 (London: Harvill Press, 1951).
2 (Tel Aviv: Yariv and Hadar, 1978).
3 The first article, "My Brother Ishmael: On the Visit of Anwar Sadat," appeared in *At* within a special section of essays welcoming the Egyptian president at the time of his visit. The second article, "Welcome, Sadat" Kahanoff composed as an afterword to *From East the Sun* published in 1978. Kahanoff also personally sent copies of this essay and the book to Egyptian first lady Jihane Sadat.
4 Ronit Matalon, "*Tlushah me-ha-mizrah*," *Ha'aretz* Musaf (1 Aug 1986), 14–15, 24.
5 *Zeh 'im ha-panim elenu* [*The One Facing Us*] (Tel Aviv: 'Am'Oved, 1995); *The One Facing Us*. Marsha Weinstein, trans. (New York: Metropolitan, 1998).
6 Included in Matalon's novel are excerpts from "Childhood in Egypt" and "Europe from Afar." The published English translation of the novel omits the embedded portions of "Europe from Afar." As a result of this and other liberties taken in the English version, while I have consulted with the published translations of Marsha Weinstein, all translations are my own.
7 "Childhood in Egypt," *The Jerusalem Quarterly* 36 (Summer 1985), 40.
8 Ibid.
9 Ibid.
10 Ibid.
11 Kahanoff, "Europe from Afar" (Unpublished ms.), 3, 8. *Mi-mizrah*, 25, 29.
12 Kahanoff, "Israel," 21. This passage appears in the extant English ms. but not in the version published in Hebrew. The manuscript may represent a later version of the essay dating from the late 1960s when Kahanoff appears to have been preparing to publish her essays in a collected volume in English. Some have suspected that Aharon Amir may have tinkered with the translations so as better to adhere to his own ideologies; however, I have found no evidence to support this claim.
13 Kahanoff, "Israel," 25; *Mi-mizrah*, 59.
14 This tendency is echoed in Kahanoff's characterization of Levantine history, "Islam at the height of its influence was a Levantine empire, for it was shaped by the civilizing influence of Byzantium on the Arabian conqueror." Kahanoff, "Israel," 24; *Mi-mizrah*, 59.
15 Kahanoff, *Mi-mizrah*, 35.
16 Kahanoff, *Mi-mizrah*, 46.
17 Dolly Benhabib, "*Hatza'iyot ha-nashim hitkatzru: ha'arot 'al zehut nashit levantinit Etzel Jacqueline Kahanoff*," *Te'oryah u-viqoret* 5 (Fall 1994), 164.
18 Kahanoff, *Mi-mizrah*, 46.
19 Matalon makes this point in an interview. Yitzhaq Levtov, "*Kismah shel ha-optziyah ha-levantinit*." *Davar* Masa (28 April 1995), 2.
20 Stacy Beckwith, "The Conceptual State of Israel: Textual Bases for Dominant and Alternative Impressions of the Nation" (Ph.D. diss., University of Minnesota, 1997), 254.
21 Joel Beinin, *The Dispersion of Egyptian Jewry*, (Berkeley: University of California Press, 1998), 227.
22 Matalon, *Zeh 'Im ha-panim elenu*, 192.
23 Matalon, *Zeh 'Im ha-panim elenu*, 193.
24 Matalon, *Zeh 'Im ha-panim elenu*, 38.
25 Matalon, *Zeh 'Im ha-panim elenu*, 189.
26 Matalon, *Zeh 'Im ha-panim elenu*, 167–68.
27 Beckwith, "The Conceptual State," 262.
28 Matalon, *Zeh 'Im ha-panim elenu*, 25.
29 Matalon, *Zeh 'Im ha-panim elenu*, 25.
30 Matalon, *Zeh 'Im ha-panim elenu*, 162.
31 English in the original. Matalon, *Zeh 'Im ha-panim elenu*, 158.
32 Matalon, *Zeh 'Im ha-panim elenu*, 77.

33 Matalon, *Zeh 'im ha-panim elenu*, 147.
34 Matalon, *Zeh 'im ha-panim elenu*, 147–48.
35 Matalon, *Zeh 'im ha-panim elenu*, 157.
36 Ibid.
37 Ammiel Alcalay, *After Jews and Arabs: Remaking of Levantine Culture* (Minneapolis: University of Minnesota Press, 1993), 254.
38 Ella Shohat, *Israeli Cinema: East/West and the Politics of Representation* (Austin: U. Texas Press, 1987), 115.
39 Matalon, *Zeh 'im ha-panim elenu*, 157.
40 Ibid.
41 Matalon, *Zeh 'im ha-panim elenu*, 28.
42 Ibid.
43 Matalon, *Zeh 'im ha-panim elenu*, 106–7. This passage echoes a similar incident in Yaakov Shabtai's *Zikharon devarim* [*Past Continuous*] (1977) in which Goldman's father, a figure representing Zionist ideology of the past and a man who "believed fanatically in a world order with good and bad and no neutral ground between them," killed the neighbor's dog to punish its owner for her corrupt, carefree lifestyle. (Tel Aviv; Ha-Sifriya ha-hadasha, 1994), 13–15; Trans. Dalya Bilu (New York: Shocken Books, 1985), 12–14.
44 Matalon, *Zeh 'im ha-panim elenu*, 106–7.
45 Matalon, *Zeh 'im ha-panim elenu*, 123.
46 Matalon, *Zeh 'im ha-panim elenu*, 62.
47 Matalon, *Zeh 'im ha-panim elenu*, 254.
48 Matalon, *Zeh 'im ha-panim elenu*, 285.
49 Matalon, *Zeh 'im ha-panim elenu*, 311.
50 Matalon, *Zeh 'im ha-panim elenu*, 312.
51 Matalon, *Zeh 'im ha-panim elenu*, 306.
52 Matalon, *Zeh 'im ha-panim elenu*, 52.
53 French in the original. Matalon, *Zeh 'im ha-panim elenu*, 313.
54 Matalon, *Zeh 'im ha-panim elenu*, 238–39.
55 Matalon, *Zeh 'im ha-panim elenu*, 84.
56 French in the original. Matalon, *Zeh 'im ha-panim elenu*, 234.
57 Homi Bhabha, *The Location of Culture* (London: Routledge, 1994), 83.
58 Matalon, *Zeh 'im ha-panim elenu*, 83.
59 Matalon, *Zeh 'im ha-panim elenu*, 213.
60 Matalon, *Zeh 'im ha-panim elenu*, 83. The animal could also stand in for Esther's perception of blacks as less than human. On more than one occasion, Esther likens the Cicurel's elderly, black gatekeeper, Augustin, to a gorilla (Matalon, *Zeh 'im ha-panim elenu*, 92, 185). It is worth noting that some of the racial tension—including the first gorilla reference for which Jean-Luc rebukes her—is "white-washed" from the English version of the book. In the English version, Esther is rather portrayed as a naïve do-gooder, her deeply rooted ambivalence toward race erased in the translation.
61 Matalon, *Zeh 'im ha-panim elenu*, 215.
62 Bhabha, *The Location of Culture*, 81.
63 Matalon, *Zeh 'im ha-panim elenu*, 51.
64 Matalon, *Zeh 'im ha-panim elenu*, 219.
65 Matalon, *Zeh 'im ha-panim elenu*, 248.
66 Cited in Alcalay, *After Jews and Arabs*, 29.
67 Like their American counterparts, the Black Panthers in Israel agitated for social equality. They were responsible for organizing several high-profile protests between 1971 and the outbreak of the 1973 war. For details about the movement see: G. N. Giladi, *Discord in Zion: Conflict Between Ashkenazi and Sephardi Jews in Israel* (London: Scorpion Publishing, 1990), 254–73. The movement is also the subject of the

documentary film *Ha-Panterim ha-shehorim medabrim* [*The Black Panthers (in Israel) Speak*], Dir. Eli Hamo and Sami Shalom Chetrit (Israel, Kedma, 2003).

9 Conclusion

1 http://salatabaladi.blogspot.com/ (accessed 9 Jan 2008).
2 One journalist who positively reviewed *House Salad* underscored this point, "it is a film on the nation in the deepest sense of nationalism." Samir Farid, "Salata baladi *filim misri wahid fi mahrajan Locarno*," *Al-Jumhuriyya*, Aug 8, 2007, http://212.103.160.28/ algomhuria/2007/08/08/arts/detail00.shtml (accessed 9 Jan 2008).
3 For example, the Egyptian director Muhammad Khan called it "a very special, personal film," dismissing the controversy by flatly stating that "there is no semblance of normalization." "*Al-sinima alan tuqadim 'hals'..wa al-nujum 'bitu' al-i'lanat*," *Al-Badil* 6 Nov 2007. http://www.elbadeel.net/index.php?option=com_content&task=view&id=2 513&Itemid=40. Accessed 10 Jan 2008.
4 I discuss this topic at greater length elsewhere. See Starr "Egyptian Representation of Israeli Culture: Normalizing Propaganda or Propagandizing Normalization?" *Review Essays in Israel Studies*, Books on Israel, vol. 5, eds. Laura Eisenberg and Neil Caplan, (Albany: SUNY Press, 2000), 263–82.
5 Muhammad 'Abd al-Rahman, "*Al-sinima al-misriyya ta'ud ila mahrajan al-qahira*," *al-Akhbar* 24 Nov 2007. http://www.al-akhbar.com/ar/node/54582 (accessed 10 Jan 2008).
6 Dir. Eran Kolirin.
7 'Abd al-Rahman, "*Al-sinima al-misriyya*."
8 'Ala al-Shaf'i, "*Nadia Kamal la tara fi filmiha da'wa ila al-tatbi'*, "*al-Hayat*, 9 Nov 2007 http://www.daralhayat.com/culture/movie/11–2007/Item-20071108-1fb859 aa-c0a8–10ed-00a4–2c31fde6c66e/story.html (accessed on 10 Jan 2008).
9 An article on the website of the Arabic satellite news network MBC discusses all three normalization scandals together: "*Uburali misri yughani fi ma'bad yahudi bi-kalimat Salah Jahin*," *MBC.net*, 4 Nov 2007 http://www.mbc.net/portal/site/mbc/menuitem. cec41c4faec6734497b11b101f10a0a0/?vgnextoid=652d8cb0dfa06110VgnVCM100 0008420010aRCRD&vgnextchannel=94fde30e61801110VgnVCM100000f1010a0a RCRD (accessed 9 Jan 2008).
10 Diane Singerman and Paul Amar, "Contesting Myths, Critiquing Cosmopolitanism, and Creating the New Cairo School of Urban Studies," *Cairo Cosmopolitan* (Cairo: American University in Cairo Press, 2006), 10.
11 Mona Abaza, "Saad Kamel: Leper of the Light," *Al-Ahram Weekly* 728 (3–9 Feb 2005).

Bibliography

Books and Articles

'Abd al-Majid (Abdel Meguid), Ibrahim. *La ahad yanam fi al-iskandariyya.* Cairo: Dar al-Hilal, 1996. Translated by Farouk Abdel Wahab as *No One Sleeps in Alexandria* (Cairo: American University in Cairo Press, 1999).

——. *Tuyur al-'anbar.* Cairo: Dar al-Hilal, 2000. Translated by Farouk Abdel Wahab as *Birds of Amber* (Cairo: American University in Cairo Press, 2005).

'Abd al-Rahman, Muhammad. "*Al-sinima al-misriyya ta'ud ila mahrajan al-qahira.*" *al-Akhbar* (24 Nov 2007). http://www.al-akhbar.com/ar/node/54582 (accessed 10 Jan 2008).

'Ali, Shwikar. "*Wa-azma hawl timthal al-iskandar bil-iskandariyya.*" *al-Ahram* (12 May 2000).

——"Inter-faith Conference Opens in Cairo to Boost Islam's Image." *Agence France Presse.* (24 Jul 1996).

——"Italian Gift to Alexandria." *Times* (London) (5 Dec 1938): 14e.

——"*Uburali misri yughani fi ma'bad yahudi bi-kalimat salah jahin.*" *MBC.net* (4 Nov 2007). http://www.mbc.net/portal/site/mbc/menuitem.cec41c4faec6734497b 11b101f10a0a0/?vgnextoid=652d8cb0dfa06110VgnVCM1000008420010aRCRD& vgnextchannel=94fde30e61801110VgnVCM100000f1010a0aRCRD (accessed 9 Jan 2008).

Abaza, Mona. "Saad Kamel: Leper of the Light." *Al-Ahram Weekly* 728 (3–9 Feb 2005).

Abu-Lughod, Janet. *Cairo: 1001 Years of the City Victorious.* Princeton: Princeton University Press, 1971.

Aciman, André. *Out of Egypt.* New York: Riverhead Books, 1994.

Adonis, *A Time Between Ashes and Roses.* Edited and translated by Shawkat Toorawa. Syracuse: Syracuse University Press, 2004.

Agstner, Rudolf. "Ein Wiener Ansichtkartenverleger in Ägypten." *Biblos* (Vienna) 50, no. 1 (2001): 5–14.

Aharoni, Ada. *The Second Exodus: A Historical Novel.* Bryn Mawr: Dorrance, 1983.

Ahmed, Leila. *A Border Passage.* New York: Farrar, Straus and Giroux, 1999.

Alcalay, Ammiel. *After Jews and Arabs: The Remaking of Levantine Culture.* Minneapolis: University of Minnesota Press, 1993.

Alloula, Malek. *The Colonial Harem.* Translated by Myrna Godzich and Wlad Godzich. Minneapolis: University of Minnesota Press, 1986.

Anderson, Amanda. "Cosmopolitanism, Universalism, and the Divided Legacies of Modernity." In Cheah and Robbins, *Cosmopolitics,* 265–89.

Anderson, Benedict. *Imagined Communities.* London: Verso, 1983.

Anger, Cedric, and Thierry Jousse. "Produire Chahine: Propos de Humbert Balsan." *Cahiers du cinéma* special supplement (Oct 1996): 36–37.

al-'Aris, Ibrahim. *Rihla fi al-sinima al-'arabiyya wa-dirasat ukhra* [A tour of Arab film and other studies]. Beirut: Dar al-Farabi, 1979.

Armbrust, Walter. *Mass Culture and Modernism in Egypt.* Cambridge: Cambridge University Press, 1996.

——. "New Cinema, Commercial Cinema, and the Modernist Tradition in Egypt." *Alif* 15 (1995):81–129.

Asad, Talal. *Formations of the Secular: Christianity, Islam, Modernity.* Stanford: Stanford UP, 2003.

al-Aswani (Al Aswany), 'Ala'. *'Imarat ya 'qubiyyan* [Yacoubian building]. Cairo: Mirit lil-nashr wa-al-ma'lumat, 2002. Translated by Humphrey Davies as *The Yacoubian Building* (Cairo: American University in Cairo Press, 2004).

Baer, Gabriel. *Studies in the Social History of Modern Egypt.* Chicago: University of Chicago Press, 1969.

Ballas, Shimon. *Solo.* Tel Aviv: Sifriyat Po'alim, 1998.

Baron, Dvorah. *Le-'et 'atah* [For the Time Being]. Tel Aviv: 'Am 'oved, 1943.

——. *Me-emesh* [Since Yesterday]. Tel Aviv: 'Am 'oved, 1955.

Beckwith, Stacy. "The Conceptual State of Israel: Textual Bases for Dominant and Alternative Impressions of the Nation." Ph.D. diss., University of Minnesota, 1997.

Beinin, Joel. The Dispersion of Egyptian Jewry: Culture, Politics, and the Formation of a Modern Diaspora. Berkeley: University of California Press, 1998.

Benhabib, Dolly. "*Hatza'iyot ha-nashim hitkatzru: ha'arot 'al zehut nashit levantinit etzel Jacqueline Kahanoff.*" *Te'oryah u-vikoret* 5 (Fall 1994): 164.

Ben Habib, Seyla. *The Rights of Others: Aliens, Residents and Citizens.* Cambridge: Cambridge University Press, 2004.

Ben-Ner, Yitzhaq. *Ha-ish mi-sham.* Tel Aviv: 'Am 'oved, 1967. Translated by Dorothea Shefer as *The Man from There* (New York: Sabra Books, 1970).

Berg, Nancy. "Sephardi Writing: From the Margins to the Mainstream." In Mintz, *The Boom in Contemporary Hebrew Literature*, 114–42.

——. *Exile from Exile: Israeli Writers from Iraq.* Albany: SUNY Press, 1996.

Bhabha, Homi. *The Location of Culture.* London: Routledge, 1994.

——, ed. *Nation and Narration.* London; New York: Routledge, 1990.

Booth, Marilyn. *Bayram al-Tunisi's Egypt: Social Criticism and Narrative Strategies.* Exeter: Ithaca Press, 1990.

Braude, Benjamin, and Bernard Lewis, ed. *Christians and Jews in the Ottoman Empire: The Functioning of a Plural Society.* Vol. 1. New York: Holmes and Meier, 1982.

Brennan, Timothy. *At Home in the World: Cosmopolitanism Now.* Cambridge: Harvard University Press, 1997.

Brenner, Yosef Hayyim. *'Atzabim* [Nerves]. Tel Aviv: Shalekhet, 1910. Reprint, in *Ketavim*, vol. 2, 1229–61. Tel-Aviv : Hotza'at ha-qibutz ha-me'uhad, 1977. Translated by Hillel Halkin as "Nerves" in *Eight Great Hebrew Short Novels*, edited by Allan Lelchuk and Gershon Shaked (New Milford, CT: The Toby Press, 2005), 33–66.

Brown, Wendy. *Regulating Aversion: Tolerance in the Age of Identity and Empire.* Princeton: Princeton University Press, 2006.

Butler, Judith. *Gender Trouble: Feminism and the Subversion of Identity.* New York and London: Routledge, 1990.

Castel-Bloom, Orly. *Sevivah 'oyenet* [Hostile Surroundings]. Tel Aviv: Zemora-Bitan, 1989.

Catta, Amal Choucri. "Dancing the Sirtaki." *Al-Ahram Weekly* 710 (30 Sept – 6 Oct 2004). http://weekly.ahram.org.eg/2004/710/cu2.htm (accessed 30 Sept 2005).

——. "Greek Delight." *Al-Ahram Weekly* 578 (19–24 Feb 2004). http://weekly.ahram.org. eg/2004/678/cu4.htm (accessed 26 Sept 2005).

Cheah, Pheng, and Bruce Robbins, ed. *Cosmopolitics: Thinking and Feeling Beyond the Nation.* Minneapolis: University of Minnesota Press, 1998.

Chedid, Andrée. *Le sixième jour.* Paris: Julliard, 1960.

Cialente, Fausta *Ballata Levantina* (Milan: Feltrineli, 1961). Translated by Isabel Quigly as *The Levantines* (Cambridge: The Riverside Press, 1962).

Coffin, Edna Amir. "The Binding of Isaac in Modern Israeli Literature." *Michigan Quarterly Review* 22, no. 3 (1983): 429–44.

Cole, Juan. *Colonialism and Revolution in the Middle East: The Social and Cultural Origins of Egypt's 'Urabi Movement.* Princeton: Princeton University Press, 1993.

Dalal, Jenine Abbushi. "The Perils of Occidentalism: How Arab Novelists are Driven to Write for Western Readers." *Times Literary Supplement* (24 April 1998).

Dimendberg, Edward. "Kiss the City Goodbye." In *Sites and Stations: Provisional Utopias*, edited by Stan Allen and Kyong Park, 56–66. New York: Lusitania Press, 1995.

Driessen, Henk. "Mediterranean Port Cities: Cosmopolitanism Reconsidered." *History and Anthropology* 16, no.1 (March 2005): 129–41.

Dumont, Paul, and François Georgeon, ed. *Villes ottomanes à la fin de l'empire.* Paris: Editions l'Harmattan, 1992.

Durrell, Lawrence. *Balthazar.* 1958. New York: Penguin, 1991.

——. *Clea.* 1960. New York: Penguin, 1991.

——. *Justine.* 1957. New York: Penguin, 1991.

——. *Mountolive.* 1958. New York: Penguin, 1991.

Eakin, John Paul. *Fictions in Autobiography.* Princeton: Princeton University Press, 1985.

El Kadi, Galila, and Dalila El Kerdany, "Belle-Époque Cairo: The Politics of Refurbishing the Downtown Business District." In Singerman and Amar, *Cairo Cosmopolitan*, 345–71.

Empereur, Jean-Yves. *Alexandria Rediscovered.* Translated by Margaret Maehler. London: British Museum Press 1997.

Errera, Eglal. "The Dream of Alexander and the Literary Myth." In Ilbert and Yanakakis, *Alexandria 1860–1960*, 128–43.

Ezrahi, Sidra. *Booking Passage.* Berkeley: University of California Press, 2000.

Fahmy, Khaled. "For Cavafy with Love and Squalor: Some Critical Notes on the History and Historiography of Modern Alexandria," In Hirst and Silk, *Alexandria Real and Imagined*, 263–80.

——. "Towards a Social History of Modern Alexandria." In Hirst and Silk, *Alexandria, Real and Imagined*, 281–306.

——. *All the Pasha's Men: Mehmed Ali, His Army, and the Making of Modern Egypt.* Cambridge: Cambridge University Press, 1997.

Fahmy, Ziad. "Francophone Egyptian Nationalists, Anti-British Discourse, and European Public Opinion, 1885–1910: The Case of Mustafa Kamil and Ya'qub Sannu'." *Comparative Studies of South Asia, Africa and the Middle East* 28, no. 1 (2008): 170–83.

Farid, Samir "*Salata baladi* filim misri wahid fi mahrajan Locarno." *Al-Jumhuriyya* (Aug 8, 2007). http://212.103.160.28/algomhuria/2007/08/08/arts/detail00.shtml (accessed 9 Jan 2008).

Fawal, Ibrahim. *Youssef Chahine.* World Directors Series. London: British Film Institute, 2001.

Fawaz, Leila, and C. A. Bayly, ed., Modernity and Culture: From the Mediterranean to the Indian Ocean. New York: Columbia University Press, 2002.

Gabara, Rachel. "Mixing Impossible Genres: David Achkar and African AutoBiographical Documentary." *New Literary History* 34, no. 2 (2003): 331–52.

Gendzier, Irene. *The Practical Visions of Ya'qub Sanu'*. Cambridge: Harvard University Press, 1966.

Gershoni, Israel, and James Jankowski. *Redefining the Egyptian Nation, 1930–1945*. Cambridge: Cambridge University Press, 1995.

Giladi, G. N. *Discord in Zion: Conflict Between Ashkenazi and Sephardi Jews in Israel*. London: Scorpion Publishing, 1990.

Gilman, Sander. *Difference and Pathology: Stereotypes of Sexuality, Race and Madness*. Ithaca: Cornell University Press, 1985.

Gordon, Joel. *Revolutionary Melodrama: Popular Film and Civic Identity in Nasser's Egypt*. Chicago: Middle East Documentation Center, 2002.

Goren, Yitzhaq Gormezano. *Ba-derekh la-itztadyon*. Tel Aviv: Kedem, 2003.

——. *Blansh* Tel Aviv: 'Am 'oved, 1986.

——. *Qayitz Alexsandroni*. Tel Aviv: 'Am 'oved, 1978.

Gover, Yerach. *Zionism: The Limits of Moral Discourse in Israeli Hebrew Fiction*. Minneapolis: University of Minnesota Press, 1994.

Govrin, Nurit. "The Encounter of Exiles from Palestine with the Jewish Community of Egypt During World War I, as Reflected in their Writings." In Shamir, *Jews of Egypt*, 177–91.

Greek Ministry of Foreign Affairs. *Bilateral Relations-Egypt*. http://www2.mfa.gr/ www.mfa.gr/en-US/Policy/Geographic+Regions/Mediterranean+-+Middle+East/ Bilateral+Relations/Egypt (accessed 23 July 2006).

Haag, Michael. *Alexandria: City of Memory*. New Haven: Yale University Press, 2004.

Halim, Hala "Alexandria Re-Inscribed." Review of *No One Sleeps in Alexandria*, by Ibrahim 'Abd al-Majid. *Al-Ahram Weekly* 472 (9–15 March 2000). http://weekly.ahram. org.eg/2000/472/bk1_472.htm.

——. "Dance to the Music of Time." *Al-Ahram Weekly* (2–8 July 1998). http://weekly. ahram.org.eg/1998/384/cu1.htm.

——. "On Being Alexandrian." *Al-Ahram Weekly* 581 (11–17 April 2002). http://weekly. ahram.org.eg/2002/581/cul.htm (accessed 17 October 2005).

Halperin, Hagit. *Shalekhet kokhavim: Aleksander Pen, hayyav v-yetzirato 'ad 1940* [Falling Stars: Alexander Penn, His Life and Works to 1940]. Tel Aviv: Papyrus, 1989.

Hardman, Esther Zimmerli. *Kleopatra, Kranzler und Kolibris*. Allschwill: E. Zimmerli Hardman, 1999. Translated by Muhammad Abu Rahma as *Hayati fi misr* [My Life in Egypt]. Alexandria: Green Leaf, 1998.

Hardt, Michael, and Antonio Negri, *Empire*. Cambridge: Harvard University Press, 2000.

Harel-Dagan, Anda. *Po'ema qahirit [Cairo Poem]*. Tel Aviv: 'Eked, 1981.

Hartman, Michelle. "'Besotted with the Bright Lights of Imperialism'?: Arab Subjectivity Constructed Against New York's Many Faces." *Journal of Arabic Literature* 35, no. 3 (2004): 270–328.

Harvey, David. "Cosmopolitanism and the Banality of Geographical Evils." *Public Culture* 12, no. 2 (2000): 529–64.

Hesiod. *Theogony*. Translated by Dorothea Wender. London: Penguin, 1987.

Hess, Andrew. "*Millet.*" In *The Oxford Encyclopedia of the Modern Islamic World*, edited by John Esposito, vol. 3, 107–8. New York: Oxford University Press, 1995.

Hever, Hanan. "Yitzhak Shami: Ethnicity as an Unresolved Conflict." *Shofar* 24, no.2 (2006): 124–39.

Hirst, Anthony, and Michael Silk, ed. *Alexandria, Real and Imagined*. Aldershot, Hampshire: Ashgate Publishing, 2004.

Hollinger, David. *Postethnic America: Beyond Multiculturalism*. New York: Basic Books, 1995.

Ibrahim, Jamil 'Atiyyah. *Awraq sakandariyya [Alexandria Papers]*. Cairo: Dar al-hilal, 1997.

Ilbert, Robert, and Ilios Yanakakis, ed. *Alexandria 1860–1960: The Brief Life of a Cosmopolitan Community*. Alexandria: Harpocrates Press, 1997.

Ilbert, Robert. "A Certain Sense of Citizenship." In Ilbert and Yanakakis, *Alexandria 1860–1960*, 18–34.

——"Alexandrie, cosmopolite?" In Dumont and Georgeon, *Villes ottomanes à la fin de l'empire*, 171–85.

——. "Cités cosmopolites: la fin d'un modèle?" *Qantara: le magazine de l'Institute de monde arabe* (April 1994): 36–38.

al-Imam, Muhammad Rif'at. *al-Arman fi misr (1896–1961)* [Armenians in Egypt (1896–1961)]. Cairo: Jam'iyyat al-qahira al-khayriyya al-armaniyya al-'amma, 2003.

Issawi, Charles. "The Transformation of the *Millets* in the Nineteenth Century," In Braude and Lewis, *Christians and Jews in the Ottoman Empire*, vol. 1, 261–86.

Jabès, Edmond. *Le Livre des Questions*. Paris: Gallimard, 1963.

Jacquemond, Richard. *Entre Scribes et Écrivains: Le Champ Littéraire dans L'Égypte Contemporaine*. Paris: Acts Suds, 2003.

Jaron, Stephen. *Edmond Jabès: The Hazard of Exile*. Oxford: Legenda, European Humanities Research Centre, University of Oxford, 2003.

Jasanoff, Maya. "Cosmopolitan: A Tale of Identity from Ottoman Alexandria." *Common Knowledge* 11:3 (2005): 393–409.

al-Jayar, Amal. "*Abu al-haul raqdan taht qadmay al-iskandar.*" *al-Ahram* (24 Aug 2001).

Jousse, Thierry. "Visite de la maison Chahine: Propos de Gabriel Khoury." *Cahiers du cinéma* special supplement (Oct 1996): 22.

Jubril, Muhammad. *al-Shati' al-akhar* [The Other Shore]. Cairo: Maktabat misr, 1996.

Kahanoff, Jacqueline. (Shohet). "Such is Rachel." *The Atlantic Monthly* 10 (1946): 113–16.

——(Shohet). *Jacob's Ladder*. London: Harvill Press, 1951.

——. "*Ahi ha-mored*" ["Rebel, My Brother"]. *Keshet* 1, no. 4 (Summer 1959): 52–62. Reprinted in Kahanoff, *Mi-mizrah shemesh*, 35–46.

——. "*Eropa mi-rahoq*" ["Europe from Afar"] *Keshet* 1, no. 3 (Spring 1959): 50–59. Reprinted in Kahanoff, *Mi-mizrah shemesh*, 24–34.

——. "*Shahur 'Al gabe lavan*" ["Black on White"] *Keshet* 2, no. 1 (Fall 1959),:121–32. Reprinted in Kahanoff, *Mi-mizrah shemesh*, 47–59.

——. "*Tarbut nefel,*" *Masa*, (25 May 1973): 2, 6.

——. *Mi-mizrah shemesh* [From East the Sun] (Tel Aviv: Yariv and Hadar, 1978).

——. "Childhood in Egypt." *Jerusalem Quarterly* 36 (Summer 1985): 31–41. Translated as "*Yaldut ba-mitzrayim*" ["Childhood in Egypt"] *Keshet* 1, no. 2 (Winter 1959): 72–79. Reprinted in Kahanoff, *Mi-mizrah shemesh*,11–19.

——. "Passover in Egypt," *Bulletin of the Israeli Academic Center in Cairo* 23 (June 1998): 26–29. Translated as "*Pesah ba-mitzrayim,*" in Kahanoff, *Mi-mizrah shemesh*, 20–23.

Kararah, Azza. "Egyptian Literary Images of Alexandria." In Hirst and Silk, *Alexandria, Real and Imagined*, 313–20.

Karpat, Kemal. "*Millets* and Nationality: The Roots of the Incongruity of Nation and State in the Post-Ottoman Era." In Braude and Lewis, *Christians and Jews in the Ottoman Empire*, vol. 1, 141–70.

Kartun-Blum, Ruth. *Profane Scriptures: Reflections on Dialogue with the Bible in Modern Hebrew Poetry*. Cincinnati: Hebrew Union College Press, 1999.

Kehr, David. "Youssef Chahine." *Film Comment* 32, no. 6 (1996): 24–27.

Kendall, Elisabeth. *Literature, Journalism and The Avant-Garde: Intersection in Egypt.* London; New York: Routledge, 2006.

Khalid, 'Ala. "*Iskandariyya nihayat 'asr, bidayat 'asr.*" *Akhbar al-adab*, al-Bustan 388, (17 December 2000): 1–8.

Khalid, 'Ala. "*Sirat maqha.*" *Akhbar al-adab*, al-Bustan. 439, (9 December 2001): 1–8.

Khan, Muhammad. "*Al-sinima alan tuqadim 'hals'..wa al-nujum 'bitu'' al-i'lanat.*" *Al-Badil* (6 November 2007). http://www.elbadeel.net/index.php?option=com_content&task=view&id=2513&Itemid=40. (Accessed 10 Jan 2008.)

al-Kharrat, Edwar. "Alexandria, My Mediterranean." Translated by Jean Burrell. *Diogenes* 52 (May 2005): 19–20.

——. "Cultural Authenticity and National Identity." *Diogenes* 52 (May 2005): 21–24.

——. *al-Hassasiyya al-jadida: maqalat fi al-zahira al-qissasiyya* [New Sensitivity: Essays on The Narrative Phenomenon]. Beirut: Dar al-Adab, 1993.

——. *Hitan 'Aliya* [High Walls] Cairo: Matba'at Atlas, 1959.

——. "*Iskandariyyati ... madinat za'faran.*" In *Iskandariyyati: madinati al-qudsiyya wa-al-hushiyya.* [My Alexandria: My Strange and Holy City] Cairo and Alexandria: Dar wa-matabi' al-mustaqbal, 1994. 5–14.

——. *al-Kitaba 'Abra al-Naw'iyya* [Writing beyond genre]. Cairo: Dar Sharqiyyat, 1994.

——. *Rama wa-al-tinnin.* Beirut: al-Mu'assasa al-'arabiyya lil-dirasat wa-al-nashr, 1980. Translated by Ferial Ghazoul and John Verlenden as *Rama and the Dragon* (Cairo: American University in Cairo Press, 2002).

——. *Turabuha za'faran.* Beirut: Dar al-mustaqbal al-'arabi, 1985. Translated by Frances Liardet as *City of Saffron* (London: Quartet, 1989).

——. *Ya banat iskandariyya.* Beirut: Dar al-adab, 1990. Translated by Frances Liardet as *Girls of Alexandria* (London: Quartet, 1993).

al-Khatib, Waddah. "Rewriting History, Unwriting Literature: Shawqi's Mirror-Image Response to Shakespeare." *Journal of Arabic Literature* 32, no. 3 (2001): 256–83.

Khurays, Ahmad. *Thuna'iyyat Idwar al-Kharrat al-nassiyya* [Idwar al-Kharrat's Textual Duets]. Amman: Azmina, 1998.

Kiernan, Maureen. "Cultural Hegemony and National Film Language: Youssef Chahine." *Alif* 15 (1995): 145.

Kitroeff, Alexander. The Greeks in Egypt 1919–37: Ethnicity and Class. Oxford: Ithaca Press, 1989.

Krämer, Gudrun. *The Jews in Modern Egypt, 1914–1952.* Seattle: University of Washington Press, 1989.

Kristeva, Julia. *Nations without Nationalism.* Translated by Leon Roudiez. New York: Columbia University Press, 1993.

Labib, Husni Sayid. *Riwa'i min bahri* [Novelist from Bahri]. Kitabat naqdiyya 113. Cairo: al-hai'a al-'amma li-qusur al-thaqafa, 2001.

Lagnado, Lucette. *Man in the White Sharkskin Suit.* New York: Harper Collins, 2007.

Lançon, Daniel. *Jabès L'Égyptien.* Paris: Jean Michel Place, 1998.

Landau, Jacob. *Jews in Nineteenth-Century Egypt.* New York: New York University Press, 1969.

Landes, David. *Bankers and Pashas: International Finance and Economic Imperialism in Egypt.* Cambridge: Harvard UP, 1958.

Laskier, Michael. *The Jews of Egypt, 1920–1970: In the Midst of Zionism, Anti-Semitism, and the Middle East Conflict.* New York: New York University Press, 1992.

Lazarev, Anouchka. "Italians, Italianity and Fascism." Translated by Colin Clement. In Ilbert and Yanakakis, *Alexandria 1860–1960*, 72–92.

Lejeuke, Philippe. *On Autobiography*. Translated by Katherine Leary. Minneapolis: University of Minnesota Press, 1989.

Lejeune, Philippe. *On Autobiography*, trans. Katherine Leary. Minneapolis: University of Minnesota Press, 1989.

Lentz, Ellen. "Germans Sweep Film Festival." *New York Times* (6 March 1979): C7.

Levtov, Yitshaq. "*Kismah shel ha-optziyah ha-levantinit.*" *Davar, Masa* (28 April 1995): 2.

Litvin, Margaret. "Vanishing Intertexts in the Arab *Hamlet* Tradition." *Critical Survey* 19, no. 3 (2007): 74–94.

Mabro, Robert. "Alexandria 1860–1960: The Cosmopolitan Identity." In Hirst and Silk, *Alexandria Real and Imagined*, 247–62.

Mabro, Robert. "Nostalgic Literature on Alexandria." In *Historians in Cairo*, edited by J. Edwards, 237–63. Cairo: American University in Cairo Press, 2002.

Maccabi, Rahel. *Mitzrayim sheli.* Merhavyah: Sifriyyat Po'alim, 1968.

Mahfuz (Mahfouz), Najib. *Al-Summan wa al-kharif.* 2nd ed. Cairo: Maktabat Misr, 1964. Translated by Roger Allen and John Rodenbeck as *Autumn Quail* (New York: Anchor Books, 1990).

——. *Miramar.* Cairo: Maktabat Misr, 1967. Translated by Fatma Moussa-Mahmoud (Washington: Three Continents Press, 1991).

Malcolmson, Scott. "The Varieties of Cosmopolitan Experience." In Cheah and Robbins, *Cosmopolitics.*

——. "*Al-malik yuzih al-sitar 'an timthal jadihi isma'il.*" *al-Ahram* (5 Dec 1938): 1–2.

Massad, Joseph. "Art and Politics in the Cinema of Youssef Chahine." *Journal of Palestine Studies* 28, no.2 (1999): 77–93.

Masters, Bruce. *Christians and Jews in the Ottoman Arab World: The Roots of Sectarianism.* New York: Cambridge University Press, 2001.

Matalon, Ronit. "*Tlushah me-ha-mizrah,*" *Ha'aretz* Musaf (1 Aug 1986): 14–15, 24.

Matalon, Ronit. *Zeh 'im ha-panim elenu.* Tel Aviv: 'Am 'Oved, 1995. Translated by Marsha Weinstein as *The One Facing Us* (New York: Metropolitan, 1998).

Mayer, Thomas. "The Image of Egyptian Jewry in Recent Egyptian Studies," in Shamir, *The Jews of Egypt: A Mediterranean Society in Modern Times*, 199–212.

Mehrez, Samia. "Experimentation and the Institution: The Case of *Ida'a 77* and *Aswat.*" In *The View from Within: Writers and Critics on Contemporary Arabic Literature*, edited by Ferial Ghazoul and Barbara Harlow, 177–96. Cairo: American University of Cairo Press: 1994.

Meijer, Roel, ed. *Cosmopolitanism, Identity and Authenticity in the Middle East.* (Surrey: Curzon Press, 1999).

Mignolo, Walter. "The Many Faces of Cosmo-polis: Border Thinking and Critical Cosmo-politanism." *Public Culture* 12, no. 3 (2000): 721–48.

Mintz, Alan, ed. *The Boom in Contemporary Hebrew Literatur.* Hanover, N.H.: Brandeis University Press, 1997.

Mitchell, Timothy. *Colonising Egypt.* Berkeley: University of California Press, 1988.

——. *Rule of Experts.* Berkeley: University of California Press, 2002.

Mohamed Awad, "The Metamorphoses of Mansheyah," *Mediterraneans*, 8/9 (1996): 42–58.

Muwafi, 'Abd al-'Aziz. "*Asatir wa-bahith 'an zaman da'i'.*" *al-Hayat* (23 August 1996), 16.

Myntti, Cynthia. *Paris along the Nile: Architecture in Cairo from the Belle Epoque.* Cairo: American University in Cairo Press, 1999.

Nasri, Samir. "The battles of Youssef Chahine." *al-Nahar* (29 Oct 1979). Cited in *Cahiers du cinéma*, special supplement (Oct 1996): 46–47.

al-Nowaihi, Magda. "Memory and Imagination in Edwar al-Kharrat's *Turabuha Za'afaran.*" *Journal of Arabic Literature* 25 (1994): 34–57.

Nussbaum, Martha. "Patriotism and Cosmopolitanism." *Boston Review* 19, no. 5 (Oct–Nov 1994). http://www.bostonreview.net/BR19.5/nussbaum.html.

Oppenheim, Jean-Marc. "Egypt and the Sudan." In Simon, Laskier, and Regeur, *The Jews of the Middle East and North Africa in Modern Times*, 409–30.

Ostle, Robin "Alexandria: A Mediterranean Cosmopolitan Center of Cultural Production." In Fawaz and Bayly, *Modernity and Culture From the Mediterranean to the Indian Ocean*, 314–29.

———. "Alexandrian Iconography: Muhammad Nagi," *Mediterraneans*, 8/9 (Autumn 1996): 168–71.

Philipp, Thomas. *The Syrians in Egypt 1725–1975.* Stuttgart: Franz Steiner Verlag, 1985.

Plutarch, *The Life of Alexander the Great.* Edited by A. Clough. Translated by J. Dryden. New York, Modern Library, 2004.

Powell, Eve Troutt. *A Different Shade of Colonialism: Egypt, Great Britain, and the Mastery of the Sudan.* Berkeley: University of California Press, 2003.

al-Qabani, 'Abd al-'Alim. "*Kafafis ... sha'ir al-iskandariyya al-'alami fi al-'asr al-hadith.*" *Amwaj* (June 1978): 35–48.

Qisas sakandariyya [Alexandrian Stories]. Alexandria: al-hay'a al-mahalliyya li-ri'ayat al-funun wa-al-adab wa-al-'ulum al-ijtima'iyya, 1967.

al-Qusas, Jamal. *al-Iskandariyya: ruba'iyya shi'riyya* [Alexandria: A poetic quartet]. Cairo: al-hay'a al-misriyya al-'amma lil-kitab, maktabat al-usra, 2002.

Raab, Ester. "*Ribat-shoshanim.*" *Moznayim* 44, no. 4 (1933). Reprinted in Esther Raab, *Kol ha-prozah.* Edited by Ehud Ben-Ezer, 308–11. Hod Ha-Sharon: Astrolog, 2001. Translated by Y.L.H. as "Rose Jam" *Sleepwalkers and Other Stories: The Arab in Hebrew Fiction*, edited by Ehud Ben-Ezer (Boulder: Lynne Rienner, 1998), 37–40.

Raafat, Samir. "R.I.P. Annie Gismann 1911–96." *Egyptian Mail* (23 March 1996). http://www.egy.com/people/96-03-23.shtml.

———. *Cairo, the Glory Years: Who Built What, When, Why and For Whom.* Alexandria: Harpocrates Press, 2003.

———. *Maadi 1904–1962: Society and History in a Cairo Suburb.* Cairo: Palm Press, 1995.

Raymond, André. "The Role of the Communities (*tawa'if*) in the Administration of Cairo in the Ottoman Period." In *The State and its Servants: Administration in Egypt from Ottoman Times to the Present*, edited by Nelly Hanna, 32–43. Cairo: American University in Cairo Press, 1995.

Rayyan, Amjad. *Riwayat al-rahawwulat al-ijtima'iyya: La ahad yanam fi al-iskandariyya l-ibrahim 'abd al-majid namudhajan* [The Novel of Social Change: The Example of Ibrahim 'Abd al-Majid's No One Sleeps in Alexandria]. Kitabat naqdiyya 99. Cairo: al-hai'a al-'amma li-qusur al-thaqafa, 2000.

Reimer, Michael. *Colonial Bridgehead: Government and Society in Alexandria 1807–1882.* Boulder: Westview Press, 1997.

Renan, Ernest. "What is a Nation?" Translated by Martin Thom. In Bhabha, *Nation and Narration*, 8–22.

Reynolds, Dwight, ed. *Interpreting the Self: Autobiography in the Arabic Literary Tradition.* Berkeley: University of California Press, 2001.

Rizk, Yunan Labib. "Close to Italy." *al-Ahram Weekly* 670 (25–31 December 2003). http://weekly.ahram.org.eg/2003/670/chrncls.htm.

Rizq, 'Abd al-Fattah. *Iskandariyya 47* [Alexandria 47]. Cairo: Dar al-hilal, 1984.

Robbins, Bruce. *Feeling Global: Internationalism in Distress.* New York: New York University Press, 1999.

Rodenbeck, John. "Literary Alexandria." *The Massachusetts Review* 42, no. 4 (Winter 2001–2): 524–72.

Roessel, David. "A Passage through Alexandria: The City in the Writing of Durrell and Forster, in Hirst and Silk, *Alexandria, Real and Imagined*, 323–36.

Said, Edward. *Orientalism.* New York: Random House, 1978.

——. *The World, The Text and The Critic.* Cambridge: Harvard University Press, 1983.

——. *Culture and Imperialism.* New York: Alfred A. Knopf, 1993.

——. *Out of Place.* New York: Alfred A. Knopf, 1999.

Schwartz, Nat, and Bruce Pollock, ed. *Popular Music, 1920–1979: A Revised Cumulation.* Detroit: Gale Research Co., 1985.

Scott, James Harry. *The Law Affecting Foreigners in Egypt.* Revised edition. Edinburgh: William Green and Sons, 1908.

Serageldin, Samia. *The Cairo House.* Syracuse: Syracuse University Press, 2000.

Shabtai, Yaakov. *Zikharon devarim.* Tel Aviv; Ha-Sifriyah ha-hadashah, 1994. Translated by Dalya Bilu as *Past Continuous* (New York: Shocken Books, 1985).

al-Shaf'i, 'Ala'. "*Nadia Kamal la tara fi filmiha da'wa ila al-tatbi'.*" *al-Hayat,* 9 Nov 2007. http://www.daralhayat.com/culture/movie/11–2007/Item-20071108-1fb859aa-c0a8–10-ed-00a4–2c31fde6c66e/story.html (accessed on 10 Jan 2008).

Shaked, Gershon. *Modern Hebrew Fiction.* Translated by Yael Lotan. Bloomington: Indiana UP, 2000.

Shami, Yitzhaq. *Nikmat ha-avot.* Tel Aviv: Hotza'at yahdav, 1975. Translated by Richard Flanz as "The Vengeance of the Fathers," in *Eight Great Hebrew Short Novels*, edited by Allan Lelchuk and Gershon Shaked (New Milford, CT: The Toby Press, 2005), 69–185.

Shamir, Shimon. "The Evolution of the Egyptian Nationality Laws and their Application to the Jews in the Monarchy Period." In Shamir, *Jews of Egypt*, 33–67.

——, ed. *The Jews of Egypt: A Mediterranean Society in Modern Times.* Boulder and London: Westview Press, 1987.

Shamit, Walid. *Yusuf Shahin: Haya lil-sinima* [Youssef Chahine: A Life of Cinema]. Beirut: Riyyad al-Rayyis lil-Kutub wa-al-Nashr, 2001.

Shammas, Maurice. *'Azza, hafidat nifirtiti* ['Azza, Nefertiti's Granddaughter]. Shafa'amru: Matba'at dar al-mashriq lil-tarjama wa-al-tiba'a wa-al-nashr, 2003.

——. *Al-Shaykh shabtay wa-hikayat min harat al-yahud* [Sheik Shabbtai and Stories from Harat al-Yahud]. Shafa'amru: Matba'at dar al-mashriq lil-tarjama wa-al-tiba'a wa-al-nashr, 1979.

Shenhav, Yehouda. *The Arab Jews: A Postcolonial Reading of Nationalism, Religion, and Ethnicity.* Stanford: Stanford UP, 2006.

Shawqi, Ahmad. *Masra' kilyubatra* [The Death of Cleopatra]. 1927. Cairo: al-Maktaba al-tijariyya al-kubra, 1964.

Shohat, Ella. "Sephardim in Israel: Zionism from the Standpoint of Its Jewish Victims." *Social Text* 19/20 (1988): 1–35.

——. Israeli Cinema: East/West and the Politics of Representation. Austin: U. Texas Press, 1987.

Shohat, Ella, and Robert Stam, "The Cinema After Babel: Language, Difference, Power." *Screen* 26, no. 3–4 (1985): 35–58.

Silberstein, Laurence. The Postzionism Debates: Knowledge and Power in Israeli Culture. New York: Routledge, 1999.

Simon, Reeva, Michael Laskier, and Sara Regeur, ed. *The Jews of the Middle East and North Africa in Modern Times*. New York: Columbia University Press, 2003.

Singerman, Diane, and Paul Amar, "Contesting Myths, Critiquing Cosmopolitanism, and Creating the New Cairo School of Urban Studies." In Singerman and Amar, *Cairo Cosmopolitan*, 3–43.

——. *Cairo Cosmopolitan*. Cairo: American University in Cairo Press, 2006.

Snir, Reuven. "'We Are Arabs Before We Are Jews': The Emergence and Demise of Arab-Jewish Culture in Modern Times." *EJOS* 8, no.9 (2005): 1–47.

Somekh, Sasson. "Participation of Egyptian Jews in Modern Arabic Culture, and the Case of Murad Faraj." In Shamir, *Jews of Egypt*, 130–40.

Srivastava, Neelam. *Secularism in the Postcolonial Indian Novel: National and Cosmopolitan Narratives in English*. Routledge: London, 2008.

Stagh, Marina. *The Limits of Freedom of Expression*. Stockholm: Almqvist & Wiksell International, 1993.

Starr, Deborah. "Egyptian Representation of Israeli Culture: Normalizing Propaganda or Propagandizing Normalization?" In *Review Essays in Israel Studies*. Books on Israel, vol. 5, edited by Laura Eisenberg and Neil Caplan, 263–82. Albany: SUNY Press, 2000.

——. "Recuperating Cosmopolitan Alexandria: Circulation of Narratives and Narratives of Circulation." *Cities* 22, no. 3 (2005): 217–28.

——. "Sensing the City: Representations of Cairo's *Harat al-Yahud*." *Prooftexts* 26, no. 1–2 (2006): 138–62.

Stille, Alexander. *The Future of the Past*. New York: Farrar Straus and Giroux, 2002.

Stillman, Norman. *The Jews of Arab Lands in Modern Times*. Philadelphia: Jewish Publication Society, 1991.

Swirski, Shlomo. "The Oriental Jews in Israel: Why Many Tilted toward Begin." *Dissent* 30 (1984): 77–91.

Tantawi, Salah. *Rihlat hubb ma'a Layla Murad* [A Journey of Love with Layla Murad]. Cairo: Rose al-Yusuf, 1979.

Telpaz, Gid'on. *Me Veradim mi-Port Sa'id* [Port Said Rose Water]. Jerusalem: Agudat Shalem, 1972.

Tignor, Robert. "The Economic Activities of Foreigners in Egypt, 1920–50: From Millet to Haute Bourgeoisie." *Comparative Studies in Society and History* 22, no.3 (Jul 1980): 416–49.

Toledano, Ehud. *State and Society in Mid-Nineteenth Century Egypt*. Cambridge: Cambridge UP, 1990.

University of Alexandria. "Historical Background," *http://www.alex.edu.eg/history.jsp* (accessed 27 December 2005).

Vatikiotis, P. J. *The History of Modern Egypt*. 4th edition. Baltimore: Johns Hopkins University Press, 1991.

Viswanathan, Gauri. *Outside the Fold: Conversion, Modernity, and Belief*. Princeton: Princeton University Press, 1998.

Vitalis, Robert. "Alexandria Without Illusions." In *Cosmopolitan Alexandria*, edited by Deborah Starr (Forthcoming).

——. *When Capitalists Collide: Business Conflict and the End of Empire in Egypt*. Berkeley: University of California Press, 1995.

Volait, Mercedes. "La Communauté Italienne et ses édiles." *Revue de l'Occident Musulman et de la Méditerranée* 46, no. 4 (1987): 137–55

Walkowitz, Rebecca. *Cosmopolitan Style*. New York: Columbia University Press, 2006.

Williams, Daniel. "Anti-Americanism a Hit With Egyptian Audiences." *Washington Post* (20 August 2004): A1.
Wilson, Rob. "A New Cosmopolitanism Is in the Air: Some Dialectical Twists and Turns." In Cheah and Robbins, *Cosmopolitics*, 351–61.

Selected Filmography

Barakat, Henri. *Shati' al-gharam* [Shore of Love] Cairo: 1950.
Bishara, Khayri. *Ice Cream fi glim* [Ice Cream in Glym] Cairo: 1992.
Buka'i, Rafi. *Avanti Popolo.* Israel: TTG Productions and Kastel Communications, 1986.
Capra, Frank. and Anatole Litvak. *The Nazis Strike.* USA: U.S. Army Signal Corps and First Motion Picture Unit, 1943.
Chahine, Youssef *Ibn al-nil* [Nile boy]. Cairo: Mary Queeny Films, 1951.
——. *Sira 'fi al-wadi* [The blazing sun]. Cairo: Gabriel Talhami Films, 1954.
——. *Jamila al-jaza'iriyya* [Jamila]. Cairo: Magda Films, 1958.
——. *Nasir Salah al-Din* [Saladin]. Cairo: Asia Films, 1963.
——. *al-Usfur* [The Sparrow]. Cairo and Algiers: Misr International Films and National Office of Cinema Industry, 1973.
——. *Iskadariyya ... lih?* [Alexandria ... Why?]. Cairo and Algiers: Misr International Films and National Office of Cinema Industry, 1978.
——. *Hadduta misriyya* [An Egyptian story]. Cairo: Misr International Films, 1982.
——. *Wada'ya Bonaparte* [Adieu Bonaparte] Cairo and Paris: Misr International Films and Lyric International, 1985.
——. *Iskandariyya kaman wa-kaman* [Alexandria again and forever]. Cairo and Paris: Misr International Films and Paris Classics Productions, 1989.
——. *al-Qahira munawwara bi-ahliha* [Cairo as seen by chahine]. Cairo and Paris: Misr International Films and Mirroirs, 1992.
——. *al-Muhajir* [The Emigrant] Cairo and Paris: Misr International Films and Mirroirs, 1994.
——. *al-Masir* [Destiny]. Cairo and Paris: Misr International Films and Ognon Pictures, 1997.
——. *al-Akhar* [The other]. Cairo and Paris: Misr International Films and Ognon Pictures, 1999.
——. *Skut ... Hansawar* [Silence ... We're rolling]. Cairo and Paris: Misr International Films and Ognon Films, 2001.
——. *Iskadariyya..New York* [Alexandria..New York]. Cairo and Paris: Misr International Films and Ognon Pictures, 2004.
Goren, Amit. *66 Was a Good Year for Tourism.* Israel, 1992.
Hamo, Eli, and Sami Shalom Chetrit. *Ha-Panterim ha-Shehorim Medabrim* [The Black Panthers (in Israel) Speak]. Israel: Kedma, 2003.
Ilióu, Maria. *Alexandria.* Greece: 2001.
Kamal, Hussayn. *Abi fawq al-shajara* [My father is up a tree] Cairo: 1969.
Kamel, Nadia. *Salata baladi* [House salad]. Cairo: Snooze Productions, 2007.
Kelley, Gene. *That's Entertainment, Part II.* Los Angeles: Metro-Goldwyn-Mayer, 1976.
Kolirin, Eran. *Bikor ha-tizmoret* [The band's visit]. Tel Aviv, Los Angeles, and Paris: July-August Productions, Bleiberg Entertainment, and Sophie Dulac Productions, 2007.
Riefenstahl, Leni. *Triumph des Willens* [Triumph of the will]. Berlin: Leni Riefenstahl-Produktion and Reichspropagandaleitung der NSDAP, 1935
Samir. *Forget Baghdad.* Germany and Switzerland: Dschoint Ventschr Filmproduktion AG and TAG/TRAUM Filmproduktion, 2002.

Index